For Renewal and Retreat

Be present with those who gather for _____ at _____:

Teach us in all things to seek first Your honor
and glory;

Guide us to perceive the ways in which You are
calling us;

and grant us grace and courage to accomplish
them . . .

For the Right Use of Leisure

In the course of this busy life, You give us times of
rest and refreshment;

Grant that we may use such time
(especially _____),

to rest our bodies and renew our minds,

that our spirits may be opened to the goodness
of Your creation . . .

VENITE

VENITE

A BOOK OF
DAILY PRAYER

Robert Benson

JEREMY P. TARCHER / PUTNAM
A MEMBER OF
PENGUIN PUTNAM INC.
NEW YORK

Most Tarcher/Putnam books are available at special quantity discounts for bulk
purchases for sales promotions, premiums, fund-raising, and educational needs.
Special books or book excerpts also can be created to fit specific needs.
For details, write Putnam Special Markets, 375 Hudson Street, New York, NY 10014.

Jeremy P. Tarcher/Putnam
a member of
Penguin Putnam Inc.
375 Hudson Street
New York, NY 10014
www.penguinputnam.com

Library of Congress Cataloging-in-Publication Data
Benson, R. (Robert), date.
Venite : a book of daily prayer / Robert Benson.
p. cm.
Includes bibliographical references and index.
ISBN 1-58542-013-1
1. Divine office—Texts. I. Title
BV199.D3 B46 2000   99-046211
264'.15—dc21

Printed in the United States of America
1   3   5   7   9   10   8   6   4   2

This book is printed on acid-free paper. ∞

Book design by Deborah Kerner

By tradition going back to early Christian times,
    the Divine Office is arranged so that
the whole course of the day and night is made holy . . .
    it is the very prayer which Christ Himself,
together with His body,
    addresses to the Almighty God.
      THE CATHOLIC ENCYCLOPEDIA

This book is offered in thanksgiving
   for all who have,
all who do,
   and all who will pray such prayer.

CONTENTS

THE PREFACE   ix

THE PRACTICE   1

THE OFFICE   6
Notes for Saying the Office
   FOR MORNING   8
   FOR MIDDAY   10
   FOR EVENING   12
   FOR NIGHT   14
   FOR TABLE   16
   FOR COMMUNION   18
   FOR COMMEMORATION   20

THE SEASONS   22
Notes for Saying the Collects for the Seasons
   1. ADVENT THROUGH CHRISTMASTIDE   24
   2. EPIPHANY THROUGH THE BEGINNING OF LENT   25
   3. LENT TO PALM SUNDAY   26
   4. HOLY WEEK   27
   5. EASTER WEEK   28
   6. EASTERTIDE THROUGH ASCENSIONTIDE   29
   7. PENTECOST TO CORPUS CHRISTI   30
   8. ORDINARY TIME THROUGH KINGDOMTIDE   31

THE REMEMBRANCES   32
Notes for Saying the Prayers of Remembrance

THE CANTICLES   94
Notes for Saying the Canticles

THE PSALTER   126
Notes for Saying the Psalter

THE GOSPEL   188
Notes for Saying the Gospel

APPENDIX   251
LITURGICAL CALENDAR   251
GLOSSARY   255
BIBLIOGRAPHY AND RESOURCE NOTES   261
INDEX   263
ACKNOWLEDGMENTS   271

THE PREFACE

This book was never really meant for you to hold in your hands. It began as a private book and later, much later, began to become something else, something that seemed to hold the possibility of its becoming and being a companion to others. And so I have let it go.

If it is pretentious, forgive me. If it has errors, have mercy. It is one pilgrim's attempt to find a way to participate in the ancient prayer. Perhaps it is best if I tell you how the book came to be at all.

Some years ago, I found myself participating in a community of prayer whose practice it was to say the Office three times each day when we were together— morning, evening, and night. For two years, we gathered once a quarter for a week at a time. For those twenty-four days each year, we lived our days framed by the rhythm of the ancient daily prayers of the Church. Participating in those rhythms—beginning the day with prayer that sanctified the day; ending the day's work with Psalms and prayers and thanksgiving; committing ourselves to the darkness and silence of the night with confession and forgiveness and confidence—gave shape and a sense of completion and wholeness to the day that was altogether new and wondrous to me. I found that I wanted to participate in such prayer when I was away from the community as well.

I was raised in the evangelical tradition where reciting the Office is not practiced. And even though my own journey has now taken me deeper and deeper into the liturgical tradition, at the time I had little or no frame of reference from which to discover how to go about praying such prayer.

The first thing I discovered is that it is very hard to find a world of people who pray this way. Not many of us live in close proximity to, or have the time every day to travel to, churches or other communities where we can participate in saying or singing the Office with others. If we are to join in such prayer, then we are going to have to do it alone most days. Our opportunities to share it with others will be relatively few. And they will be a gift, a precious gift, but it is not likely that they will be given to us very regularly.

The second thing I discovered is that the prayerbooks that one finds to use are in many ways marvelously unhelpful to a lay person who wants to practice this daily prayer in their own solitude. They contain very little instruction about how to practice such prayer, they are generally structured for corporate prayer rather than private prayer, and they are generally written as though a "leader" will always be there to know what to do so that Seasons are observed, holy days are remembered, the liturgical calendar is observed, and so forth. Finding your way to the daily practice of the ancient daily prayer through these books is so difficult that almost anyone who attempts it on their own is usually discouraged and likely to finally give it up.

The last thing I discovered is that more often than not these prayerbooks require the use of another book or two if you want to follow the Office properly. For example, saying the daily prayer using the Book of Common Prayer requires that you also have your Bible to be able to read the Scripture, which is best done with the three-volume set of daily Scripture and another book with the prayers for lesser feasts and fasts. If you do not find the cost prohibitive—well over one hundred dollars—you may find that carrying three or four books back and forth to the office or on your travels becomes a bit burdensome. Enough so that one's desire to participate in the ancient prayer can be overwhelmed by the sheer practicalities of trying to do so.

We no longer live in a time when the structure or the geography of our culture is very conducive to the observance of the daily Office. It is not offered at our churches, our work does not allow the time and freedom to do so anyway, and we have by and large not been taught anything at all about the necessity and importance of such prayer. The prayer that sanctifies the day, the prayer that Christ Himself prays through his Body, has been left to priests and monks and nuns. Is it any wonder that our days seem to be something less than holy, our churches seem to be something less than prayerful, and our lives seem something less than sanctified?

But we also live in a time when the call to practice such prayer seems to be clearly drawing more and more Christians to its practice. It is an ancient call, with its roots in the Jewish faith, and in the early Christian communities, and the desert where our fathers and mothers kept the faith alive. It is a call that seems to be crying out for some new ways to think about this prayerful discipline, and so you hold this book in your hands.

The one who made this book is neither priest nor scholar nor monk. I am a pilgrim. I was drawn to pray to try to take my place alongside the faithful who have tried to answer the call to pray without ceasing, to pray the prayer of Christ Himself, to participate in the prayer that sanctifies the day.

I am neither a holy man nor a saint. I am not as faithful as I would like to be or as devout as this book implies. I am simply a man who wants to pray. And I have found these prayers helpful.

VENITE. It is an invitation given to us all. An invitation to pray the prayer of Christ. An invitation to pray the ancient prayer, until our lives become a prayer, one that is prayed without ceasing.

Venite adoremus.

THE FEAST OF THE EPIPHANY 2000
NASHVILLE, TENNESSEE

VENITE

THE PRACTICE

To attempt to tell someone else how to pray is frightening, presumptuous by its very nature. I cannot do that. However, I can tell you how best to use this book. Or, at least, how best to begin to use it.

At some point, you may well discover things that make sense for you that I have not yet recognized. When that happens, ignore what I have written and follow what you know. Leave out whole sections if you want, or supplement them with new things. I myself have not finished making this book; I have only, as a friend of mine said, taken a snapshot of it in its present state.

The book is divided into six parts—*The Office, The Seasons, The Remembrances, The Canticles, The Psalter,* and *The Gospel.* At the beginning of each section you will find some additional notes regarding the individual section, notes that you might find beneficial from time to time in helping you to understand or modify your practice a bit. And in the *Appendix,* there is a note or two about other things that will deepen your understanding of the meaning of certain words, books to read, resources to explore, and so forth.

THE OFFICES

There are four daily Offices in this prayerbook—*Morning* (*Lauds*), *Midday* (*None*), *Evening* (*Vespers*), and *Night* (*Compline*). The structures for all four of them are parallel, mirroring the rhythm of the mass, the basic pattern for worship in the liturgical tradition. That basic pattern—praise, confession, hearing the Word, going forth—is vital to begin to hold in your heart.

Each *Office* begins with a *Versicle,* a short sentence or two that is meant to be said aloud as a call to worship, and followed by a moment of silence.

Next is the *Venite*—the invitation to prayer. It is a Psalm that has been traditionally used in this way for a particular *Office.* It is followed by the *Gloria.*

Then come the *Collects* for the Season, the Day, and the specific Office. These prayers are to be said one right after the other, as a way to place ourselves within the Season of the Story, the Communion of Saints, and the particular part of the Day. The Collects themselves are found in the sections for *Seasons* and *Remembrances.* One need not say all of the Collects at every Office, but should say all three Collects throughout the course of the day.

The *Canticle,* either for the Day or for the Office, is said next. The Canticle for the Day is found in the *Canticles* section, the one for the specific Office is found within each Office.

The *Lessons* for the Day are to be read next—from the *Psalter,* the Canticles, the *Gospel,* or from other texts. There are separate sections for each set of readings, organized into a thirty-day cycle. One need not read all of the Lessons at each Office; one must determine one's own habits based on time, circumstance, and the kind of Scripture reading to which one is drawn at a particular point in one's journey.

Then the *Prayers of the People* are said, a set of thanksgivings, petitions, and intercessions for the day, for the various activities of one's life, and for people and concerns that are a part of your everyday life. The prayers are written in such a way that one can easily add in intercessions and petitions for people and concerns. This part of the Office always ends with the *Our Father*.

Finally, there is a *Blessing,* one especially for the particular Office.

There are three other "Offices" included here, and they follow the same basic structural pattern, though the Collects for the Season and the Day are not used, and the Lessons may or may not be read, as you choose.

The first is a *Table Office* (*Gratia*) to be used at the evening meal alone or with family and friends on a regular basis on special days. The second is a Communion service. The third is an office of *Commemoration* that can be said in solitude upon the news of the death of a friend or loved one.

Each of us must begin to practice as well as we can, perhaps with one Office or two; perhaps reading all of the texts from the book at one Office each day and then simply saying the Office itself at other times because of the pressures of time and circumstance. Each of the Offices can be said in as little as five to ten minutes, depending on the number of readings and the amount of time spent in silence and other variables.

For example, a person may choose to spend a longer time with the Morning Office, reading the Collects for the Day, the Canticle, all of the Psalms, and the readings before the day begins when there is more quiet. Another person may find their schedule is such that this reading is best done at night. Someone may choose to do only the Office itself and use the additional time for prayer or meditation or journaling. Some may find that the reading of some texts at each Office makes the most sense.

We are admonished by St. Paul to "work out our own salvation with fear and trembling." The same could be said of working out our prayer.

THE SEASONS

In the Church, there are two calendars. One is known as the *Temporale,* the calendar of Days and Seasons whose calendar dates vary according to Easter or according to other festival days. In order for you to pray with the communion of the faithful, a seasonal arrangement of these prayers is helpful.

In each of the four daily Offices, there is a place for the Collect of the Season. These are prayers that lead us through the movements of the liturgical calendar, giving us words by which our prayer converts us continually to the Story of us all.

The other calendar of the Church is known as the *Sanctorale,* the calendar of festival days, feasts, and other remembrances that have fixed dates during the year. Saying these prayers, within the *Office,* connects our prayer with the Communion of Saints in a way that allows us to give thanks for all of the faithful of time past, as well as to remind us of our own calling and vocation to build the kingdom.

The prayers of Remembrance in this book are on thirty two-page spreads, one spread for each day of each month. (The last spread includes Remembrances for both the 30th and the 31st days of the month.)

There are prayers for major feasts of the Church, as well as for specific saints or groups whose contributions to the Church have shaped the lives of all the faithful. There are also prayers for events or for specific intentions that will make it possible for you to join your prayer with others around the world.

THE CANTICLES

Canticles, the songs of praise, are included in this section. There are thirty of them and they are meant to be used in addition to or in the place of the opening or closing Canticle that is specific to the Office itself.

These ancient songs of praise and worship contain within them the foundational truths of Christianity. They carry within them many of the statements that we not only cling to most tenaciously but also, from time to time, find the hardest to believe or even understand. Who among us has not found ourselves taking a deep breath when we come to certain statements in the creeds?

To offer the Canticles as part of our prayer, whether read or chanted, is to continually expose ourselves to their truths and their claims on our hearts and minds, and to continually offer up our praise with the Communion of Saints who have gone before.

THE PSALTER

The ancient tradition of praying the Psalms goes back hundreds of years before the time of Christ. To pray the Psalms in a regular pattern, in this case a thirty-day cycle, is to pray the prayerbook of the Bible, to pray the prayer that the people of the Hebrew and Christian traditions have always prayed, and it is to allow these deep prayers to begin to shape us and to transform us.

As is found in many traditions, the *Psalter* for the Office is arranged so that there are Psalms for the morning and Psalms for the evening, although the decision to say all of them at once or not, or to say one or two at each of the Offices, is up to each person.

THE GOSPEL

The *Gospel* is a thirty-day cycle of thematically arranged quotations of Jesus from the Gospels. A somewhat longer explanation is helpful here.

In the tradition, the readings for every day include passages from the Gospels, the Letters, and other New Testament works, as well as extra-canonical gospels written in the first century after Christ. There are various systems for arranging those readings so that they engage the reader, if followed faithfully, in the whole of the Story of God's people. This book does not, for reasons of space and ease of use, incorporate that basic pattern. (You will find references to them in the bibliography.)

Instead, the premise here is that those who are drawn to such a significant practice of prayer as this one are likely to be mighty familiar with the Story, part of a worshiping community whose practice includes the regular reading of the Story, and, not least, likely to be at a place in their journey where the questions are more about what it means to follow Christ than about wrestling with the Story as a whole.

For better or worse, the choice has been made here to provide a cycle of readings that focuses on the teachings of Christ for those who would follow him, in such a way that we are compelled to hear clearly and repeatedly his call and claim on our lives.

All of that said, there are some other things that you should know about this book and how to use it in your prayer.

THE OCCASIONAL PRAYERS

On the endsheets of this book, both front and back, there is a selection of prayers that can be used at various times or in various circumstances. They can also be used as Collects in any of the Offices.

THE LANGUAGE

The words that are here are paraphrases and adaptations of the words from several sources. They are acknowledged and referenced in the back of the book. The choices of the principles guiding the paraphrasing and language should be clarified.

First is that all of the material, save the *Gospel*, is written in the first person plural. We do not pray alone, neither do we pray just for ourselves. One of the keys to the discipline of the prayer of the *Office* is the realization that when we pray the *Office*, we are joining our voices with a great multitude unknown to us who are marking the same *Office* at the same time each day. Another key is the understanding that when we pray, we do so for, on behalf of, and in the place of those who cannot pray or do not pray, for whatever the reason.

A second guiding principle concerns the use of the second person when addressing God, and the subsequent capitalization of certain words. Our addressing of God directly in this way helps to personalize a way of prayer whose formality is often a discouragement to those who would pray it. The capitalization of the pronouns that refer to God, and certain nouns, is a reminder of Whom we are addressing. Hence, you will find throughout a combination of the familiar and the formal.

The third guiding principle addresses the question of inclusive language. There are few exceptions to a strict insistence on making the language inclusive and they occur in places where the sheer poetics, history, tradition, and other considerations rendered the author helplessly torn between the great and beautiful language of the tradition and some new way of expressing the same without being poetic enough. Even though newer and more inclusive words have become more and more commonly used as time has gone by, and rightly so, in many ways, it seems to me that in some cases the older words carry rich meaning that we are wise to hold on to.

Whenever possible, a combination of using first lines only, or ellipses, or some other literary device was used to allow you to insert your own names for God so that the overall work is as inclusive as possible. For any shortcomings, I ask forgiveness.

THE WORD OF CAUTION

There is a great temptation to succumb to the notion that one can go from saying no Office at all to saying all of the four daily Offices, complete with all of the Collects and all of the Lessons, in one gigantic leap. Unless one joins a community where that is part of the practice, and where, therefore, everything about the daily life is arranged for that purpose, such a leap is seldom possible. Indeed, even thinking that one might make such a leap is to create an enormous potential for failure and frustration.

The experience of many who, as individuals drawn to pray the daily prayer on their own, have traveled this way before is that the best approach is to begin slowly, and to add to your practice as you become more familiar with the ways of the liturgy. Begin with one Office, the one that speaks to you most clearly, and work with it for a time until it has become part of your habit. Read only the Psalter at the Lessons until it has begun to be comfortable to you. Say only the seasonal Collects for a time to avoid the frustration of drowning in a sea of page-turning. There is no hurry, this is not a contest. We are called to pray, not to achieve.

One of my friends once reminded me, "The Rule that you cannot keep just might be someone else's Rule." Find your own way, and be gentle with yourself. Pray as you can, not as you ought.

These pages have been good companions to me, and to some of my fellow pilgrims, over the course of my journey. They are offered to you, humbly, and in prayer, that they might become agreeable companions to you as well.

—THE AUTHOR

Notes for Saying the Office

Read slowly, breathing between lines and phrases, with reverence and care for the art of the prayer.

The roman type is said by the leader, the italics are said as responses by everyone else. Of course, the italic information in brackets is not said by anyone. Some parts of the Office—the Canticle or the *Our Father,* for example—are best said in unison. Let your tradition and your own intuition be your guide. If you say the Office alone, then you say all of the words, including the italicized ones.

The *Gloria*—Glory be to the . . .—is deliberately left unfinished to allow you to use the traditional words—Father, Son, and Holy Spirit—or other words if you choose. The mark [†] indicates making the sign of the cross, which may or may not be done, depending on your own practice.

The Collect for the Office itself can be preceded by the proper Collect(s) for the Season or the Day as found in the Seasons and Remembrances sections. The only exceptions are the Table Office and the Office of Commemoration: only the Collect for that Office is to be said.

The Canticle to be read at the Office can be either the particular Canticle that has been included in the Office or the one for the Day as found in the Canticles section. Or both can be said, with one of them used between Lessons, or as a Lesson itself.

The choice of Lessons, as well as the number of them for any one of the Offices, is up to you. They can be taken from the Canticles, the Psalter, the Gospel, or, to be sure, any other recommended sequence of readings to which you subscribe. For example, you may choose to read all of the Psalms at the Morning Office, or to space them out over the course of all the Offices. You may choose to read both parts of the Gospel at once, or perhaps one part at Morning prayer and the other at Vespers. Let your own rhythms, time frames, and experience be your guide. Whatever guidelines you use to govern your reading of Scripture, maintain silence after each reading to allow the Word to resonate within you.

In the Prayers of the People, the designation [*n*] is a reminder to say names or particular petitions aloud or silently.

If there is to be Communion in conjunction with any of the Offices, it should begin after the *Our Father.*

Finally, remember that you do not make these prayers alone, neither do you make them for yourself. At any time that you say an Office, there is a great host of the community of the faithful making the same prayer at the same time. And there is a great host of your brothers and sisters who cannot, for various reasons, offer these prayers: your prayer is offered on their behalf and in their place.

THE OFFICE

May the lifting of our hands be as a sacrifice;
   may our prayer rise as incense before You.
      —FROM THE PSALMS

Deliver us when we draw near to You,
   from coldness of heart and wanderings of mind:
Grant that with steadfast thoughts and kindled affections,
   we may worship You in spirit and in truth. *Amen.*
      —A COLLECT BEFORE WORSHIP

I must say my Office with great care.
   It is my daily offering of fresh flowers to the Beloved Spouse.
      —CHARLES DE FOUCAULD

[Versicle]
God said: "Let there be light"; and there was light,
   And God saw that the light was good.
This very day the Lord has acted.
   May God's Name be praised.

[Venite : Venite, exultemus : Psalm 95]
Come, let us raise a joyful song,
   a shout of triumph to the rock of our salvation.
Let us come into Your presence with thanksgiving,
   singing songs of triumph.
For You are a great God, a great king over all gods.
   The depths of the earth are in Your hands; mountains belong to You.
The sea is Yours, for You made it;
   and the dry land Your hands fashioned.
Let us bow down in worship, let us kneel before the One who made us.
   For You are our God, and we are the flock that You shepherd.
We will know Your power and presence this day,
   if we will but listen for Your voice.
   [†] *Glory be to . . . Amen.*

[Collect : Of the Season, the Day, and the Office]
Drive far from us all wrong desires,
   and incline our hearts to keep Your ways:
Grant that having cheerfully done Your will this day,
   we may, when night comes, rejoice and give You thanks;
through the One Who lives and reigns with You and the Holy Spirit,
   one God, now and for ever.
   Amen.

[Canticle: Benedictus : Zechariah's Song (or the Canticle for the Day)]
Blessed be God, who has turned to His people and saved us and set us free.
   You have raised up for us a strong deliverer, and so You promised:
Age after age You proclaimed by the lips of Your holy prophets,
   that You would deliver us, calling to mind Your solemn covenant.
This was the promise that You made: To rescue us and free us from fear,
   so that we might worship You with a holy worship,
in Your holy presence our whole life long.
   In Your tender compassion, the morning sun has risen upon us—
to shine on us in our darkness, to guide our feet into the paths of peace.

[Lessons to be chosen from the Psalter, Canticles, Gospel, or other texts]

[Prayers of the People]

We give You thanks, Almighty God: For all Your gifts
    so freely bestowed upon us and all whom You have made:
We bless You for our creation, preservation, and all the blessings of life;
    above all, for the redemption of the world by our Lord Jesus Christ,
for the hope of glory and for the means of grace.
    We thank You, O Lord.

Grant us such an awareness of Your mercies, we pray,
    that with truly thankful hearts, we may give You praise,
not only with our lips, but in our lives, by giving ourselves to Your service,
    and by walking before You in holiness and righteousness all our days.
    Hear us, O Lord.

We offer prayers for all those with whom we share the Journey:
For our loved ones, those who have been given to us,
    and to whom we have been given: [*n*].
    Lord, have mercy; *Christ, have mercy.*
For those whom we have loved who are now absent from us: [*n*].
    Lord, have mercy; *Christ, have mercy.*
And for those we know who face particular trials and tests this day: [*n*].
    Lord, have mercy; *Christ, have mercy.*
We entrust all who are dear to us to Your never-failing love and care,
    for this life and the life to come;
knowing that You will do for them
    far more than we can desire or pray for.
    Amen.

Now with all your people on earth, we pray the prayer
    that Jesus taught those He called brothers and sisters and friends:
    Our Father . . . Amen.

[Blessing]

[†] Thanks be to God—Creator, Redeemer, and Giver of Life.
    We go in peace to serve the Lord,
and may the grace of the Lord Jesus Christ go with us all.
    Amen.

[*Versicle*]
Let the words of our mouths, and the meditations of our hearts,
   be acceptable in Your sight, O Lord, our strength and our redeemer.

   [*Venite : In quo corrigit? : Psalm 119, Beth*]
How shall we cleanse our ways?
   By keeping Your word.
With our whole hearts we seek You;
   let us not stray from Your commandments.
We treasure Your promises within us, that we may not sin against You.
   Blessed are You, O Lord; instruct us in Your ways.
We take greater delight in the way of Your decrees
   than in all manner of riches.
Our delight is in You, O Lord, we will not forget Your word.
   [†] *Glory be to . . . Amen.*

   [*Collect : Of the Season, the Day, and the Office*]
Deliver us from the service of self alone,
   that we may do the work You have given us to do,
in truth and beauty, and for the common good;
   for the sake of the One who comes among us as one who serves;
and Who lives and reigns with You and the Holy Spirit,
   one God, now and for ever.
   Amen.

   [*Canticle : Gloria in excelsis (or the Canticle for the Day)*]
Glory to God in the highest, and peace to His people on earth.
   Lord God, Heavenly king, Almighty God and Father:
We worship You, we give You thanks, we praise You for Your glory.
   Lord Jesus Christ, only Son of the Father, Lord God, Lamb of God:
You take away the sins of the world, have mercy on us;
   You are seated at the right hand of the Father, receive our prayer.
For You alone are the Holy One, You alone are the Lord;
   You alone are the Most High, Jesus Christ,
with the Holy Spirit, in the glory of God the Father.

   [*Lessons to be chosen from the Psalter, Canticles, Gospel, or other texts*]

[Prayers of the People]

We give You thanks, Almighty God,
    for the gift of the Church and its people and its work:
For the mothers and fathers of the faith, and all the faithful of time past;
    for Your holy prophets and apostles,
and all martyrs and saints in every age and in every land;
    for all who serve You as servants and stewards of Your divine mysteries,
and those who have taught us Your Story and shown us Your ways.
      We thank You, O Lord.
You have made us one with Your saints in heaven and earth:
    Grant that in our pilgrimage, we may always be supported
by this fellowship of love and prayer, and know ourselves
    to be surrounded by their witness to Your power and mercy.
      Hear us, O Lord.
We offer prayers for the holy catholic Church, and all who seek the Truth:
    For the holy communities of which we are a part: [*n*].
      Lord, have mercy; *Christ, have mercy.*
For all bishops, priests, ministers, and leaders: [*n*].
      Lord, have mercy; *Christ, have mercy.*
For the companions to whom we have promised
    our faithfulness and prayers: [*n*].
      Lord, have mercy; *Christ, have mercy.*
Accept the prayers of Your people, we pray, and in Your mercy,
    look with compassion on all who turn to You for help:
Grant that we may find You and be found by You;
    that our divisions may cease; that we may be united in Your truth;
and walk together in love to bear witness to Your glory in the world.
      Amen.
Now with all your people on earth, we pray the prayer
    that Jesus taught those He called brothers and sisters and friends:
      Our Father . . . Amen.

[Blessing]

[†] Thanks be to God—Creator, Redeemer, and Giver of Life.
    May the grace of the Lord Jesus Christ, and the love of God,
and the fellowship of the Holy Spirit be with us all, for evermore.
      Amen.

[*Versicle*]
Send out Your light and Your truth that they may lead us,
and bring us to Your holy hill and dwelling.

[*Venite: Levavi, oculos : Psalm 121*]
We lift our eyes to the hills, where shall our help come from?
Our help comes from the Lord, the maker of heaven and earth.
You are our defense, our guardian Who never slumbers and never sleeps.
How could the One Who guards us sleep, or let our feet stumble?
You will guard us against all evil, guard us body and soul;
the sun will not strike us by day, nor the moon by night
You will guard our going out and our coming home,
from this time forth, for evermore.
[†] *Glory be to . . . Amen.*

[*Collect : Of the Season, the Day, and the Office*]
You made this day for the works of the light,
and this night for the refreshment of our minds and bodies:
Keep us now in Christ; grant us a peaceful evening,
and a night free from sin, and bring us at last to eternal life;
through the One Who lives and reigns with You and the Holy Spirit,
one God, now and for ever.
Amen.

[*Canticle : Magnificat : Mary's Song (or the Canticle for the Day)*]
Our souls proclaim the glory of the Lord;
our spirits rejoice in God, our Saviour,
For You have looked with favor upon Your lowly servant.
You have done great things and holy is Your Name.
You have mercy on those who fear You;
You have cast down the mighty, and lifted the lowly;
You have filled the hungry with good things,
and sent the rich away empty.
You have come to Your children and set them free,
for You have remembered Your promise of mercy
to our mothers and fathers, and to all Your children forever.

[*Lessons to be chosen from the Psalter, Canticles, Gospel, or other texts*]

We give You thanks, Almighty God,
    for all Your gifts and graces to us this day:
For the splendor of the whole creation and the beauty of this world;
    for the wonder of life and the mystery of love;
for the blessings of family and friends,
    and the loving care that surrounds us on every side.
We are grateful for this day's work,
    for the things that demanded our best, and things that delighted us;
and for disappointments and failures that lead us to depend on You truly.
    We thank You, O Lord.
Stay with us, O LORD, for evening is at hand and the day is done.
    Be our light in the darkness, we pray,
and in Your great mercy,
    defend us from all perils and dangers of this night.
    Hear us, O Lord.
We offer prayers for the welfare of the whole world,
    and for all people in their daily life and work:
For all who hold authority,
    and all who work for freedom, justice and peace: [*n*].
    Amen.
For all who suffer,
    and for all who remember and care for them: [*n*].
    Lord, have mercy; *Christ, have mercy.*
And for all those in whom we have seen the Christ this day,
    in joy and in sorrow [*n*].
    Amen.
Now with all your people on earth, we pray the prayer
    that Jesus taught those He called brothers and sisters and friends:
    Our Father . . . Amen.

    [Blessing]
[†] Thanks be to God—Creator, Redeemer, and Giver of Life.
    May the Lord be with us, may the holy angels bring us peace,
and may the grace of the Lord Jesus Christ be always with us.
    Amen.

[*Versicle*]
May the Lord grant us a quiet night,
a quiet night and peace at the last.

[*Venite : Domine, investigasti: Psalm 139*]
Lord, You have examined us and know us well;
    You know everything about us.
You know our thoughts;
    there is not a word on our lips that You do not know.
You are familiar with all our paths;
    You have traced our journeys and our resting places.
You have kept close guard on us,
    And You have spread Your hand over us.
Such knowledge is beyond our understanding;
    it is so high and so deep that we cannot grasp it.
Examine us, O God: Know our thoughts and understand our fears.
    Watch over us, lest we take any path that grieves You,
And guide us in the Ancient and everlasting ways.
    [†] *Glory be to . . . Amen.*

[*Collect : Of the Season, the Day, and the Office*]
Almighty God: Look down from on high;
    and illumine this night with Your light:
that by night as by day your people may glorify Your holy Name;
    through the One Who lives and reigns with You and the holy Spirit,
one God, now and for ever.
    Amen.

[*Canticle : Nunc dimittis : Simeon's Song (or the Canticle for the Day)*]
Lord, now let Your servants depart in peace, as You have promised:
    For with our own eyes we have seen the Saviour,
the One You prepared for all the world to see,
    The Light to enlighten all the earth,
and to bring glory to Your people for evermore.

[*Lessons to be chosen from the Psalter, Canticles, Gospel, or other texts*]

[Prayers of the People]

We give you thanks, Almighty God, for the gift of Your divine Son:
    For the truth of His word and the example of His life;
for His steadfast obedience, by which He overcame temptation;
    for His dying, through which he overcame death;
and for His rising to life again, through which we are raised to new life.
      We thank You, O Lord.
We confess that we have sinned against You this day:
    some of our sin we know, and some is known only to You . . .
    (silence)
We are truly sorry and we humbly repent.
    For the sake of Your Son Jesus Christ,
[†] have mercy on us and forgive us,
    that we may delight in Your will, and walk in Your ways,
to the glory of Your Name.
    Amen.
Into Your hands, we commit our spirits;
    for You have redeemed us.
Keep us as the apple of Your eye,
    and hide us in the shadow of your wings.
      Lord, have mercy; *Christ, have mercy.*
Keep watch, dear LORD, with all who work or watch or weep this night,
    and give Your angels charge over those who sleep.
Tend the sick, we pray, and give rest to the weary;
    soothe the suffering and bless the dying;
pity the afflicted and shield the joyous;
    and all for Your love's sake.
    Amen.
Now with all your people on earth, we pray the prayer
    that Jesus taught those He called brothers and sisters and friends:
    Our Father . . . Amen.

[Blessing]

[†] Thanks be to God—Creator, Redeemer, and Giver of Life.
    May the LORD guide us waking, and guard us sleeping;
that awake we may watch with Christ and asleep we may rest in peace.
    Amen.

[*Versicle*]

Blessed are You, O God, Maker of all things:

For You give us food to sustain our lives and to make our hearts glad.

[*Venite: Laudate Dominum: Psalm 146*]

Happy are they whose help and hope is in the Almighty God:

For You made heaven and earth, and You keep faith for ever.

You give food to the hungry and justice to the oppressed.

You set prisoners free, open eyes that are blind,

And You lift up those who are bowed down.

You love the righteous, care for the stranger, and sustain the lonely.

And You shall reign for ever—alleluia.

[†] *Glory be to . . . Amen.*

[*Collect*]

We praise and thank You, O God,

for You are without beginning and without end.

Through Christ, You created the whole world;

through Christ, You preserve it.

You made this day for the works of the light,

and this night for the refreshments of our minds and bodies.

Keep us now in Christ;

grant us a peaceful evening and a night free from sin,

and bring us at last to eternal life;

through the One Who lives and reigns with You and the Holy Spirit,

one God, now and for ever.

Amen.

[*Canticle : Phos hilaron*]

O gracious Light, pure brightness of the ever living God in heaven;

O Jesus Christ, holy and blessed!

Now as we come to the setting of the sun,

and our eyes behold the vesper light, we sing Your praises.

You are worthy at all times to be praised by happy voices,

[†] Creator, Redeemer, and Giver of life

and to be glorified throughout the world.

[*Lessons to be chosen from the Psalter, Canticles, Gospel, or other texts*]

[Prayers of the People]

We give you thanks, Almighty God, for all Your goodness to us:
    Bless all Your gifts to our use and to Your service;
make us ever mindful of the needs of others,
    and ever grateful for Your providence.
For these and all Your mercies—
        We thank You, O Lord.
Keep watch, dear Lord, with all who work or watch or weep this night,
    and give Your angels charge over those who sleep:
Tend the sick, we pray, and give rest to the weary;
    bless the dying and soothe the suffering;
pity the afflicted and shield the joyous;
    and all for Your love's sake.
        Hear us, O Lord.
We offer prayers for those in whom
    we have seen the face and heard the voice of Christ this day,
in joy and in sorrow: [*n*].
        Lord, have mercy; *Christ, have mercy.*
Now with all Your people on earth, we pray the prayer
    that Jesus taught those he called brothers and sisters and friends:
        Our Father . . . Amen.

[Blessing]

[†] Thanks be to God—Creator, Redeemer, and Giver of Life.
    May the Lord be with us, may the holy angels bring us peace,
and may the grace of the Lord Jesus Christ be always with us.
        Amen.

[*Versicle*]

Be present to us, O Christ, as you were present to your disciples;
  that we may know You as You are revealed to us in the breaking of this Bread.

[*Confession of Sin, if one has not been said.*]

Most merciful God, we confess that we have sinned against You this day,
  in thought, word, and deed;
by what we have done, and by what we have left undone.
  We have not loved You with our whole hearts;
we have not loved our neighbors as ourselves.
  We are truly sorry and we humbly repent.
For the sake of Your Son Jesus Christ, have mercy on us and forgive us,
  that we may delight in Your will, and walk in Your ways,
to the glory of Your Name.
  Amen.
Grant to Your people pardon and peace,
  [†] that in Your great mercy, we may be forgiven all our sins,
and serve You with a quiet and contrite heart.
  Amen.

[*Great Thanksgiving*]

Let us give thanks to the Lord.
  It is right to give our thanks and praise.
It is right, and a good and joyful thing, always and everywhere
  to give thanks to You, Almighty God, Creator of heaven and earth.
Therefore we praise You, joining our voices with Angels and Archangels
  and with all the company of heaven,
who for ever sing this hymn to proclaim the glory of Your Name:
  Holy, holy, holy Lord, God of power and might:
  Heaven and earth are full of Your glory, hosanna in the highest.
  [†] *Blessed is he who comes in the Name of the Lord;*
  Hosanna in the highest.

Holy and gracious God:
  In Your infinite love You made us for Yourself;
and when we had fallen into sin and become subject to evil and death,
  You, in Your mercy, sent Jesus Christ, Your only and eternal Son,
to share our human nature, to live and die as one of us,
  to reconcile us to You, the God and Father of all.
He stretched out his arms upon the cross,
  and offered himself in obedience to Your will,
a perfect sacrifice for the whole world.

On the night he was handed over to suffering and death,
  our Lord Jesus Christ took bread;
and when He had given thanks to You,
  he broke it, and gave it to his disciples, and said,
"Take, eat: This is my Body, which is given for you.
  Do this for the remembrance of Me."
After supper he took the cup of wine;
  and when he had given thanks, he gave it to them, and said,
"Drink this, all of you: This is my Blood of the new Covenant,
  which is shed for you and for many for the forgiveness of sins.
Whenever you drink it, do this for the remembrance of Me."
  Therefore we proclaim the mystery of faith:
    Christ has died; Christ is risen; Christ will come again.

We celebrate the memorial of our redemption, O Father,
  in this sacrifice of praise and thanksgiving.
Recalling his death, resurrection, and ascension, we offer You these gifts.
  Sanctify them by Your Spirit
to be for Your people the Body and Blood of Your Son,
  the holy food and drink of new and unending life in him.
Sanctify us also that we may faithfully receive this holy Sacrament,
  and serve You in unity, constancy, and peace; and at the last day
bring us with all Your saints into the joy of Your eternal kingdom. Amen.
  All this we ask through Your Son Jesus Christ.
By him, and with him, and in him, in the unity of the Holy Spirit
  all honor and glory is Yours, Almighty Father, now and for ever.
    Amen.

  [*Breaking of the Bread*]
Christ our Passover was sacrificed for us.
  Therefore, let us keep the feast.
These are the gifts of God for the people of God.
  Take them in remembrance that Christ died for you,
and feed on Him in your hearts, with thanksgiving.

  [*Prayer after Receiving*]
Eternal God : *You have graciously accepted us*
  as living members of Your Son our Saviour, Jesus Christ;
and You have fed us with spiritual food in this holy Sacrament.
  Send us now into the world in peace, and grant us strength and courage
to love and serve You with gladness and singleness of heart.
    Amen.

  [*Blessing to be chosen from any of the Offices*]

[*Versicle*]

Give rest, O Lord, to all Your saints, where sorrow and pain are no more;
  where there is neither sighing, but life everlasting.

[*Venite : Dominus, pascit me : Psalm 23*]

You are our shepherd; we shall not want.
  You make us to lie down in green pastures; You lead us by still waters.
You restore our souls; and You guide us along the paths of righteousness.
  Though we travel the valley of the shadow of death, we will fear no evil;
For You are with us; Your rod and Your staff will comfort us.
  You have spread a table before us in the presence of our enemies.
You anoint us with Your blessing; our cup is running over.
  Surely goodness and mercy will follow us all of our days;
And we will dwell in Your house for ever.
  [†] *Glory be to . . . Amen.*

[*Collect*]

We commend [*n*] to You as (*he/she*) journeys beyond our sight:
  Receive [*him/her*] into the arms of Your mercy,
into the blessed rest of everlasting peace,
  and into the glorious company of Your saints.
Grant [*him/her*] entrance into the land of light and joy,
  and a place at Your table,
so to rejoice in Your presence and eternal glory,
  through the One Who lives and reigns with You and the Holy Spirit,
  one God, now and for ever.
    Amen.

[*Canticle*]

"I am Resurrection and I am Life," says the Lord.
  "Whoever has faith in me shall have life, even though they die.
Everyone who has life, and has committed themselves to me in faith,
  shall not die, for ever."
As for us, we know that our Redeemer lives,
  and that at the last He will stand upon the earth.
After our waking, He will raise us up; and we shall see You.
  We ourselves shall see, and our eyes behold,
the One Who is our friend and not a stranger.
  For none of us has life in ourselves;
none of us becomes our own master when we die.
  For if we have life, we are alive in You; and if we die, we die in You.
So then, whether we live or die, we belong to You.

[*Lessons to be chosen from the Psalter, Canticles, Gospel, or other texts*]

We give You thanks, Almighty God,
    for the good examples of all Your servants who,
having finished their course, now find true rest and refreshment.
    And we thank You for giving [*n*] to us
and to [*his/her*] family and friends,
    to know and to love as a companion on this earthly pilgrimage.
We remember the times and places and ways
    in which [*he/she*] was Christ to us,
their life shining forth with Your love and grace.
    We thank You, O Lord.
God of all mercies and Giver of all comfort:
    Deal graciously, we pray,
with all who mourn this death, especially: [*n*].
    Surround them with Your love
that they may not be overwhelmed by their loss,
    but have confidence in Your goodness,
to meet the days ahead with steadfastness and patience;
    not sorrowing as those without hope,
but in thankful remembrance and in joyful expectation
    of eternal life with all those that they love.
    Lord, have mercy; *Christ, have mercy.*
You brought us into being, Almighty God, and into Your arms we die:
    Hold us and comfort us in our grief; embrace us with Your love;
grant us hope in our confusion and sorrow;
    and grace to let go into new life.
    Lord, have mercy; *Christ, have mercy.*
And now, with all Your people, we pray the prayer that Jesus taught
    those he called brothers and sisters and friends:
    Our Father in heaven . . . Amen.

[Blessing]
Go forth upon Your journey, dear friend [*n*]:
    May your portion this day be in peace,
and your dwelling in the City of God,
    [†] In the Name of the One Who created you;
in the Name of the One Who suffered for you;
    and in the Name of the One Who strengthened you.
    Amen.
And may the Lord bless us and keep us:
    May the Lord make His face to shine upon us and be gracious unto us;
and may the Lord lift up His countenance upon us, and give us peace.
    Amen, and amen.

Notes for Saying the Collects for the Seasons

These are Collects to be said during the liturgical seasons and appointed days for feasts, fasts, and other commemorations. They are in the order of their appearance in the calendar year, though the specific date varies from year to year.

The length of the seasons, in many cases, is variable, depending on the date of Easter in a given year, and so we have done our best to provide a general frame for the seasons that you can use to follow the liturgical calendar. Let your practice be guided by that of your community from year to year. Such rules should guide your choices as to colors, other names for the Seasons or feast days, and so forth.

The *Collect for the Season* is meant to be used following the *Venite* during the Office, though you certainly may choose to only use the Collect for the Season once each day. If one were to say all of the Collects following the Venite, there would be three of them—one for the Season, one for the Remembrance, and the Collect for the specific Office (the Collect that is found in the text for each Office). To be sure, you will want to try different patterns—perhaps the seasonal Collect always at Midday, for example, or the Remembrance at the beginning of the day—to discover the one that seems best to you.

The numbers that appear in parentheses are for specific Psalms that are generally read at particular Remembrances or during particular Seasons. You may want to change your Scripture reading for the Day or the Season to include the particular Psalm.

The ellipsis (. . .) is to remind you to finish the Collect as you would like in order to lead to the next prayer or to lead to the *Canticle*. For example, one may want to close the prayer by simply saying *Amen,* or by saying *In the Name of* . . . , or by using some other closing phrase.

Finally, if you have not followed the liturgical calendar before, it may take some getting used to. Be patient, both with the calendar and with yourself. The Story is meant to unfold over time, and if you are faithful to the practice, you may be assured that it will begin to do so.

THE SEASONS

We shall speak of Your mighty acts, and tell of Your greatness,
    We shall publish the remembrance of Your goodness,
and sing of Your righteousness.
        —FROM THE PSALMS

You wonderfully created, Almighty God,
    and yet more wonderfully restored the dignity of our human nature:
Grant that we who remember the story of the One You sent,
    the One Who humbled himself to share in our humanity,
may come to share in his divine life. *Amen.*
        —A COLLECT FOR THE SEASONS

Let us be attentive to enter into the meaning of the liturgical action;
    let us seek to perceive something of the invisible reality of the kingdom.
        —FROM THE RULE OF TAIZÉ

A Collect for Advent : *Daily to O Sapienta, 17 December (85)*
You sent Your messengers, the prophets,
    to preach repentance and to prepare the way for our salvation:
Give us grace to heed their warnings, and to forsake our sins,
    that we may greet with joy the coming of our Redeemer . . .

Winter Ember Days : *Wednesday after 13 December (135)*
In Your providence, You have appointed various orders in Your Church:
    Grant Your grace to all who are called to any office and ministry,
and so fill them with truth, and clothe them with holiness of life,
    that they may faithfully serve You to the glory of Your Name . . .

Winter Ember Days : *Friday after 13 December (63)*
You led Your holy apostles to ordain ministers in every place:
    Grant that Your Church, by Your Spirit,
may choose suitable persons for the ministry of Word and Sacrament,
    and may uphold them in their work for the building of Your kingdom . . .

Winter Ember Days : *Saturday after 13 December (15)*
By Your Spirit, the whole body of Your faithful people is sanctified:
    Receive our prayers and supplications,
which we offer for all Your people,
    that in their vocation they may truly and devoutly serve You . . .

A Collect for Christmastide : *Daily until Twelfth Night, 5 January (96)*
You make us glad by the yearly festival
    of the birth of Your Divine Son Jesus Christ:
Grant that we who joyfully revere him as our Saviour,
    may behold him with sure confidence when he comes to be our judge . . .

The Feast of the Holy Family : *First Sunday after Christmas (132)*
Your Divine Son shared at Nazareth in a life like our own,
    the life of an earthly home:
Help us to live as the holy family, united in love and obedience,
    and bring us at last to our home in heaven . . .

A COLLECT FOR EPIPHANY : *Daily until Ash Wednesday (72)*
In the work of Your creation, Almighty God,
    You commanded the Light to shine out of the darkness:
Grant that the light of the gospel of Christ may shine into the hearts of all,
    dispelling the darkness of unbelief, and revealing Your glory in the world . . .

THE FEAST OF THE BAPTISM OF OUR LORD : *First Sunday of Epiphany (89)*
At the baptism of Jesus in the River Jordan,
    You proclaimed him Your beloved Son, anointing him with the Spirit:
Grant that we, who are baptized in his name, may keep our covenant,
    and boldly confess him as Lord and Saviour . . .

ASH WEDNESDAY : *About fifty Days before Easter Sunday (103)*
You hate nothing that You have made, and You forgive the sins
    of all who are truly penitent: Create in us new hearts that we,
worthily lamenting our sins and acknowledging our wickedness,
    may obtain of You, God of all mercy, perfect remission and forgiveness . . .

THURSDAY AFTER ASH WEDNESDAY *(1)*
Direct us in all our doings with Your most gracious favor,
    and further us with Your continual help:
Grant that in all our works, begun, continued, and ended in You,
    we may glorify Your Name and, by Your mercy, obtain everlasting life . . .

FRIDAY AFTER ASH WEDNESDAY *(51)*
Support us with Your gracious favor,
    throughout the fast that we have begun:
Grant that as we observe it by bodily self-denial,
    so may we fulfill it by inner sincerity of heart . . .

SATURDAY AFTER ASH WEDNESDAY *(86)*
Mercifully look on all our infirmities,
    and in all our dangers and necessities,
stretch forth Your right hand to help and defend us . . .

A COLLECT FOR LENT : *Daily to Palm Sunday (51)*
You alone bring order to the unruly wills and affections of sinners:
    May we love what You command, and desire what You promise,
so that, among the swift and varied changes of this world,
    our hearts may be fixed where true joy is to be found . . .

SPRING EMBER DAYS : *Wednesday after the First Sunday of Lent (135)*
In Your providence, You have appointed various orders in Your Church:
    Grant Your grace to all who are called to any office and ministry,
and so fill them with truth and clothe them with holiness of life,
    that they may faithfully serve You to the glory of Your Name . . .

SPRING EMBER DAYS : *Friday after the First Sunday of Lent (63)*
You led Your holy apostles to ordain ministers in every place:
    Grant that Your Church, by Your Spirit,
may choose suitable persons for the ministry of Word and Sacrament,
    and may uphold them in their work for the building of Your kingdom . . .

SPRING EMBER DAYS : *Saturday after the First Sunday of Lent (15)*
By Your Spirit, the whole body of Your faithful people is sanctified:
    Receive our prayers and supplications,
which we offer for all Your people,
    that in our vocation we may truly and devoutly serve You . . .

PALM SUNDAY : THE FEAST OF THE PASSION OF OUR LORD *(118)*
In Your tender love for the human race, You sent Your Divine Son,
    to take upon him our nature, showing us his great humility:
Grant that we may walk in the way of his suffering,
    and share in the joy of his resurrection . . .

Holy Monday *(36)*

Your most dear Son went not up to joy but first he suffered pain,
 and entered not into glory but first he was crucified:
Grant that we, walking in the way of the cross,
 may find it none other than the way of life and peace . . .

Holy Tuesday *(71)*

By the passion of Your Divine Son,
 You caused an instrument of shameful death to be for us the means of life:
Grant us so to glory in the cross of Christ,
 that we may gladly suffer shame and loss for the sake of Your Son . . .

Holy Wednesday *(69)*

Your Divine Son gave his body to be whipped,
 and his face to be spat upon:
Give us grace to accept joyfully the sufferings of our time,
 confident of the glory that shall be revealed . . .

Maundy Thursday *(78)*

Your Divine Son, on the night before he suffered death,
 instituted the sacrament of his Body and Blood:
Grant that we may receive it thankfully, in remembrance of him,
 who in these holy mysteries gives to us a pledge of eternal life . . .

Good Friday *(22)*

We pray You graciously to uphold this Your family,
 for whom Jesus was willing to be betrayed,
and to suffer death upon the cross . . .

Holy Saturday *(130)*

The crucified body of Your Divine Son
 was laid in the tomb and rested on this holy sabbath:
give us grace to await with him the coming of the third day,
 and rise with him into newness of life . . .

Easter Eve : The Vigil for the Resurrection of Our Lord *(36)*

You made this most holy night to shine with the glory of the resurrection,
 and have bestowed upon us the brightness of Your light:
Sanctify this fire within us, and grant that we may so burn with holy desire
 that with pure minds we may attain to the festival of everlasting light . . .

EASTER SUNDAY : THE FEAST OF THE RESURRECTION OF OUR LORD *(118)*
Through Your Divine Son, You overcame death
   and opened to us the gates of the life that does not end:
Grant that we who celebrate this day with joy
   may be raised from the death of sin by Your life-giving spirit . . .

EASTER MONDAY *(36)*
Your most dear Son went not up to joy but first he suffered pain,
   and entered not into glory but first he was crucified:
Grant that we, walking in the way of the cross,
   may find it none other than the way of life and peace . . .

EASTER TUESDAY *(33)*
By the glorious resurrection of Your Divine Son,
   You destroyed death and brought life and immortality to light:
Grant that we, who have been raised with him,
   may abide in his presence and rejoice in the hope of eternal glory . . .

EASTER WEDNESDAY *(105)*
Your blessed Son made himself known to his disciples
   in the breaking of bread:
Open the eyes of our faith, we pray,
   that we may behold him in all his redeeming work . . .

EASTER THURSDAY *(8)*
In the Paschal mystery,
   You established the new covenant of reconciliation:
Grant that all who have been reborn into the fellowship of Christ's Body
   may show forth in our lives what we profess by our faith . . .

EASTER FRIDAY *(116)*
You gave Your Divine Son to die for our sins
   and to rise for our justification:
Grant us grace so to put away the leaven of malice and wickedness
   that we may always serve You in purity of living and truth . . .

EASTER SATURDAY *(118)*
We thank You that You have delivered us from the dominion of sin and death,
   and brought us into the kingdom of Your Son:
Grant we pray that, as by his death he has recalled us to life,
   so by his love he may raise us to eternal joy . . .

A COLLECT FOR EASTERTIDE : *Daily until Ascension Eve (8)*
In the Paschal mystery,
   You established the new covenant of reconciliation:
Grant that all who have been reborn into the fellowship of Christ's Body
   may show forth in our lives what we profess by our faith . . .

ROGATION DAYS : *Monday after the Sixth Sunday of Easter (147)*
We pray that Your gracious providence may give
   and preserve to our use the harvest of the land and of the seas:
Prosper all who labor to gather them, that we,
   to whom You constantly give good things, may always give You thanks . . .

ROGATION DAYS : *Tuesday after the Sixth Sunday of Easter (107)*
Your Son shared our toil and hallowed our labor:
   Be present with us where we work;
may those who carry on our industries and commerce be responsive to Your will;
   and give us all a pride in what we do, and a just return for our labor . . .

ROGATION DAYS : *Wednesday after the Sixth Sunday of Easter (104)*
Your hand is open wide to satisfy the needs of every living creature:
   Make us always thankful for Your providence;
and grant that we, remembering the account that we must one day give,
   may be faithful stewards of Your good gifts . . .

THE VIGIL FOR THE FEAST OF THE ASCENSION OF OUR LORD *(47)*
Grant, we pray, that as we believe Your divine Son
   to have ascended into heaven on this holy day to which we draw nigh,
so may we also in heart and mind there ascend,
   and with him continually dwell . . .

THE FEAST OF THE ASCENSION OF OUR LORD: *Forty Days after Easter (110)*
Your blessed Son ascended far above the heavens
   that he might fill all things:
Mercifully grant us faith to perceive that, according to his promise,
   he abides with us here on earth, even to the end of all ages . . .

A COLLECT FOR ASCENSIONTIDE : *Daily until Whitsunday (68)*
You have exalted Your divine Son with great triumph
   to Your kingdom in heaven:
Do not leave us comfortless, but send Your Spirit to strengthen us,
   and exalt us to the place where the Christ has gone before . . .

WHITSUNDAY : THE FEAST OF PENTECOST *(130)*
On this day, You taught the hearts of Your people,
 by sending them the light of Your Spirit:
Grant us, by the same Spirit, to have a right judgment in all things,
 and to evermore rejoice in Your holy comfort . . .

A COLLECT FOR PENTECOST : *Daily until Holy Cross Day (130)*
You opened Your Way to every race and to every nation,
 by the promised gift of Your Holy Spirit:
Shed abroad this power throughout the world, by the preaching of the Gospel,
 that it may reach to the ends of the earth . . .

SUMMER EMBER DAYS : *Wednesday after Whitsunday (135)*
In Your providence, You have appointed various orders in Your Church:
 Grant Your grace to all who are called to any office and ministry,
and so fill them with truth and clothe them with holiness of life,
 that they may faithfully serve You to the glory of Your Name . . .

SUMMER EMBER DAYS : *Friday after Whitsunday (63)*
You led Your holy apostles to ordain ministers in every place:
 Grant that Your Church, by Your Spirit,
may choose suitable persons for the ministry of Word and Sacrament,
 and may uphold them in their work for the building of Your kingdom . . .

SUMMER EMBER DAYS : *Saturday after Whitsunday (15)*
By Your Spirit, the whole body of Your faithful people is sanctified:
 Receive our prayers and supplications,
which we offer for all Your people,
 that in their vocation they may truly and devoutly serve You . . .

TRINITY SUNDAY : *First Sunday after Whitsunday (93)*
You have given us grace to acknowledge the glory of the eternal Trinity,
 and in Your power to worship its unity:
Keep us steadfast in faith and worship, we pray,
 and bring us at last to see You in Your one and eternal glory . . .

CORPUS CHRISTI : *Thursday after Trinity Sunday (116)*
You have given to us this memorial of the passion of Your Divine Son,
 the sacrament of his Body and Blood:
Grant us so to reverence this sacred mystery, that we may know within ourselves
 and show forth in our lives the glorious fruits of Your redemption . . .

THE FEAST OF THE DIVINE COMPASSION : *Twelve days after Whitsunday (36)*
Your Divine Son was moved with compassion for all who had gone astray,
    and with indignation for all who had suffered wrong:
Inflame our hearts with Your love that we may seek out the lost,
    have mercy on the fallen, and stand fast for truth and righteousness . . .

A COLLECT FOR ORDINARY TIME : *Daily until All Saints (145)*
You have taught us to keep Your commandments by loving You
    and our neighbor: Grant us the grace of Your Spirit
that we may be devoted to You with our whole heart,
    and united to one another in pure affection . . .

AUTUMN EMBER DAYS : *Wednesday after Holy Cross Day (135)*
In Your providence, You have appointed various orders in Your Church:
    Grant Your grace to all who are called to any office and ministry,
and so fill them with truth and clothe them with holiness of life,
    that they may faithfully serve You to the glory of Your Name . . .

AUTUMN EMBER DAYS : *Friday after Holy Cross Day (63)*
You led Your holy apostles to ordain ministers in every place:
    Grant that Your Church, by Your Spirit,
may choose suitable persons for the ministry of Word and Sacrament,
    and may uphold them in their work for the building of Your kingdom . . .

AUTUMN EMBER DAYS : *Saturday after Holy Cross Day (15)*
By Your Spirit, the whole body of Your faithful people is sanctified:
    Receive our prayers and supplications,
which we offer for all Your people,
    that in our vocation we may truly and devoutly serve You . . .

A COLLECT FOR KINGDOMTIDE : *Daily until Advent Sunday (146)*
By Your command, the order of time runs its course:
    Forgive our impatience, we pray,
and preserve our faith while we await the fulfillment of Your promises;
    and grant to us a good hope because of Your Word . . .

Notes for Saying the Prayers of Remembrance

This section is laid out in thirty two-page spreads, where you will find particular prayers for particular people, groups, and events that are remembered throughout various parts of the Church. To pray these Collects as they come around during the passing of time is to become a participant in the history and in the intercessory prayer of all faithful people of time past.

The Collect for the Day, the *Remembrance* as the term is used here, is meant to be used following the *Venite* during the office, though you certainly may choose to only use the collect for the Season on a particular day.

The numbers that appear in parentheses are for specific psalms that are generally read at a particular *Remembrance* or during particular seasons. You may want to change your Scripture reading for the day to include the particular Psalm.

The ellipsis (. . .) is to remind you to finish the collect as you would like in order to lead into the Collect for the Office. For example, one may want to close the prayer by simply saying *"Amen,"* or by saying *"In the Name of . . . ,"* or by using some other closing phrase.

Some of these people and holy days will be unfamiliar to you, and the hope is that you will do some digging on your own to learn more about the stories themselves. Some resources for that study are listed in the Appendix.

This is not a complete list of all the prayers for all of the holy days from every tradition within the Church, though it does provide a Collect for each day of each month with the exception of some prayers for days 30 and 31, and no prayer for February 29. Some selection was inevitable, and the choices have been made as carefully as possible to provide something of the width and breadth of the history and the ongoing practice of such prayer. In addition, you may well find that certain dates for specific *Remembrances* are different from the dates in the tradition with which you are most familiar. By virtue of the fact that this book reflects a range of traditions, such problems were simply unavoidable, and every effort was made to be as faithful to the ancient practice as possible.

THE REMEMBRANCES

You have declared Your word to Your children;
    And you have made Your ways known to them.
        —FROM THE PSALMS

You have made us one with your saints in heaven and earth:
    Grant that in our pilgrimage,
we may always be supported by this fellowship of love and prayer:
    And know ourselves to be surrounded
by their witness to Your power and mercy. *Amen*
        —A COLLECT FOR THE COMMUNITY OF SAINTS

The prayer of the Office is in the communion of saints.
    But to make real this communion of the faithful through the ages,
we must give ourselves up to ardent intercession
    for men and women and for the Church.
        —FROM THE RULE OF TAIZÉ

JAN • THE FEAST OF THE HOLY NAME OF OUR LORD *(8)*
You gave to Your Divine Son the holy name of Jesus
    to be the sign of our salvation:
Plant in every heart, we pray,
    the love of Him Who is the Saviour of the world . . .

FEB • THE VIGIL FOR CANDLEMAS, THE PRESENTATION OF OUR LORD *(84)*
Grant that our remembrance of this holy day to which we are drawing nigh,
    the day on which Your Divine Son was presented to You in Your temple,
may deepen our devotion and make us ever more prepared
    to come into Your holy presence . . .

MAR • DAVID : *Patron Saint of Wales, c. 544*
You called Your servant David to be a faithful and wise steward
    of Your divine mysteries for the people of Wales:
Grant that we, following his purity of life and zeal for the Gospel,
    may receive with him our heavenly rewards . . .

APR • HUGH OF GRENOBLE : *Bishop, France, 1053*
You raised up Your servant Hugh of Grenoble, Almighty God,
    to be a faithful shepherd of Your people:
Grant Your Spirit, we pray, to all bishops, priests, ministers, and leaders,
    that they also may serve You as true stewards of Your divine mysteries . . .

MAY • THE FEAST OF ST. PHILIP AND ST. JAMES *(119, Heth)*
You gave to Your apostles Philip and James grace and strength
    to bear witness to the Truth:
Grant that we, being mindful of their faith,
    may glorify in life and death the name of Our Lord Jesus Christ . . .

JUN • JUSTIN THE MARTYR : *Martyred at Rome, c. 167*
You found Your servant Justin wandering from teacher to teacher
    seeking You, and You revealed to him the sublime wisdom
of Your eternal Word: Grant that all who seek You,
    or a deeper knowledge of You, may find and be found by You . . .

JUL • OLIVER PLUNKET: *Bishop and Martyr, London, 1681*
In every age, You send those who give their lives for Your sake:
    Inspire us, we pray, with the memory of Your holy martyr Oliver Plunket,
Whose faithfulness led him in the way of the Cross,
    and give us courage to bear witness to Your love with our lives . . .

AUG • JOSEPH OF ARIMETHEA : *Disciple and Friend of Our Lord*
You gave Joseph of Arimethea the compassion and courage
    to provide for the burial of the body of Your Divine Son:
Grant to us hearts of compassion for our friends who are in need,
    and the courage to give generously to them no matter the cost . . .

SEP • GILES THE HERMIT: *Monk, Provence, c. 710*
Your Divine Son became poor that through His poverty we might become rich:
    Deliver us, we pray, from an inordinate love of this world, that we,
inspired by the devotion of Your servant Giles, may serve You with pure hearts,
    and attain to the riches of the world to come . . .

OCT • ST. THERESA OF LISIEUX : *Carmelite Mystic, France, 1897*
You have surrounded us with a great cloud of witnesses:
    Grant that we may be encouraged by Your servant Theresa,
and persevere in running the race that is set before us,
    until at last we may with her attain to Your eternal joy . . .

NOV • THE FEAST OF ALL SAINTS *(149)*
You have knit Your people together in one fellowship and communion
    in the mystical Body of Your Divine Son, Our Lord: Give us grace
so to follow Your blessed saints in all virtues and godly living,
    that we may come to the joy You have prepared for all who love You . . .

DEC • CHARLES DE FOUCAULD : *Founder of the Little Brothers of Jesus, 1916*
You built Your Church through the love and devotion of Your saints,
    and we give You thanks for Your servant Charles:
Inspire us to follow his example that we in our generation
    may rejoice with him in the vision of Your glory . . .

JAN • MACARIUS THE YOUNGER : *Desert Monk, Upper Egypt, c. 300*
Your Blessed Son became poor that through His poverty we might become rich:
  Deliver us, we pray, from an inordinate love of this world, that we, inspired by
Your servant Macarius the Younger, may serve You with singleness of heart,
  and attain to the riches of the age to come . . .

FEB • CANDLEMAS : **THE FEAST OF THE PRESENTATION OF OUR LORD** *(84)*
As Your Divine Son was this day presented in the temple:
  Grant, we pray, that we who celebrate this feast
may be presented to You with clean hands and pure hearts,
  by the grace of Our Lord Jesus Christ . . .

MAR • CHAD : *Bishop of Lichfield, England, 672*
Your servant Chad cheerfully relinquished the honors that had been given him:
  Keep us, we pray, from thinking more highly of ourselves than we should,
and ready at all times to step aside for others,
  that the cause of Christ might be advanced . . .

APR • FRANCIS OF PAOLA : *Founder of the Order of Minim Friars, France, 1507*
By Your grace, Francis of Paola, kindled with the flame of Your love,
  became a burning and shining light among Your people:
Grant that we also may be aflame with a spirit of love and discipline,
  and walk before You as children of light . . .

MAY • ATHANASIUS : *Bishop and Advisor to the Nicene Council, 373*
As You upheld Your servant Athanasius to proclaim boldly the Catholic faith:
  Uphold Your Church to proclaim the same,
trusting solely in the grace of Your eternal Word,
  who took on our humanity that we might share in His divinity . . .

JUN • MARTYRS OF LYON : *France, 177*
Grant that we who remember the sacrifice of Your holy martyrs of Lyons
  may be rooted and grounded in love of You:
and we pray that we may endure the sufferings of this life
  for the glory that is to be revealed in us . . .

JUL • SIMEON OF SALUS : *Monk and Hermit of Palestine, c. 590*
Your blessed Son became poor that through His poverty we might become rich:
     Deliver us, we pray, from an inordinate love of this world, that we, inspired by
the devotion of blessed Simeon of Salus, may serve You with singleness of heart,
     and attain to the riches of the age to come . . .

AUG • ALPHONSUS LIGUORI : *Founder, Congregation of the Most Holy Redeemer, 1781*
You kindled in Your servant Alphonsus
     a burning zeal for the salvation of souls:
Grant that we, taught by his doctrine and strengthened by his example,
     may happily attain to Your kingdom . . .

SEP • THE MARTYRS OF NEW GUINEA : *Martyred During World War II, 1942*
We remember before You this day the blessed martyrs of New Guinea
     who lay down their lives for their friends:
And we pray that we who honor their memory
     may imitate their loyalty and faith . . .

OCT • THE FEAST OF THE HOLY GUARDIAN ANGELS *(103)*
In Your unspeakable providence,
     You send Your holy angels for our safekeeping:
Grant unto us, we pray, that we may ever be defended by their protection,
     and rejoice in their eternal fellowship . . .

NOV • ALL SOULS' DAY *(130)*
Your Divine Son is the resurrection and the life of all the faithful:
     Raise us, we pray, from the death of sin to the life of righteousness,
that at the last, with the company of all faithful people,
     we may come into Your eternal joy . . .

DEC • NICHOLAS FERRAR : *Founder of Little Gidding, 1637*
You call Your witnesses from all peoples to reveal Your glory in their lives:
     Make us thankful for the example of Nicholas and all at Little Gidding,
and strengthen us by the memory of their community,
     that we may be faithful in the service of Your kingdom . . .

JAN • **GENEVIEVE** : *Nun and Patron of Paris, c. 435*
You created us in Your image, Almighty God:
Grant us grace to contend fearlessly against all evil and oppression.
Help us, as You did Your servant Genevieve to use our freedom
to bring justice to Your peoples, for the glory of Your Name . . .

FEB • **ANSKAR** : *Missionary to Denmark and Sweden, 865*
You sent Anskar as an apostle to Scandinavia, enabling him to lay a foundation
for their conversion, though he did not see the fruits of his labors:
Keep us from discouragement, knowing that when you have begun a good work,
You will bring it to a fruitful conclusion . . .

MAR • **JOHN AND CHARLES WESLEY** : *Priests and Missionaries, England, 1791, 1798*
You inspired Your servants John and Charles with a burning zeal
for the salvation of souls, and endowed them with eloquence:
Kindle us with such fervor, we pray, that those whose faith has cooled
may be warmed, and those who have not known You may be saved . . .

APR • **RICHARD** : *Bishop of Chichester, England, 1253*
We thank You for all the benefits You have given us through Your Divine Son,
and for all the pain that he has borne for us: And we pray that,
following the example of Your servant Richard, we may see Christ more clearly,
love him more dearly, and follow him more nearly . . .

MAY • **THEODOSIUS OF THE CAVES** : *Abbot of the Caves of Kiev, Russia, 1074*
Almighty God, we thank You for Your servant Theodosius of the Caves,
who was faithful in the care and nurture of Your flock:
Grant, we pray, that following this example of such a holy life,
we may grow in Your grace and into the fullness of life in Christ . . .

JUN • **POPE JOHN XXIII** : *Inspirer of Renewal in the Church, 1963*
You have called us to continue Your Son's work of reconciliation
and reveal You to all the world: Forgive us the sins that keep us apart,
give us courage to overcome our fears,
and to seek that unity that is Your gift and Your will . . .

JUL • THE FEAST OF ST. THOMAS THE APOSTLE *(126)*
You strengthened Your servant Thomas
  with a firm and certain faith in the resurrection of Your Divine Son:
Grant us so perfectly and without doubt to believe in Christ, our Lord,
  that our faith may never be found wanting in Your sight . . .

AUG • PETER EYMARD : *Founder, Priests of the Blessed Sacrament, Paris, 1868*
By Your grace Your servant Peter Eymard, kindled with the flame of Your love,
  became a burning and shining light among Your people:
Grant that we also may be aflame with a spirit of love and discipline,
  and walk before You as children of light . . .

SEP • CUTHBURGA : *Abbess, Founder of the Nunnery at Wimborne, Britain, c. 725*
By Your grace Your servant Cuthburga, kindled with the flame of Your love,
  became a burning and shining light among Your people:
Grant that we also may be aflame with a spirit of love and discipline,
  and walk before You as children of light . . .

OCT • GEORGE KENNEDY BELL : *Ecumenist and Peacemaker, England, 1958*
Almighty God, whose peace passes all understanding: Grant that,
  as Your servant George Kennedy Bell toiled for peace in the world,
we too may become instruments of Your peace among all Your children,
  as befits the followers of the Prince of Peace . . .

NOV • THE SAINTS AND MARTYRS OF ASIA *(33)*
You call witnesses from every nation to reveal Your glory in their lives:
  Make us thankful for the example of the saints and martyrs of Asia,
and strengthen us by their fellowship that we, like them,
  may be faithful in the service of Your kingdom . . .

DEC • FRANCIS XAVIER : *Missionary to Asia, 1552*
You called Your servant Francis Xavier
  to lead many to know Your Divine Son as their Redeemer:
Bring us, we pray, to the new life of glory that is promised
  to all who follow in Your ways . . .

JAN • **ELIZABETH SETON** : *Founder, American Sisters of Charity, New York, 1821*
You call Your witnesses from every land, to reveal Your glory in the world:
    We give You thanks this day, for the example and the devotion of
Elizabeth Seton and the American Sisters of Charity;
    strengthen us by their fellowship, that we may be faithful in service . . .

FEB • **CORNELIUS THE CENTURION** : *The First Gentile Converted to the Faith*
You called Cornelius to be the first Christian among the Gentiles:
    Grant to Your Church a ready will to go where You send
and to do what You command, that under Your guidance it may welcome
    all who turn to You in love and faith . . .

MAR • **CASIMIR** : *Prince and Patron of Poland, 1484*
You called Your servant Casimir to an earthly throne
    and You gave him a zeal for the Church and a love for Your people:
Grant that we who remember his example may be fruitful in all good works
    and attain to the glorious crown of Your saints . . .

APR • **MARTIN LUTHER KING, JR.**: *Martyr for Civil Rights, 1968*
By Your grace and power, Your holy martyr Martin
    triumphed over suffering and was faithful unto death:
Strengthen us by Your grace, that we too may endure reproach,
    and faithfully bear witness to Your Name . . .

MAY • **MONICA** : *Mother of Augustine of Hippo, 387*
You strengthened Your servant Monica to persevere in offering her love and
    prayer and tears for the conversion of her husband and their son Augustine:
Deepen our devotion, we pray, and use us to bring others, even our own kindred,
    to acknowledge Jesus Christ as their Saviour and Lord . . .

JUN • **PETROC** : *Abbot and Teacher, Britain, 6th century*
By Your Spirit You give to some the word of wisdom,
    to others the word of knowledge, and to others the word of faith:
We praise You for the gifts manifested in Your servant Petroc,
    and pray that Your people may never be destitute of such gifts . . .

JUL • INDEPENDENCE DAY : *United States of America*
In Your Name, the founders of this country
    won liberty for themselves and for us, and lit the torch of freedom for nations
then unborn: Grant that we and all the people of this land
    may have grace to maintain our liberties in righteousness and peace . . .

AUG • JOHN BAPTIST VIANNEY : *Priest and Confessor, France, 1859*
Shepherd of Your people, we thank You for Your servant John Baptist Vianney,
    who was faithful in the care and nurture of Your flock:
Grant, we pray, that following this example of such a holy life,
    we may grow in Your grace and into the fullness of life in Christ . . .

SEP • ALBERT SCHWEITZER : *Missionary to Africa, 1965*
We thank You for Your servant Albert Schweitzer,
    whom You called to preach the Gospel to the people of Africa:
Raise up in this and every land, we pray,
    men and women who will be heralds of Your kingdom . . .

OCT • FRANCIS OF ASSISI : *Friar and Founder of the Franciscans, Italy, 1226*
You are the Most High, Omnipotent Creator:
    Grant to Your people grace to renounce gladly the vanities of this world,
that, following the way of Your blessed servant Francis, we may,
    for the love of You, delight in Your whole creation with perfect joy . . .

NOV • CHARLES BORROMEO : *Bishop and Cardinal, Milan, 1584*
You raised up Your servant Charles Borromeo, Almighty God,
    to be a faithful shepherd of Your people:
Grant Your Spirit, we pray, to all bishops, priests, ministers, and leaders,
    that they also may serve You as true stewards of Your divine mysteries . . .

DEC • JOHN OF DAMASCUS : *Priest and Theologian, Syria, c.760*
Confirm our minds, O Lord, in the mysteries of the faith
    as set forth with power by Your servant John of Damascus;
that we, with him, confessing Jesus to be true God and true Man,
    and singing the praises of the risen Lord, may obtain to eternal joy . . .

JAN • **TWELFTH NIGHT** : *The Vigil for the Feast of the Epiphany (72)*
By the leading of a star, You manifested Your Divine Son
   to the peoples of this earth: Grant that our remembrance of this holy day to
which we are drawing nigh may deepen our devotion
   and make us ever more prepared to come into Your holy presence . . .

FEB • **AGATHA** : *Martyr, Sicily, 3rd century*
You kindled the flame of Your love in the heart of Your holy martyr Agatha:
   Grant to us, we pray, a like faith and power of love,
that we who remember her triumph this day
   may profit in our own lives by her example . . .

MAR • **JOHN DONNE** : *Priest and Poet, London, 1631*
Almighty God, You are the root and fountain of all being:
   Open our eyes that we may come to see,
along with Your servant John Donne,
   that whatever has any being is a mirror in which we may behold You . . .

APR • **VINCENT FERRER** : *Preacher and Renewer of the Church, Spain, 1418*
We praise You for those You have sent to call the Church to its tasks
   and renew its life, such as Your servant Vincent Ferrer:
Raise up in our own day teachers and prophets inspired by Your Spirit,
   whose voices will proclaim the reality of Your kingdom . . .

MAY • **HILARY OF ARLES** : *Monk and Bishop, France, c. 400*
By Your grace Your servant Hilary of Arles, kindled with the flame of Your love,
   became a burning and shining light among Your people:
Grant that we also may be aflame with a spirit of love and discipline,
   and walk before You as children of light . . .

JUN • **BONIFACE** : *Missionary and Martyr in Germany, 754*
You called Your servant Boniface to be a witness and martyr in Germany
   and by his labor and suffering, You raised up a people for Your own:
Pour out Your Spirit upon us, that by the service and sacrifice of many,
   Your Name may be glorified and Your kingdom enlarged . . .

JUL • ATHANASIUS THE ATHONITE : *Abbot and Teacher, Greece, c. 1003*
Almighty God, You gave Your servant Athanasius the Athonite
 special gifts of grace to understand and teach Your truth:
Grant that by this teaching we may know You
 and the One Whom You have sent . . .

AUG • THE VIGIL FOR THE FEAST OF THE TRANSFIGURATION OF OUR LORD *(99)*
On Your holy mountain, to Your chosen witnesses,
 You revealed Your Divine Son transfigured: Grant that our remembrance of
this mighty act to which we draw nigh, may deepen our devotion
 and make us ever more prepared to come into Your holy presence . . .

SEP • LAWRENCE GIUSTINIANI : *Bishop and Reformer, Venice, 1455*
We praise You, Almighty God, for those, like Your servant Lawrence Giustiniani,
 whom You have sent to call the Church to its true work and to renew its life:
Raise up in our day, we pray, men and women whose voices will
 give strength to Your people and proclaim the reality of Your ways . . .

OCT • PLACID : *Monk, Italy, 6th century*
Your blessed Son became poor that through His poverty we might become rich:
 Deliver us, we pray, from an inordinate love of this world, that we, inspired by
the devotion of Your servant Placid, may serve You with singleness of heart,
 and attain to the riches of the age to come . . .

NOV • ELIZABETH AND ZECHARIAH : *Companions of the Blessed Mother*
In Your wisdom and power, You raised up Elizabeth and Zechariah
 to be companions to the Blessed Mary and the parents of Your prophet John:
Give us grace, we pray, to be watchful in our times
 for the coming of Your kingdom . . .

DEC • CLEMENT OF ALEXANDRIA : *Priest and Apologist for the Faith, Egypt, c. 210*
O God of unsearchable wisdom, You gave Your servant Clement the grace
 to understand and teach the truth as it is in Christ, the source of all truth:
Grant to Your Church the same grace to discern Your Word
 wherever truth may be found . . .

JAN • **THE FEAST OF THE EPIPHANY OF OUR LORD** *(72)*
By the leading of a star,
    You manifested Your Divine Son to the peoples of this earth:
Lead us, we pray, we who know You now by faith, to Your presence,
    where we may see Your glory face to face . . .

FEB • **DOROTHY** : *Martyr of Cappadocia, 3rd century*
By Your grace and power, Your holy martyr Dorothy
    triumphed over suffering and was faithful unto death:
Strengthen us with Your grace, that we may endure reproach and persecution,
    and faithfully bear witness to Your Name . . .

MAR • **COLETTE** : *Nun and Reformer, France, 1447*
We praise You, Almighty God, for those like Your servant Collette,
    whom You have sent to call the Church to its true work and to renew its life:
Raise up in our day, we pray, men and women whose voices will
    give strength to Your people and proclaim the reality of Your ways . . .

APR • **MICHELANGELO** : *Artist of the Renaissance, 1564*
Your saints and angels delight to worship You in heaven: Be ever present
    with Your servants who seek through art to perfect the praises of Your people,
and grant to them even now glimpses of Your beauty,
    and make them worthy at length to behold it unveiled for evermore . . .

MAY • **FLORIAN** : *Martyr, Noricum (Austria), 304*
Almighty God, You gave to Your servant Florian the boldness
    to confess Christ in this world, and the courage to die for his faith:
Grant that we may always be ready to give a reason for the hope that is in us,
    and to suffer gladly for the sake of our Lord Jesus Christ . . .

JUN • **JARLATH OF TUAM** : *Abbot and Bishop, Ireland, c. 550*
You raised up Your servant Jarlath of Tuam, Almighty God,
    to be a faithful shepherd of Your people:
Grant Your Spirit, we pray, to all bishops, priests, ministers, and leaders,
    that they also may serve You as true stewards of Your divine mysteries . . .

JUL • **THOMAS MORE AND JOHN FISHER** : *Defenders of the Faith and Martyrs, 1535*
You gave to Your martyrs Thomas More and John Fisher
   a gentleness of spirit and a firmness of faith:
Grant us strength for holding on to Your Truth that at the last,
   we may ever live and love together with all Your saints in heaven . . .

AUG • **THE FEAST OF THE TRANSFIGURATION OF OUR LORD** *(99)*
On Your holy mountain, You revealed to Your chosen witnesses,
   Your Divine Son, transfigured, in raiment white and glistening:
Mercifully grant that we, being delivered from the disquietude of this world,
   may by faith behold Him in glory . . .

SEP • **SIMONE WEIL** : *Writer and Mystic, France, 1943*
You are ever present, Almighty God, with artists like Simone Weil,
   and all those who seek through their art to perfect the praises of Your people:
Grant to them even now glimpses of Your beauty,
   and make us worthy at last to behold it unveiled for evermore . . .

OCT • **WILLIAM TYNDALE** : *Priest and Translator of Scriptures, England, 1536*
You endowed Your servant William with the gift of graceful expression
   and perseverance to bring the Scriptures to people in their native tongue:
Reveal to us, we pray, Your saving Word as we read and study the Scriptures
   and hear them calling us to repentance and to life eternal . . .

NOV • **LEONARD** : *Hermit, France, 6th century*
Your blessed Son became poor that through His poverty we might become rich:
   Deliver us, we pray, from an inordinate love of this world, that we, inspired by
the devotion of blessed Leonard, may serve You with singleness of heart,
   and attain to the riches of the age to come . . .

DEC • **NICHOLAS OF MYRA** : *Patron of Children and of Sailors, c. 342*
You gave Your servant Nicholas a name for deeds of kindness:
   Grant that we may never cease to work for the happiness of children,
the safety of sailors, the relief of the poor,
   and all those tossed about by the tempests of doubt and grief . . .

JAN • **LUCIAN OF ANTIOCH** : *Scholar and Martyr, Nicomedia, 312*
By Your grace and power, Almighty God, Your holy martyr Lucian of Antioch
   triumphed over suffering and was faithful unto death:
Grant that we, remembering him with thanksgiving,
     may be so faithful in our witness, that we too may receive the crown of life . . .

FEB • **THE SAINTS AND MARTYRS OF EUROPE** *(33)*
You call Your witnesses from every nation to reveal Your glory in their lives:
   Make us thankful for the example of the saints and martyrs of Europe,
and strengthen us by their fellowship that we, like them,
   may be faithful in the service of Your kingdom . . .

MAR • **PERPETUA AND FELICITY** : *Martyrs at Carthage, 202*
You helped Perpetua and Felicity and their friends to make a good confession,
   staunchly resisting for the cause of Christ the claims of human affection,
and encouraging one another in their trials:
   Grant that we who remember them may share their pure and steadfast
         faith . . .

APR • **JOHN BAPTIST DE LA SALLE** : *Founder, Brothers of the Christian Schools, 1719*
By Your grace, John de la Salle, kindled with the flame of Your love,
   became a burning and shining light among Your people:
Grant that we also may be aflame with a spirit of love and discipline,
   and walk before You as children of light . . .

MAY • **JOHN OF BEVERLEY** : *Teacher and Bishop, Britain, 721*
By Your spirit You give to some the word of wisdom,
   to others the word of knowledge, and to others the word of faith:
We praise You for the gifts manifested in Your servant John Beverley,
   and pray that Your people may never be destitute of such gifts . . .

JUN • **SEATTLE** : *Peacemaker and Chief of the Duwamish Confederacy, 1866*
Almighty God, whose peace passes all understanding:
   Grant that, as Your servant Seattle toiled for peace in the world,
we too may become instruments of Your peace among all Your children,
   as befits the followers of the Prince of Peace . . .

jul • THOMAS BECKET : *Archbishop of Canterbury and Defender of the Church, 1170*
You called Your servant Thomas Becket
    to be a shepherd of Your people and a defender of Your Church:
Keep Your household from all evil, we pray,
    and raise up for us faithful leaders, who are wise in the ways of the Gospel . . .

aug • JOHN MASON NEALE : *Priest and Hymn Writer, England, 1866*
You are ever present, Almighty God, with artists like John Mason Neale,
    and all those who seek through their art to perfect the praises of Your people:
Grant to them even now glimpses of Your beauty,
    and make us worthy at last to behold it unveiled for evermore . . .

sep • CLOUD : *Prince, France, c. 560*
You called Your servant Cloud to an earthly throne
    and You gave him a zeal for the Church and a love for Your people:
Grant that we who remember his example may be fruitful in all good works
    and attain to the glorious crown of Your saints . . .

oct • HENRY MUHLENBERG : *Missionary to America, 1727*
We thank You for Your servant Henry Muhlenberg,
    whom You called to preach the Gospel to the people of the West:
Raise up, we pray, in this and every land, heralds of Your kingdom,
    that Your people may proclaim the unsearchable riches of Your ways . . .

nov • WILLIBRORD : *Archbishop of Utrecht, Missionary to Frisia, 739*
You sent Your servant Willibrord as apostle to the Low Countries,
    to turn the people there from the worship of idols to serve the living God:
Preserve us from the temptation to exchange the perfect freedom of Your service
    for servitude to the false gods of our making . . .

dec • AMBROSE : *Bishop of Milan, 397*
You gave Ambrose the grace to eloquently proclaim Your righteousness:
    Mercifully grant to all bishops and ministers such excellence in preaching
and such faithfulness in ministering Your Word,
    that we may be partakers with them of the glory that shall be revealed . . .

JAN • **ABO** : *Martyr, Georgia, 786*
In every age, Almighty God, You send those who give their lives for Your sake:
    Inspire us, we pray, with the memory of Your holy martyr Abo
whose faithfulness led him in the way of the Cross,
    and give us courage to bear witness to Your love with our lives . . .

FEB • **JOHN OF MATHA** : *Founder of the Order of Trinitarian Friars, France, 1213*
By Your grace Your servant John Matha, kindled with the flame of Your love,
    became a burning and shining light among Your people:
Grant that we also may be aflame with a spirit of love and discipline,
    and walk before You as children of light . . .

MAR • **JOHN OF GOD** : *Founder of Order of Hospitallers, Spain, 1550*
By Your grace, Your servant John of God, kindled with Your love,
    became a burning and shining light in Your Church:
Grant that we also may be aflame with a spirit of love and discipline,
    and walk before You as children of light . . .

APR • **THE SAINTS AND MARTYRS OF THE AMERICAS** *(33)*
You call Your witnesses from every nation to reveal Your glory in their lives:
    Make us thankful for the example of the saints and martyrs
of the Americas, and strengthen us by their fellowship that we, like them,
    may be faithful in the service of Your kingdom . . .

MAY • **JULIAN OF NORWICH** : *Anchorite and Mystic, England, c. 1417*
In Your compassion, You granted to the Lady Julian
    many revelations of Your nurturing and sustaining love:
Move our hearts, like hers, that we may love You in all things;
    for in giving us Yourself, You give us all things . . .

JUN • **MELANIA THE YOUNGER** : *Married Woman, Jerusalem, 439*
You have graciously surrounded us with a great cloud of witnesses:
    Grant that we, encouraged by the good example of Melania the Younger,
may persevere in running the race that is set before us,
    until we too at last attain to Your eternal joy . . .

JUL • ELIZABETH OF PORTUGAL : *Queen and Peacemaker, Portugal, 1336*
You called Your servant Elizabeth of Portugal to an earthly throne
    and You gave her a zeal for the Church and a love for Your people:
Grant that we who remember her example may be fruitful in all good works
    and attain to the glorious crown of Your saints . . .

AUG • DOMINIC : *Friar and Founder of the Dominicans, Italy, 1221*
You opened the eyes of Your servant Dominic to perceive a famine of the
    hearing of the Word of the Lord, and moved him to satisfy that hunger:
Grant that we, in our time, may be attentive to the hungers of the world,
    and quick to respond to those who are perishing . . .

SEP • THE FEAST OF THE NATIVITY OF THE BLESSED MOTHER *(138)*
With special grace, You made the Blessed Mary
    to be the mother of Your Divine Son:
By the same grace, make us holy in body and soul,
    and ever preserve us in Your gifts of humility and love . . .

OCT • SERGIUS AND BACCHUS : *Martyrs, Syria, c. 303*
In every age, Almighty God, You send those who give their lives for Your sake:
    Inspire us, we pray, with the memory of Your holy martyrs Sergius and
        Bacchus,
whose faithfulness led them in the way of the Cross,
    and give us courage to bear witness to Your love with our lives . . .

NOV • THE SAINTS AND MARTYRS OF THE BRITISH ISLES *(33)*
You call Your witnesses from every nation to reveal Your glory in their lives:
    Make us thankful for the example of the saints and martyrs
of the British Isles, and strengthen us by their fellowship that we, like them,
    may be faithful in the service of Your kingdom . . .

DEC • THE FEAST OF THE IMMACULATE CONCEPTION OF MARY *(113)*
Hear the supplication of Your servants, O Lord:
    Grant that we who honor the conception of the Blessed Mother of God
may, through her intercession,
    be delivered by You from the perils that beset us . . .

JAN • **ADRIAN** : *Abbot and Teacher, Canterbury, 710*
You have surrounded us with a great cloud of witnesses:
    Grant that we may be encouraged by Your servant Adrian,
and persevere in running the race that is set before us,
    until at last we may with him attain to Your eternal joy . . .

FEB • **APOLLONIA** : *Martyr of Cappadocia, 3rd century*
By Your grace and power, Your holy martyr Apollonia
    triumphed over suffering and was faithful unto death:
Strengthen us with Your grace, that we may endure reproach and persecution,
    and faithfully bear witness to Your Name . . .

MAR • **GREGORY OF NYSSA** : *Bishop and Cappadocian Father, c. 394*
You have revealed Your eternal Being as one God in the Trinity of Persons:
    Grant us grace that we, like Your servant Gregory,
may continue steadfast in the confession of this faith,
    and constant in our worship of You . . .

APR • **DIETRICH BONHOEFFER** : *Pastor and Martyr, Germany, 1945*
By Your grace and power, Your holy martyr Dietrich Bonhoeffer
    triumphed over suffering and was faithful unto death:
Strengthen us with Your grace, that we may endure reproach and persecution,
    and faithfully bear witness to Your Name . . .

MAY • **GREGORY OF NAZIANZEN** : *Bishop and Cappadocian Father, 389*
You have revealed Your eternal Being as one God in the Trinity of Persons:
    Grant us grace that we, like Your servant Gregory,
may continue steadfast in the confession of this faith,
    and constant in our worship of You . . .

JUN • **COLUMBA** : *Patron of Scotland, 597*
By the preaching of Your blessed servant Columba,
    You caused the light of the Gospel to shine in Scotland:
Grant, we pray, that having his life and labors in remembrance,
    we may show our thankfulness to You by following his example . . .

JUL • **VERONICA GIULIANI** : *Nun and Mystic, Italy, 1727*
You built Your Church through the love and devotion of Your saints,
    and we give thanks for Your servant Veronica Giuliani this day:
Inspire us to follow her example
    that we in our generation may rejoice with her in the vision of Your glory . . .

AUG • **OSWALD OF NORTHUMBRIA** : *Martyr, 642*
You so kindled the faith of Your servant Oswald of Northumbria
    that he set up the sign of the Passion in his kingdom
and turned his people to Your light: Grant that we, fired with the same spirit,
    may ever be found faithful servants of the gospel . . .

SEP • **CONSTANCE AND HER COMPANIONS** : *Martyred at Memphis, 1878*
We give You thanks, for the heroic witness of Constance and her companions,
    who in a time of plague and pestilence were steadfast in their care of the dying,
and loved not their own lives, even unto death:
    Inspire in us a like love and commitment to those of Your children in need . . .

OCT • **DENIS OF PARIS** : *Bishop and Martyr, France, 258*
In every age, You send those who give their lives for Your sake:
    Inspire us, we pray, with the memory of Your holy martyr Denis,
whose faithfulness led him in the way of the Cross,
    and give us courage to bear witness to Your love with our lives . . .

NOV • **NECTARIUS KEPHALAS** : *Bishop, Greece, 1920*
You raised up Your servant Nectarius Kephalas, Almighty God,
    to be a faithful shepherd of Your people:
Grant Your Spirit, we pray, to all bishops, priests, ministers, and leaders,
    that they also may serve You as true stewards of Your divine mysteries . . .

DEC • **HIPPARCHUS AND PHILOTHEUS** : *Martyrs at Samosata, Syria, 297*
Almighty God, You gave to Your servants Hipparchus and Philotheus
    the boldness to confess Christ, and the courage to die for this faith:
Grant that we may always be ready to give a reason for the hope that is in us,
    and to suffer gladly for the sake of our Lord Jesus Christ . . .

JAN • **WILLIAM LAUD** : *Archbishop of Canterbury and Martyr, England, 1645*
Keep us, Almighty God, constant in faith and zealous in witness,
 that we, like Your servant William Laud,
may live in Your fear, die in Your favor,
 and rest in Your peace . . .

FEB • **SCHOLASTICA** : *Sister of St. Benedict, Italy, 542*
You caused the soul of Your blessed servant Scholastica
 to enter heaven in the likeness of a dove that You might show us
the way of the undefiled: Grant us by the aid of her merits and prayers
 to so innocently live that we may attain to life eternal . . .

MAR • **FORTY MARTYRS OF ENGLAND AND WALES,** *16th and 17th centuries*
In every age, Almighty God, You send those who give their lives for Your sake:
 Inspire us with the memory of Your holy martyrs of England and Wales,
whose faithfulness led them in the way of the Cross,
 and give us courage to bear witness to Your love with our lives . . .

APR • **PIERRE TEILHARD DE CHARDIN** : *Visionary, France, 1955*
You have enlightened Your Church
 by the teaching of Your servant Teilhard:
Enrich it ever more with Your grace and raise up faithful witnesses who,
 by their life and their teaching, may proclaim Your Truth . . .

MAY • **ISIDORE THE FARMER-SERVANT** : *Patron of Madrid, Spain, 1130*
You built Your Church through the love and devotion of Your saints,
 and we give You thanks for Your servant Isidore whom we remember this day:
Inspire us to follow his example
 that we in our generation may rejoice with him in the vision of Your glory . . .

JUN • **EPHREM** : *Deacon, Odessa, 373*
Pour out on us, we pray, that same Spirit by which Your servant Ephrem
 rejoiced to proclaim in song the mysteries of faith;
and so gladden our hearts that we, like him,
 may be devoted to You alone . . .

JUL • **THE SEVEN BROTHERS** : *Martyred at Rome, c. 150*
Almighty God, You gave to the Seven Brothers of Rome the boldness
    to confess Christ in this world, and the courage to die for this faith:
Grant that we may always be ready to give a reason for the hope that is in us,
    and to suffer gladly for the sake of our Lord Jesus Christ . . .

AUG • **LAWRENCE** : *Deacon and Martyr of Rome, 258*
You called Your servant Laurence to serve You with deeds of love
    and You gave to him the crown of martyrdom:
Grant that we, following his example, may fulfill Your commandments
    by defending the poor, and loving You with our whole heart . . .

SEP • **ALEXANDER CRUMMELL** : *Missionary and Educator, Liberia, 1898*
You called Your servant Alexander Crummell,
    to preach the Gospel to those who were far away and those who were near:
Raise up in this and every land evangelists and heralds of the Good News,
    that Your people may proclaim the riches of Your Truth . . .

OCT • **PAULINUS OF YORK** : *Missionary Bishop, Britain, 644*
Almighty God, You raised up Your servant Paulinus of York
    to be a light in this world: Shine in our hearts, we pray,
that we also in our generation may show forth Your praise,
    because You have called us out of darkness into Your marvelous light . . .

NOV • **LEO THE GREAT** : *Bishop at Rome, 461*
Grant that Your Church, following the teaching of Your servant Leo,
    may hold fast to the great mystery of our redemption,
and adore the one Christ, true God and true Man, neither divided
    from our human nature nor separate from Your Divine Being . . .

DEC • **THOMAS MERTON** : *Monk and Writer, Kentucky, 1968*
By Your grace, Your servant Thomas, kindled with Your love,
    became a burning and shining light in Your Church:
Grant that we also may be aflame with a spirit of love and discipline,
    and walk before You as children of light . . .

JAN • **THEODOSIUS THE CENOBITE** : *Abbot, Palestine, c. 423*
You raised up Your servant Theodosius the Cenobite, Almighty God,
    to be a faithful shepherd of Your people:
Grant Your Spirit, we pray, to all bishops, priests, ministers, and leaders,
    that they also may serve You as true stewards of Your divine mysteries . . .

FEB • **BENEDICT OF ANIANE** : *Abbot and Reformer, France, 821*
We praise You, Almighty God, for those like Your servant Benedict of Aniane,
    whom You have sent to call the Church to its true work and to renew its life:
Raise up in our day, we pray, men and women whose voices will
    give strength to Your people and proclaim the reality of Your ways . . .

MAR • **SOPHRONIUS** : *Bishop of Jerusalem, 638*
You raised up Your servant Sophronius, Almighty God,
    to be a faithful shepherd of Your people:
Grant Your Spirit, we pray, to all bishops, priests, ministers, and leaders,
    that they also may serve You as true stewards of Your divine mysteries . . .

APR • **GEORGE AUGUSTUS SELWYN** : *Missionary Bishop of New Zealand, 1878*
We thank You for Your servant George Augustus Selwyn,
    whom You called to preach the Gospel to the people of the Pacific:
Raise up, we pray, in this and every land, heralds of Your kingdom,
    that Your people may proclaim the unsearchable riches of Your ways . . .

MAY • **FRANCIS DE GIROLAMO** : *Jesuit Preacher, Italy, 1716*
Almighty God, You gave Your servant Francis de Girolamo
    special gifts of grace to understand and teach Your truth:
Grant that by such teaching we may know You
    and the One Whom You have sent . . .

JUN • **THE FEAST OF ST. BARNABAS THE APOSTLE** *(112)*
Grant that we may follow the example of Your faithful servant Barnabas who,
    not seeking his own renown, but the well-being of Your Church,
gave generously of his life and substance
    for the relief of the poor and the spread of the Good News . . .

jul • **Benedict** : *Abbott of Monte Cassino, Italy, c. 540*
Your precepts are the wisdom of a loving father:
  Give us grace, we pray, following the example of Your servant Benedict,
to walk with loving and willing hearts in the school of Your service;
  let Your ears be open to our prayers; and bless the work of our hands . . .

aug • **Clare** : *Abbess at Assisi, Italy, 1253*
Your Divine Son became poor that through his poverty we might become rich:
  Deliver us, we pray, from an inordinate love of this world, that we,
inspired by the devotion of Clare, may serve You with pure hearts,
  and attain to the riches of the world to come . . .

sep • **Protus and Hyacinth** : *Martyrs at Rome, 3rd century*
By Your grace and power Your holy martyrs Protus and Hyacinth
  triumphed over suffering and were faithful unto death:
Grant that we, remembering them with thanksgiving,
  may be so faithful in our witness, that we too may receive the crown of life . . .

oct • **Bruno** : *Founder of the Carthusians, France, c. 1100*
You call Your witnesses from every land, to reveal Your glory in the world:
  We give You thanks this day, for the example and the devotion of
Bruno and all the members of the Order of the Carthusians;
  strengthen us by their fellowship, that we may be faithful in service . . .

nov • **Martin of Tours** : *Bishop and Patron of France, 397*
You clothed Your servant Martin the soldier with the spirit of sacrifice,
  and set him as bishop to be a defender of the Catholic faith:
Give us grace to follow in his footsteps, that at the last,
  we may be found clothed with righteousness in the dwellings of peace . . .

dec • **Daniel the Stylite** : *Monk and Hermit, Constantinople, 493*
Your blessed Son became poor that through His poverty we might become rich:
  Deliver us, we pray, from an inordinate love of this world, that we,
inspired by the devotion of Daniel, may serve You with singleness of heart,
  and attain to the riches of the age to come . . .

JAN • **AELRED** : *Abbot of Rievaulx, England, 1167*
Through Your servant Aelred of Rievaulx,
    You drew many to Your community of love:
Pour into our hearts, we pray, the gift of love,
    that we may share in the joy of true friendship . . .

FEB • **MARINA** : *Woman Monk, Germany, date unknown*
Your blessed Son became poor that through His poverty we might become rich:
    Deliver us, we pray, from an inordinate love of this world, that we, inspired by
the devotion of Your servant Marina, may serve You with singleness of heart,
    and attain to the riches of the age to come . . .

MAR • **GREGORY THE GREAT:** *Bishop at Rome, 604*
You raised up Your servant Gregory to be a servant of the servants of God,
    and inspired him to send missionaries to the English people:
Preserve in us the faith that they taught, that being faithful in every good work,
    we may receive the crown of glory that never fades away . . .

APR • **TERESA OF THE ANDES** : *Novice, Chile, 1920*
Your blessed Son became poor that through His poverty we might become rich:
    Deliver us, we pray, from an inordinate love of this world, that we, inspired by
the devotion of Teresa of the Andes, may serve You with singleness of heart,
    and attain to the riches of the age to come . . .

MAY • **SIMON OF CYRENE** : *Bearer of the Cross of Christ*
You chose a stranger to help Your Divine Son
    to bear the burden of the cross on his way to death:
Grant that we too may be ever ready to take up the cross of Christ,
    and to bear it humbly in Your service . . .

JUN • **ESKIL** : *Bishop and Missionary to Sweden, c. 1080*
We thank You for Your servant Eskil,
    whom You called to preach the Gospel to the peoples of Sweden:
Raise up, we pray, in this and every land, heralds of Your kingdom,
    that Your people may proclaim the unsearchable riches of Your ways . . .

JUL • **JOHN THE IBERIAN** : *Abbot, Mount Athos, c. 1002*
You raised up Your servant John the Iberian, Almighty God,
　　to be a faithful shepherd of Your people:
Grant Your Spirit, we pray, to all bishops, priests, ministers, and leaders,
　　that they also may serve You as true stewards of Your divine mysteries . . .

AUG • **HIPPOLYTUS OF ROME** : *Theologian and Martyr, Sardinia, c. 235*
Almighty God, You gave to Your servant Hippolytus of Rome the boldness
　　to confess Christ in this world, and the courage to die for this faith:
Grant that we may always be ready to give a reason for the hope that is in us,
　　and to suffer gladly for the sake of our Lord Jesus Christ . . .

SEP • **CYPRIAN** : *Bishop and Martyr at Carthage, 258*
You gave Your servant Cyprian boldness and courage
　　to confess the name of Christ before the rulers of this world and to die for it:
Grant we may always be ready to give a reason for the hope that is in us,
　　and to suffer gladly for the sake of our Lord Jesus Christ . . .

OCT • **WILFRID OF YORK** : *Bishop, England, 709*
You raised up Your servant Wilfrid, Almighty God,
　　to be a faithful shepherd of Your people:
Grant Your Spirit, we pray, to all bishops, priests, ministers, and leaders,
　　that they also may serve You as true stewards of Your divine mysteries . . .

NOV • **CHARLES SIMEON** : *Priest and Reformer of the Church, England, 1836*
All things are ordered by Your wisdom and love, Almighty God:
　　Grant that in all things we may see Your hand at work,
and that, following the example of Your servant Charles Simeon, we may
　　walk with Christ in simplicity, and serve You with contented minds . . .

DEC • **JANE FRANCES DE CHANTAL** : *Founder, Order of the Visitation, France, 1641*
You enkindled Your servant Jane and made her to walk in all ways of perfection,
　　and by her You enriched Your Church with a new offspring:
Grant that we, by her merits and prayers,
　　may overcome all adversity by the help of Your grace . . .

JAN • **HILARY** : *Bishop and Teacher, Poitiers, 368*
You raised up Your servant Hilary to be a champion of the Catholic faith:
    Keep us steadfast in that faith we professed at our baptism,
that we may rejoice in having You for our Father,
    and that we may abide in Your Son, in the fellowship of the Holy Spirit . . .

FEB • **CATHERINE DEI RICCI** : *Nun and Visionary, Italy, 1590*
You built Your Church through the love and devotion of Your saints,
    and we give thanks this day for Your servant Catherine dei Ricci:
Inspire us to follow her example
    that we in our generation may rejoice with her in the vision of Your glory . . .

MAR • **EUPHRASIA** : *Nun, Egypt, c. 420*
Your blessed Son became poor that through His poverty we might become rich:
    Deliver us, we pray, from an inordinate love of this world, that we, inspired by
the devotion of Your servant Euphrasia, may serve You with singleness of heart,
    and attain to the riches of the age to come . . .

APR • **MARTIN THE FIRST** : *Pope and Martyr, Italy, 655*
In every age, Almighty God, You send those who give their lives for Your sake:
    Inspire us, we pray, with the memory of Your holy martyr Martin,
whose faithfulness led him in the way of the Cross,
    and give us courage to bear witness to Your love with our lives . . .

MAY • **ANDREW FOURNET** : *Co-Founder, Daughters of the Holy Cross of Saint Andrew, 1834*
You call Your witnesses from every land, to reveal Your glory in the world:
    We give You thanks this day, for the example and the devotion of
Andrew Fournet and the Daughters of the Cross;
    strengthen us by their fellowship, that we too may be faithful in service . . .

JUN • **ANTHONY OF PADUA** : *Franciscan Friar and Preacher, Portugal, c. 1231*
You raised up Your servant Anthony of Padua, Almighty God,
    to be a faithful shepherd of Your people:
Grant Your Spirit, we pray, to all bishops, priests, ministers, and leaders,
    that they also may serve You as true stewards of Your divine mysteries . . .

JUL • SILAS : *Companion to Saint Paul, 1st century*
You built Your Church through the love and devotion of Your saints,
    and we give You thanks for Your servant Silas whom we remember this day:
Inspire us to follow his example
    that we in our generation may rejoice with him in the vision of Your glory . . .

AUG • FLORENCE NIGHTINGALE : *Renewer of Society, U.S.A., 1910*
Your Divine Son came among us to serve:
    Lead us by his love, we pray, as You did Your servant Florence Nightingale
that we may give hope to the hopeless, love to the unloved,
    peace to the troubled, and rest to the weary . . .

SEP • THE VIGIL FOR THE FEAST OF THE HOLY CROSS OF OUR LORD *(98)*
Grant that our remembrance of this holy day to which we are drawing nigh,
    the day upon which we venerate the holy cross of Jesus Christ,
may deepen our devotion and make us ever more prepared
    to come into Your holy presence . . .

OCT • EDWARD THE CONFESSOR : *1066*
You numbered Your confessor Edward
    among the glorious company of Your saints:
Grant us grace to follow his example of a devout and godly life,
    and to a further knowledge of You and Your heavenly kingdom . . .

NOV • ALL SAINTS OF THE ORDER OF ST. BENEDICT *(119, Shin)*
By Your grace, the monks of Benedict became a shining light in Your Church:
    Grant, we pray, that we too may serve You with singleness of heart,
that we may also be aflame with the spirit of love and discipline,
    and that we may ever walk before You as children of light . . .

DEC • LUCY : *Martyr at Syracuse, 304*
For the salvation of all, Your Divine Son went up to the cross
    to give light to the world which was in darkness:
Shed that light on us, we pray, that with Your servant Lucy,
    we may come to eternal light and enjoy life with You in the world to come . . .

JAN • **GEORGE FOX** : *Founder of The Society of Friends, 1691*
Your Spirit guides us into all truth and makes us free;
    Strengthen and sustain us as You did Your servant George Fox:
Grant us vision and courage to stand against war and its violence,
    and against all that works against the peace You offer all Your children . . .

FEB • **CYRIL AND METHODIUS** : *Missionaries to the Slavic Peoples, 869 and 884*
By the power of Your Spirit, You moved Your servants Cyril and Methodius
    to bring the light of the Gospel to a hostile and divided people:
Overcome, we pray, all bitterness and strife among us by the love of Christ,
    and make us one united people under the banner of the Prince of Peace . . .

MAR • **MATILDA** : *Queen and Philanthropist, Germany, 968*
You called Your servant Matilda to an earthly throne
    and You gave her a zeal for the Church and a love for Your people:
Grant that we who remember her example may be fruitful in all good works
    and attain to the glorious crown of Your saints . . .

APR • **TIBURTIUS** : *Martyred at Rome, c. 190*
In every age, Almighty God, You send those who give their lives for Your sake:
    Inspire us, we pray, with the memory of Your holy martyr Tiburtius,
whose faithfulness led him in the way of the Cross,
    and give us courage to bear witness to Your love with our lives . . .

MAY • **MATTHIAS THE APOSTLE**, *1st century*
In the place of Judas, Almighty God,
    You chose Matthias to be among the Twelve:
Grant that Your people may be delivered from false apostles,
    and may always be guided and governed by true and faithful pastors . . .

JUN • **BASIL THE GREAT** : *Bishop and Cappadocian Father, Caesaria, 379*
You have revealed Your eternal Being as one God in the Trinity of Persons:
    Grant us grace that we, like Your servant Basil,
may continue steadfast in the confession of the faith,
    and constant in our worship of You . . .

JUL • NICODEMUS OF THE HOLY MOUNTAIN : *Monk and Writer, Mount Athos, 1809*
By Your Spirit You give to some the word of wisdom,
  to others the word of knowledge, and to others the word of faith:
We praise You for the gifts manifested in Nicodemus of the Holy Mountain,
  and pray that Your people may never be destitute of such gifts . . .

AUG • MAXIMILIAN KOLBE : *Priest and Martyr, Poland, 1941*
By Your grace and power, Almighty God, Your holy martyr Maximilian Kolbe
  triumphed over suffering and was faithful unto death:
Grant that we, remembering him with thanksgiving,
  may be so faithful in our witness, that we too may receive the crown of life . . .

SEP • THE FEAST OF THE HOLY CROSS OF OUR LORD *(98)*
Your Divine Son was lifted high upon the cross
  that he might draw the whole world unto himself:
Mercifully grant that we, who glory in the mystery of our redemption,
  may have grace to take up our cross and follow him . . .

OCT • JUSTUS OF LYONS : *Bishop, France, c. 390*
You raised up Your servant Justus of Lyons, Almighty God,
  to be a faithful shepherd of Your people:
Grant Your Spirit, we pray, to all bishops, priests, ministers, and leaders,
  that they also may serve You as true stewards of Your divine mysteries . . .

NOV • GREGORY PALAMAS : *Mystic and Theologian, Greece, c. 1359*
Almighty God, You gave Your servant Gregory Palamas
  special gifts of grace to understand and teach Your truth:
Grant that by such teaching we may know You
  and the One Whom You have sent . . .

DEC • JOHN OF THE CROSS : *Mystic and Teacher, Spain, 1591*
You gave to Your servant John of the Cross
  the gift of a mystical knowledge of You:
Grant to all who faithfully love You
  the true union of body and soul . . .

JAN • ITA : *Teacher, Ireland, 570*
By Your Holy Spirit, You gave some the word of wisdom,
 to others the word of knowledge, and to others the word of faith:
We praise You for the gifts of grace manifested in Your servant Ita,
 and we pray that Your Church will never be destitute of such gifts . . .

FEB • SIGFRID : *Missionary Bishop to Sweden and Denmark, c. 1045*
We thank You for Your servant Sigfrid,
 whom You called to preach the Gospel to the peoples of Scandinavia:
Raise up, we pray, in this and every land, heralds of Your kingdom,
 that Your people may proclaim the unsearchable riches of Your ways . . .

MAR • LOUISE DE MARILLAC : *Co-Founder of the Daughters of Charity, France, 1660*
By Your grace, Louise de Marillac, kindled with the flame of Your love,
 became a burning and shining light among Your people:
Grant that we also may be aflame with a spirit of love and discipline,
 and walk before You as children of light . . .

APR • STEPHEN HARDING : *Abbot and Cistercian Reformer, France, 1134*
We praise You, Almighty God, for those like Your servant Stephen Harding,
 whom You have sent to call the Church to its true work and to renew its life:
Raise up in our day, we pray, men and women whose voices will
 give strength to Your people and proclaim the reality of Your ways . . .

MAY • HALLVARD : *Martyr and Patron of Oslo, 1043*
Almighty God, You gave to Your servant Hallvard the boldness
 to confess Christ in this world, and the courage to die for this faith:
Grant that we may always be ready to give a reason for the hope that is in us,
 and to suffer gladly for the sake of our Lord Jesus Christ . . .

JUN • EVELYN UNDERHILL : *Mystic and Writer, England, 1941*
You enlightened Your Church
 by the teaching of Your servant Evelyn:
Enrich it evermore by Your grace, and raise up faithful witnesses,
 who by their life and their learning may proclaim Your Truth . . .

JUL • **VLADIMIR OF RUSSIA** : *First Christian Ruler of Russia, 1015*
You called Your servant Vladimir of Russia to an earthly throne
   And You gave him a zeal for the Church and a love for Your people:
Grant that we who remember his example may be fruitful in all good works
   and attain to the glorious crown of Your saints . . .

AUG • **THE FEAST OF MARY, THE BLESSED MOTHER OF OUR LORD** *(34)*
You have taken to Yourself the Blessed Mary,
   Mother of Your Divine Son, Our Lord and Savior:
Grant that we, who have been redeemed by his blood,
   may share with her in the eternal glory of the world to come . . .

SEP • **THE FEAST OF THE SEVEN SORROWS OF MARY** *(88)*
Grant that we who call to mind the suffering of the Blessed Mary
   may, through the glorious merits and prayers
of all the saints who have faithfully stood beside the cross,
   obtain to the blessed fruit of Your passion . . .

OCT • **TERESA OF AVILA** : *Mystic and Writer, Spain, 1582*
Hear us as we rejoice
   in the remembrance of the blessed Teresa:
May we be nourished with the food of her doctrine,
   and taught in the spirit of her loving devotion . . .

NOV • **ALBERT THE GREAT** : *Teacher and Theologian, Germany, 1280*
By Your Spirit You give to some the word of wisdom,
   to others the word of knowledge, and to others the word of faith:
We praise You for the gifts manifested in Your servant Albert the Great,
   and pray that Your people may never be destitute of such gifts . . .

DEC • **MARY DI ROSA** : *Founder of the Handmaids of Charity, Italy, 1855*
You call Your witnesses from every land, to reveal Your glory in the world:
   We give You thanks this day, for the example and the devotion of
Mary di Rosa and the Handmaids of Charity;
   strengthen us by their fellowship, that we may be faithful in service . . .

JAN • BERARD AND COMPANIONS : *First Franciscan Martyrs, Morocco, 1220*
By Your grace, Almighty God, Your holy martyr Berard and his companions
    triumphed over suffering and were faithful unto death:
Grant that we, remembering them with thanksgiving,
    may be so faithful in our witness, that we too may receive the crown of life . . .

FEB • ELIAS AND COMPANIONS : *Martyrs of Egypt, 309*
In every age, Almighty God, You send those who give their lives for Your sake:
    Inspire us with the memory of Your holy martyrs Elias and his companions,
whose faithfulness led them in the way of the Cross,
    and give us courage to bear witness to Your love with our lives . . .

MAR • JULIAN OF ANTIOCH : *Martyr, c. 302*
In every age, Almighty God, You send those who give their lives for Your sake:
    Inspire us, we pray, with the memory of Your holy martyr Julian of Antioch,
whose faithfulness led him in the way of the Cross,
    and give us courage to bear witness to Your love with our lives . . .

APR • BERNADETTE : *Visionary and Nun of Lourdes, France, 1879*
By Your grace, Your servant Bernadette, kindled with Your love,
    became a burning and shining light in Your Church:
Grant that we also may be aflame with a spirit of love and discipline,
    and walk before You as children of light . . .

MAY • BRENDAN : *Monk and Explorer, England, c. 577*
Your servant Brendan carried the Good News of Your Son
    to the dark places of the world:
Grant that we who commemorate his service may know
    the hope of the Gospel in our hearts and manifest its light in all our ways . . .

JUN • DAYS OF PRAYER FOR THE UNITY OF THE CHURCH : *First Day*
You call us as Your children to continue the work of reconciliation in the world:
    Forgive us the sins which keep us apart from others who bear Christ's name,
grant us courage to overcome our fear of our differences and our pasts,
    and strength to seek that unity that is Your gift to us and Your will for us . . .

JUL • **OSMUND** : *Bishop of Salisbury, England, 1099*
You raised up Your servant Osmund, Almighty God,
    to be a faithful shepherd of Your people:
Grant Your Spirit, we pray, to all bishops, priests, ministers, and leaders,
    that they also may serve You as true stewards of Your divine mysteries . . .

AUG • **STEPHEN OF HUNGARY** : *King and Reformer of Society, 1038*
You called Your servant Stephen of Hungary to an earthly throne
    and You gave him a zeal for the Church and a love for Your people:
Grant that we who remember his example may be fruitful in all good works
    and attain to the glorious crown of Your saints . . .

SEP • **NINIAN** : *Missionary to Britain, c. 430*
By the preaching of Your servant Ninian,
    You caused the light of the Gospel to shine in Britain:
Grant that we, who remember his life and labors,
    may show forth our thankfulness by following the example of his zeal . . .

OCT • **THOMAS CRANMER** : *Author, Book of Common Prayer, England, 1556*
Through Your servant Thomas,
    You restored the language of the people in the prayers of Your Church:
Make us always thankful for this heritage, and help us to pray
    with understanding, that we may worthily magnify Your Holy Name . . .

NOV • **MARGARET** : *Philanthropist, Scotland, 1083*
By Your grace, Your servant Margaret
    recognized and honored Jesus in the poor of this world:
Grant that we, following her example,
    may serve with love and gladness those in any need or trouble . . .

DEC • **ADELAIDE** : *Empress, France, 999*
You called Your servant Adelaide to an earthly throne
    and You gave her a zeal for the Church and a love for Your people:
Grant that we who remember her example may be fruitful in all good works
    and attain to the glorious crown of Your saints . . .

JAN • **ANTONY** : *Abbott and Monk of Egypt, 356*
By Your Holy Spirit, You enabled Your servant Antony
    to withstand the temptations of the world, the flesh, and the devil:
Give us grace, with pure hearts and minds,
    to follow You, our only Lord . . .

FEB • **THE SEVEN FOUNDERS**, *Florence, 13th century*
You call Your witnesses from every land, to reveal Your glory in the world:
    We give You thanks this day, for the example and the devotion
of the Seven Founders of the Servants of Mary;
    strengthen us by their fellowship, that we may be faithful in service . . .

MAR • **PATRICK** : *Missionary and Patron Saint of Ireland, 461*
You chose Your servant Patrick to be the apostle to the Irish people,
    to bring those who were wandering in darkness to the true light:
Grant us so to walk in that Light
    that we may come at last to the light of everlasting life . . .

APR • **ROBERT OF CHAISE-DIEU** : *Founder of Abbey at Chaise-Dieu, France, 1087*
By Your grace Robert of Chaise-Dieu, kindled with the flame of Your love,
    became a burning and shining light among Your people:
Grant that we also may be aflame with a spirit of love and discipline,
    and walk before You as children of light . . .

MAY • **ROBERT BELLARMINE** : *Theologian and Doctor of the Church, Rome, 1621*
Almighty God, You gave Your servant Robert Bellarmine
    special gifts of grace to understand and teach Your truth:
Grant that by such teaching we may know You
    and the One Whom You have sent . . .

JUN • **DAYS OF PRAYER FOR THE UNITY OF THE CHURCH** : *Second Day*
You call us as Your children to continue the work of reconciliation in the world:
    Forgive us the sins which keep us apart from others who bear Christ's name,
grant us courage to overcome our fear of our differences and our pasts,
    and strength to seek that unity that is Your gift to us and Your will for us . . .

JUL • **ALEXIS, THE MAN OF GOD** : *Patron of the Alexian Brothers, Rome, c. 430*
Your blessed Son became poor that through His poverty we might become rich:
  Deliver us, we pray, from an inordinate love of this world, that we, inspired by
the devotion of Alexis, the Man of God, may serve You with singleness of heart,
  and attain to the riches of the age to come . . .

AUG • **HYACINTH OF CRACOW** : *Dominican Friar, Poland, 1257*
You raised up Your servant Hyacinth of Cracow, Almighty God,
  to be a faithful shepherd of Your people:
Grant Your Spirit, we pray, to all bishops, priests, ministers, and leaders,
  that they also may serve You as true stewards of Your divine mysteries . . .

SEP • **HILDEGARD OF BINGEN** : *Mystic and Abbess, Germany, 1179*
You built Your Church through the love and devotion of Your saints,
  and we give thanks for Your servant Hildegard whom we remember this day:
Inspire us to follow her example
  that we in our generation may rejoice with her in the vision of Your glory . . .

OCT • **IGNATIUS** : *Bishop and Martyr of Antioch, c. 107*
We thank You for Your servant Ignatius who offered himself as grain
  to be eaten by wild beasts that he might become the pure bread of sacrifice:
Accept the willing tribute of our lives and grant to us
  a share in the pure and spotless offering of Your Divine Son . . .

NOV • **HUGH OF LINCOLN:** *Monk, Prior, and Bishop, England, 1200*
You endowed Your servant Hugh with wise and cheerful boldness,
  and taught him to commend the discipline of a holy life to kings and princes:
Grant that we also, rejoicing in the good news of Your mercy,
  may be bold to speak the truth in love . . .

DEC • **O SAPIENTIA** : *The Eight Days of Prayer Before Christmas (113)*
Purify our conscience we pray, by Your daily visitation:
  mercifully grant that Your Divine Son, at His coming,
may find in us a mansion prepared for Himself . . .

JAN • **THE FEAST OF THE CONFESSION OF ST. PETER** *(23)*
You inspired Simon Peter, first among Your apostles,
  to confess Jesus as the Messiah and as Your Divine Son:
Keep Your Church steadfast upon this rock of our faith,
  so that in unity and peace, we may proclaim the Truth and follow Him . . .

FEB • **MARTIN LUTHER:** *Priest and Reformer of the Church, Germany, 1546*
You raised up Your servant Martin Luther
  to reform and renew Your Church in the light of Your Word:
Defend and purify her in our own day and grant we may boldly proclaim
  the riches of Your grace that have been made known to us in Christ . . .

MAR • **CYRIL OF JERUSALEM** : *Bishop of Jerusalem, 386*
Strengthen Your bishops in their calling to be ministers of the sacraments,
  so that they, like Your servant Cyril of Jerusalem,
may effectively instruct Your people in Christian faith and practice,
  so that we may more fully celebrate the Paschal mystery . . .

APR • **LEO THE NINTH** : *Pope and Reformer of the Church, Rome, 1054*
You raised up Your servant Leo, Almighty God,
  to be a faithful shepherd of Your people:
Grant Your Spirit, we pray, to all bishops, priests, ministers, and leaders,
  that they also may serve You as true stewards of Your divine mysteries . . .

MAY • **ERIC** : *King of Sweden, c. 1160*
You called Your servant Eric of Sweden to an earthly throne
  and You gave him a zeal for the Church and a love for Your people:
Grant that we who remember his example may be fruitful in all good works
  and attain to the glorious crown of Your saints . . .

JUN • **DAYS OF PRAYER FOR THE UNITY OF THE CHURCH** : *Third Day*
You call us as Your children to continue the work of reconciliation in the world:
  Forgive us the sins which keep us apart from others who bear Christ's name,
grant us courage to overcome our fear of our differences and our pasts,
  and strength to seek that unity that is Your gift to us and Your will for us . . .

JUL • **ARNULF OF METZ** : *Bishop, France, 640*
You raised up Your servant Arnulf of Metz, Almighty God,
    to be a faithful shepherd of Your people:
Grant Your Spirit, we pray, to all bishops, priests, ministers, and leaders,
    that they also may serve You as true stewards of Your divine mysteries . . .

AUG • **HELEN** : *Empress and Mother of Constantine the Great, Nicomedia, c. 330*
You called Your servant Helen to an earthly throne
    and You gave her a zeal for the Church and a love for Your people:
Grant that we who remember her example may be fruitful in all good works
    and attain to the glorious crown of Your saints . . .

SEP • **DAG HAMMARSKJÖLD** : *Peacemaker and Writer, Norway, 1961*
Almighty God, whose peace passes all understanding:
    Grant that, as Your servant Dag Hammarskjöld toiled for peace in the world,
we too may become instruments of Your peace among all Your children,
    as befits the followers of the Prince of Peace . . .

OCT • **THE FEAST OF ST. LUKE THE EVANGELIST** *(147)*
You inspired Your servant Luke, the physician,
    to set forth in the Gospel the love and healing power of Your Divine Son:
Graciously continue in Your Church this love and power to heal,
    to the praise and glory of Your Name . . .

NOV • **HILDA** : *Abbess of Whitby, Great Britain, 680*
You endowed Hilda with the gifts of justice, prudence, and strength
    to rule as a wise mother over the nuns and monks of her household:
Give us the grace to recognize the varying gifts you bestow on men and women,
    that our common life may be enriched and Your gracious will be done . . .

DEC • **O SAPIENTIA** : *The Eight Days of Prayer Before Christmas (113)*
Purify our conscience we pray, by Your daily visitation:
    mercifully grant that Your Divine Son, at His coming,
may find in us a mansion prepared for Himself . . .

JAN • **WULFSTAN** : *Bishop of Worcester, 1095*
Multiply among us faithful pastors, we pray,
   who, like Your holy bishop Wulfstan,
will give courage to those who are oppressed and held in bondage:
   And bring us all into the true freedom of Your kingdom . . .

FEB • **THOMAS KEN** : *Bishop and Hymn Writer, England, 1711*
You are ever present, Almighty God, with artists like Thomas Ken,
   and all those who seek through their art to perfect the praises of Your people:
Grant to them even now glimpses of Your beauty,
   and make us worthy at last to behold it unveiled for evermore . . .

MAR • **THE FEAST OF ST. JOSEPH** *(89)*
You raised up Joseph from the family of Your servant David
   to be the guardian of Your Divine Son and the husband of the Blessed Mary:
Grant us grace to imitate his uprightness of life
   and obedience to Your commands . . .

APR • **ALPHEGE** : *Archbishop of Canterbury and Martyr, 1012*
Your martyred bishop Alphege of Canterbury suffered violent death
   when he refused to permit a ransom to be extorted from his people:
Grant that all pastors may pattern themselves on the Good Shepherd,
   who laid down his life for the sheep . . .

MAY • **DUNSTAN** : *Monk, Artist, and Bishop of Canterbury, 988*
You richly endowed Your servant Dunstan with skill in music and art:
   Teach us, we pray, to see in You the source of all our talents,
and move us to offer them for the adornment of worship
   and the advancement of true religion . . .

JUN • **DAYS OF PRAYER FOR THE UNITY OF THE CHURCH** : *Fourth Day*
You call us as Your children to continue the work of reconciliation in the world:
   Forgive us the sins which keep us apart from others who bear Christ's name,
grant us courage to overcome our fear of our differences and our pasts,
   and strength to seek that unity that is Your gift to us and Your will for us . . .

JUL • MACRINA : *Monastic, Theologian, and Teacher, Cappodocia, 379*
You called Your servant Macrina to reveal in her life and in her teachings
    the riches of Your grace and Your truth:
May we, following her example, seek after her wisdom
    and live according to her way . . .

AUG • JOHN EUDES : *Founder, The Sisters of Our Lady of Charity of the Refuge, 1680*
By Your grace Your servant John Eudes, kindled with the flame of Your love,
    became a burning and shining light among Your people:
Grant that we also may be aflame with spirit of love and discipline,
    and walk before You as children of light . . .

SEP • THEODORE OF TARSUS : *Archbishop of Canterbury, 690*
You called Theodore of Tarsus and gave him the grace to
    establish unity out of division, and order out of chaos among Your people:
Create in Your Church such godly union and accord that we may proclaim,
    by word and example, the Gospel of the Prince of Peace . . .

OCT • FRIDESWIDE : *Abbess and Patron of Oxford, England, c. 735*
Shepherd of Your people, we thank You for Your servant Frideswide,
    who was faithful in the care and nurture of Your flock:
Grant, we pray, that following this example of such a holy life,
    we may grow in Your grace and into the fullness of life in Christ . . .

NOV • ELIZABETH : *Philanthropist, Hungary, 1231*
By Your grace, Your servant Elizabeth
    recognized and honored Jesus in the poor of this world:
Grant that we, following her example,
    may serve with love and gladness those in any need or trouble . . .

DEC • O SAPIENTIA : *The Eight Days of Prayer Before Christmas (113)*
Purify our conscience we pray, by Your daily visitation:
    mercifully grant that Your Divine Son, at His coming,
may find in us a mansion prepared for Himself . . .

JAN • **FABIAN** : *Bishop and Martyr at Rome, 250*
Your servant Fabian, chief pastor of Your Church, led and strengthened Your
    Church so that it stood fast on the day of persecution:
Grant that those You call to ministry may be obedient to Your call in all humility,
    and be enabled to carry out their tasks with diligence and faithfulness . . .

FEB • **SHAHDOST** : *Martyred in Persia, 342*
In every age, Almighty God, You send those who give their lives for Your sake:
    Inspire us, we pray, with the memory of Your holy martyr Shahdost,
whose faithfulness led him in the way of the Cross,
    and give us courage to bear witness to Your love with our lives . . .

MAR • **CUTHBERT** : *Bishop of Lindisfarne, England, 687*
You called Your servant Cuthbert to be a shepherd of Your people:
    Grant that, as he sought in dangerous and remote places
those who had erred and strayed from Your ways,
    so we may seek the indifferent and the lost, and lead them back to You . . .

APR • **AGNES OF MONTEPULCIANO** : *Nun and Mother Superior, Tuscany, 1317*
We thank You for Your servant Agnes of Montepulciano,
    who was faithful in the care and nurture of Your flock:
Grant, we pray, that following this example of such a holy life,
    we may grow in Your grace and into the fullness of life in Christ . . .

MAY • **ALCUIN** : *Deacon and Abbott of Tours, France, 804*
In a rude and barbarous age,
    You raised up Your servant Alcuin to rekindle the light of learning:
Illumine our minds, that amid the uncertainties and confusions of our time,
    we may show forth Your eternal Truth . . .

JUN • **DAYS OF PRAYER FOR THE UNITY OF THE CHURCH** : *Fifth Day*
You call us as Your children to continue the work of reconciliation in the world:
    Forgive us the sins which keep us apart from others who bear Christ's name,
grant us courage to overcome our fear of our differences and our pasts,
    and strength to seek that unity that is Your gift to us and Your will for us . . .

JUL • SOJOURNER TRUTH : *Prophet and Campaigner for Civil Rights, 1883*
Your Spirit guides us into all truth and makes us free;
    Strengthen and sustain us as You did Your servant Sojourner Truth:
Grant us vision and courage to stand against oppression and injustice
    and all that works against the liberty to which You call all Your children . . .

AUG • BERNARD OF CLAIRVAUX : *Abbott, France, 1153*
By the life of Your servant Bernard,
    You rekindled the radiant light of Your Church:
Grant us, in our generation, to be inflamed with a spirit of love and discipline,
    and ever walk before You as children of light . . .

SEP • THE SAINTS AND MARTYRS OF THE PACIFIC *(33)*
You call Your witnesses from every nation and reveal Your glory in their lives:
    Make us thankful for the example of the saints and martyrs of the Pacific,
and strengthen us by their fellowship that we, like them,
    may be faithful in the service of Your kingdom . . .

OCT • BERTILLA BOSCARDIN : *Nursing Sister, Italy, 1922*
Your blessed Son became poor that through His poverty we might become rich:
    Deliver us, we pray, from an inordinate love of this world, that we, inspired by
Your servant Bertilla Boscardin, may serve You with singleness of heart,
    and attain to the riches of the age to come . . .

NOV • EDMUND : *King of East Anglia and Martyr, 870*
You gave grace and fortitude to the blessed King Edmund,
    that he might triumph over the enemy by dying nobly for Your Holy Name:
Bestow on all Your servants the shield of faith
    with which we can withstand the assaults of our ancient enemy . . .

DEC • O SAPIENTIA : *The Eight Days of Prayer Before Christmas (113)*
Purify our conscience we pray, by Your daily visitation:
    mercifully grant that Your Divine Son, at His coming,
may find in us a mansion prepared for Himself . . .

JAN • AGNES : *Martyr at Rome, 304*
You chose those whom the world deems powerless
    to put the powerful to shame:
Grant us so to cherish the memory of Your youthful martyr Agnes
    that we may share her pure and steadfast love for You . . .

FEB • THE SAINTS AND MARTYRS OF AFRICA *(33)*
You call Your witnesses from every nation and reveal Your glory in their lives:
    Make us thankful for the example of the saints and martyrs of Africa,
and strengthen us by their fellowship that we, like them,
    may be faithful in the service of Your kingdom . . .

MAR • NICHOLAS VON FLÜE : *Married Man and Hermit, Switzerland, 1487*
Your blessed Son became poor that through His poverty we might become rich:
    Deliver us, we pray, from an inordinate love of this world, that we,
inspired by the devotion of Nicholas von Flüe, may serve You
    with singleness of heart, and attain to the riches of the age to come . . .

APR • ANSELM : *Archbishop of Canterbury, 1109*
You raised up Your servant Anselm to teach the Church of his day
    to understand its faith in Your eternal Being, perfect justice, and saving mercy:
Provide Your Church in every age, we pray, with learned and devout scholars,
    that we may be able to give reason for the hope that is in us . . .

MAY • GODRIC : *Hermit and Poet, England, 1170*
You built Your Church through the love and devotion of Your saints,
    and we give You thanks for Your servant Godric whom we remember this day:
Inspire us to follow his example
    that we in our generation may rejoice with him in the vision of Your glory . . .

JUN • DAYS OF PRAYER FOR THE UNITY OF THE CHURCH : *Last Day*
You call us as Your children to continue the work of reconciliation in the world:
    Forgive us the sins which keep us apart from others who bear Christ's name,
grant us courage to overcome our fear of our differences and our pasts,
    and strength to seek that unity that is Your gift to us and Your will for us . . .

JUL • **ELIJAH AND ELISHA** : *Prophets and Patrons of Our Lady of Mount Carmel*
By Your Spirit You give to some the word of wisdom,
   to others the word of knowledge, and to others the word of faith:
We praise You for the gifts manifested in Your holy prophets Elijah and Elisha,
   and pray that Your people may never be destitute of such gifts . . .

AUG • **ABRAHAM OF SMOLENSK** : *Abbot, Russia, 1221*
Shepherd of Your people, we thank You for Your servant Abraham of Smolensk,
   who was faithful in the care and nurture of Your flock:
Grant, we pray, that following this example of such a holy life,
   we may grow in Your grace and into the fullness of life in Christ . . .

SEP • **THE FEAST OF ST. MATTHEW THE APOSTLE** *(119, He)*
We thank You for the witness of Your servant Matthew
   to the Gospel of Your Son, our Saviour:
And we pray that, after his example, we may, with ready wills and hearts,
   obey the calling of Our Lord to follow Him . . .

OCT • **HILARION** : *Hermit of Palestine, c. 371*
Your blessed Son became poor that through His poverty we might become rich:
   Deliver us, we pray, from an inordinate love of this world, that we, inspired by
the devotion of Your servant Hilarion, may serve You with singleness of heart,
   and attain to the riches of the age to come . . .

NOV • **GELASIUS THE FIRST** : *Pope, Rome, 496*
You raised up Your servant Gelasius, Almighty God,
   to be a faithful shepherd of Your people:
Grant Your Spirit, we pray, to all bishops, priests, ministers, and leaders,
   that they also may serve You as true stewards of Your divine mysteries . . .

DEC • **O SAPIENTIA** : *The Eight Days of Prayer Before Christmas (113)*
Purify our conscience we pray, by Your daily visitation:
   mercifully grant that Your Divine Son, at His coming,
may find in us a mansion prepared for Himself . . .

JAN • **VINCENT OF SARAGOSSA** : *Deacon and Protomartyr of Spain, 304*
Your deacon Vincent of Saragossa was upheld by Your grace,
 and was not terrified by threats nor overcome by torments:
Strengthen us that we too may endure all adversity
 with invincible and steadfast faith . . .

FEB • **MARGARET OF CORTONA** : *Penitent and Franciscan Tertiary, Italy, 1297*
By Your grace, Margaret of Cortona, kindled with the flame of Your love,
 became a burning and shining light among Your people:
Grant that we also may be aflame with a spirit of love and discipline,
 and walk before You as children of light . . .

MAR • **JONATHAN EDWARDS** : *Teacher and Missionary to the American Indians, 1758*
We thank You for Your servant Jonathan Edwards,
 whom You called to preach the gospel to the peoples of America:
Raise up in this and every land, we pray,
 men and women who will be heralds of Your kingdom . . .

APR • **THEODORE OF SYKEON** : *Monk and Bishop, Asia Minor, 613*
You raised up Your servant Theodore of Sykeon, Almighty God,
 to be a faithful shepherd of Your people:
Grant Your Spirit, we pray, to all bishops, priests, ministers, and leaders,
 that they also may serve You as true stewards of Your divine mysteries . . .

MAY • **RITA OF CASCIA** : *Married Woman and Nun, Italy, 1457*
Your blessed Son became poor that through His poverty we might become rich:
 Deliver us, we pray, from an inordinate love of this world, that we, inspired by
the devotion of Your servant Rita of Cascia, may serve You
 with singleness of heart, and attain to the riches of the age to come . . .

JUN • **ALBAN** : *Martyr, Great Britain, c. 304*
By Your grace and Your power, Your holy Martyr Alban
 triumphed over suffering and was faithful even unto death:
Grant that we, who now remember him in thanksgiving,
 may be faithful in our witness, that we too may receive the crown of life . . .

JUL • THE FEAST OF ST. MARY MAGDALENE *(42)*
Your Divine Son restored Mary to health of body and mind,
    and called her to be a witness of the Resurrection:
Mercifully grant by Your grace that we may be healed of our infirmities
    and know You in the power of unending life . . .

AUG • SYMPHORIAN : *Martyr, Gaul, 2nd century*
Almighty God, You gave to Your servant Symphorian the boldness
    to confess Christ in this world, and courage to die for this faith:
Grant that we may always be ready to give a reason for the hope that is in us,
    and to suffer gladly for the sake of our Lord Jesus Christ . . .

SEP • MARTYRS OF AGAUNUM : *Roman Soldiers and Martyrs, Gaul, 3rd century*
Almighty God, You gave to Your holy martyrs of Agaunum the boldness
    to confess Christ in this world, and courage to die for this faith:
Grant that we may always be ready to give a reason for the hope that is in us,
    and to suffer gladly for the sake of our Lord Jesus Christ . . .

OCT • PHILIP OF HERACLEA : *Bishop and Martyr, Adrianople, 304*
By Your grace and power, Almighty God, Your holy martyr Philip of Heraclea
    triumphed over suffering and was faithful unto death:
Grant that we, remembering him with thanksgiving,
    may be so faithful in our witness, that we too may receive the crown of life . . .

NOV • CECILIA : *Patron of Poets, Artists, and Musicians, Rome, c. 230*
Your saints and angels delight to worship You in heaven: Be ever present
    with Your servants who seek through art to perfect the praises of Your people,
and grant to them even now glimpses of Your beauty,
    and make them worthy at length to behold it unveiled for evermore . . .

DEC • O SAPIENTIA : *The Eight Days of Prayer Before Christmas (113)*
Purify our conscience we pray, by Your daily visitation:
    mercifully grant that Your Divine Son, at His coming,
may find in us a mansion prepared for Himself . . .

JAN • **JOHN THE ALMSGIVER** : *Bishop and Reformer of Society, Cyprus, 619*
Lead us by Your love, we pray, as You did Your servant John the Almsgiver,
 to serve all those to whom the world offers no comfort and little help:
Grant that we, like him, may give hope to the hopeless, love to the unloved,
 peace to the troubled, and rest to the weary . . .

FEB • **POLYCARP** : *Pupil of St. John the Apostle; Bishop and Martyr of Smyrna, 156*
You gave Your venerable servant, the holy and gentle Polycarp,
 boldness to confess Jesus Christ, and steadfastness to die for his faith:
Give us grace, following his example, to share the cup of Christ
 and to rise to eternal life . . .

MAR • **GREGORY THE ILLUMINATOR** : *Bishop and Martyr of Armenia, c. 332*
You raised up Your servant Gregory the Illuminator to be a light in the world,
 and to preach the Gospel to the people of Armenia:
Shine in our hearts that we in our generation may also show forth Your praise,
 Who called us out of darkness into Your marvelous light . . .

APR • **GEORGE** : *Martyr and Patron of England, c. 300*
You so kindled the flame of love in the heart of Your servant George
 that he bore witness to the Risen Lord by his life and his death:
Grant to us the same faith and power of love, that we who rejoice in his triumph
 may come to share with him in the fullness of the Resurrection . . .

MAY • **EUPHROSYNE OF POLOTSK** : *Virgin and Patron of Belarus, 1173*
You have graciously surrounded us with a great cloud of witnesses:
 Grant that we, encouraged by the example of Euphrosyne of
Polotsk, may persevere in running the race that is set before us,
 until we too at last attain to Your eternal joy . . .

JUN • **JOSEPH CAFASSO** : *Teacher, Turin, Italy, 1860*
Almighty God, You gave Your servant Joseph Cafasso
 special gifts of grace to understand and teach Your truth:
Grant that by such teaching we may know You
 and the One Whom You have sent . . .

JUL • **BRIDGET OF SWEDEN** : *Visionary and Founder of the Brigittines, 1373*
By Your grace, Your servant Bridget of Sweden, kindled with Your love,
    became a burning and shining light in Your Church:
Grant that we also may be aflame with a spirit of love and discipline,
    and walk before You as children of light . . .

AUG • **ROSE OF LIMA** : *Recluse and Dominican Tertiary, Peru, 1617*
Your blessed Son became poor that through His poverty we might become rich:
    Deliver us, we pray, from an inordinate love of this world, that we, inspired by
the devotion of Your servant Rose of Lima, may serve You
    with singleness of heart, and attain to the riches of the age to come . . .

SEP • **ADAMNAN** : *Abbot, Ireland, 704*
Shepherd of Your people, we thank You for Your servant Adamnan,
    who was faithful in the care and nurture of Your flock:
Grant, we pray, that following this example of such a holy life,
    we may grow in Your grace and into the fullness of life in Christ . . .

OCT • **THE FEAST OF ST. JAMES, THE BROTHER OF OUR LORD** *(1)*
Grant, we pray, that following the example of Your servant James the Just,
    we may give ourselves continually to prayer,
and to the reconciliation of all Your children
    who are at variance and enmity . . .

NOV • **CLEMENT** : *Bishop of Rome, c. 100*
You chose Your servant Clement to recall Your people to obedience and stability:
    Grant that we may be grounded and settled in truth by Your Spirit;
reveal to us what is not yet known; fill up what is lacking;
    confirm what has been revealed; and keep us blameless in Your service . . .

DEC • O **SAPIENTIA** : *The Eight Days of Prayer Before Christmas (113)*
Purify our conscience we pray, by Your daily visitation:
    mercifully grant that Your Divine Son, at His coming,
may find in us a mansion prepared for Himself . . .

JAN • **FRANCIS DE SALES** : *Teacher and Confessor, France, 1622*
You called Your servant Francis de Sales to a devout and holy life,
    and by his teaching You enlightened Your people:
Grant that we, by word and example,
    may reflect Your gentleness and glory to all we meet . . .

FEB • **MONTANUS AND LUCIUS:** *Martyred at Carthage, 259*
By Your grace and power, Your holy martyrs Montanus and Lucius
    triumphed over suffering and were faithful unto death:
Grant that we, remembering them with thanksgiving,
    may be so faithful in our witness that we too may receive the crown of life . . .

MAR • **THE FEAST OF ST. GABRIEL THE ARCHANGEL** *(97)*
You chose the angel Gabriel from among the other angels
    to announce the incarnation of Your Divine Son:
Grant that we who celebrate his feast here on earth
    may experience his protection from heaven . . .

APR • **EGBERT** : *Hermit and Evangelist to the German Peoples, Iona, 729*
We thank You for Your servant Egbert,
    whom You called to preach the Gospel to the peoples of Germany:
Raise up, we pray, in this and every land, heralds of Your kingdom,
    that Your people may proclaim the unsearchable riches of Your ways . . .

MAY • **JACKSON KEMPER** : *First Episcopal Missionary Bishop in the United States, 1870*
In Your providence, Jackson Kemper became a missionary bishop in America,
    and by his labors congregations were established in the settlements of the
West: Grant that Your people may always have the courage, vision,
    and perseverance to make known Your Truth to all people . . .

JUN • **THE FEAST OF THE NATIVITY OF JOHN THE BAPTIST** *(85)*
You sent John to prepare the way of Your Son by preaching repentance:
    Make us so to follow his teaching and his holy life that we may truly repent,
constantly seek the truth, boldly rebuke vice,
    and patiently suffer for the sake of the Truth . . .

JUL • THOMAS À KEMPIS : *Priest and Writer, Low Countries, 1471*
You nourished Your Church by the inspired writing of Your servant Thomas:
  Grant that we may learn from him to know what is necessary to be known,
to love what is to be loved, to praise what highly pleases You,
    and always to seek to know and to follow Your will . . .

AUG • SAINT BARTHOLOMEW THE APOSTLE
You gave to Your Servant Bartholomew
  the grace to truly believe and to preach Your Word:
Grant that we who remember him this day
  may believe what he believed and preach what he taught . . .

SEP • GERARD OF CSANAD : *Bishop and Martyr, Hungary, 1046*
You raised up Your servant Gerard of Csanad, Almighty God,
  to be a faithful shepherd of Your people:
Grant Your Spirit, we pray, to all bishops, priests, ministers, and leaders,
  that they also may serve You as true stewards of Your divine mysteries . . .

OCT • ANTONY MARY CLARET : *Bishop, Founder of Claretian Missionaries, 1870*
You raised up Your servant Antony Mary Claret, Almighty God,
  to be a faithful shepherd of Your people:
Grant Your Spirit, we pray, to all bishops, priests, ministers, and leaders,
  that they also may serve You as true stewards of Your divine mysteries . . .

NOV • MARTYRS OF VIETNAM, *18th and 19th centuries*
Almighty God, You gave to the blessed martyrs of Vietnam the boldness
  to confess Christ in this world, and the courage to die for this faith:
Grant that we may always be ready to give a reason for the hope that is in us,
  and to suffer gladly for the sake of our Lord Jesus Christ . . .

DEC • CHRISTMAS EVE: *The Vigil for the Nativity of Our Lord (98)*
You have caused this holy night to shine
  with the brightness of the True Light:
Grant that we who have known the mystery of the Light on earth
  may also enjoy him perfectly in heaven . . .

JAN • THE FEAST OF THE CONVERSION OF ST. PAUL *(67)*
By the preaching of the apostle Paul
    You have caused the light of the Gospel to shine throughout the world:
Grant we pray that we, having his wonderful conversion in remembrance,
    may show ourselves thankful to You by following his holy teaching . . .

FEB • WALBURGA : *Abbess and Missionary to Germany, 779*
We thank You for Your servant Walburga,
    whom You called to preach the Gospel to the peoples of Germany:
Raise up, we pray, in this and every land, heralds of Your kingdom,
    that Your people may proclaim the unsearchable riches of Your ways . . .

MAR • THE FEAST OF THE ANNUNCIATION OF OUR LORD *(40)*
Pour Your grace into our hearts, we pray,
    that we who have known the incarnation of Your Divine Son,
announced by an angel to the Blessed Mother Mary,
    may by His cross and passion be brought to the glory of His Resurrection . . .

APR • THE FEAST OF ST. MARK THE APOSTLE *(2)*
By the hand of Mark the evangelist
    You have given to us the Gospel of Christ:
We thank You for this witness,
    and pray that we may be firmly grounded in its truth . . .

MAY • BEDE THE VENERABLE : *Priest and Monk of Jarrow, England, 735*
You called Your servant Bede, while he was still a child,
    to devote his life to Your service in the disciplines of religion and scholarship:
Grant that as he labored to bring the riches of truth to his generation,
    we, in our various occupations, may strive to make You known . . .

JUN • THE AUGSBURG CONFESSION, *1530*
You have brought us near to an innumerable company of angels,
    and to the spirits of just men and women made perfect:
Grant us in our earthly pilgrimage to abide in their fellowship,
    and in our heavenly country to become partakers of their joy . . .

JUL • THE FEAST OF ST. JAMES THE ELDER *(67)*
We remember before You this day Your servant James,
   the first among the Twelve to suffer martyrdom for the sake of the Christ:
Pour out upon the leaders of Your Church that same spirit of self-denying service
   by which alone they may have true authority among Your people . . .

AUG • LOUIS IX : *King of France, 1270*
You called Louis to the throne that he might announce Your heavenly kingdom,
   and gave him zeal for Your Church and for Your people:
Grant that we who remember him this day may be fruitful in all good works,
   and attain to the glorious crown of Your saints . . .

SEP • SERGIUS : *Abbot and Patron of Russia, 1392*
Your blessed Son became poor that through his poverty might we become rich:
   Deliver us from an inordinate love of the things of this world, that we,
inspired by the devotion of Your servant Sergius of Moscow, may serve You
   with purity of heart, and attain to the riches of the age to come . . .

OCT • CRISPIN : *Missionary, Martyred in Rome, c. 286*
By Your grace and power, Your holy martyr Crispin
   triumphed over suffering and was faithful unto death:
Strengthen us, we pray, that we may endure reproach and persecution,
   and faithfully bear witness to Your name . . .

NOV • ISAAC WATTS : *Priest and Hymn Writer, England, 1748*
You are ever present, Almighty God, with artists like Isaac Watts,
   and all those who seek through their art to perfect the praises of Your people:
Grant to them even now glimpses of Your beauty,
   and make us worthy at last to behold it unveiled for evermore . . .

DEC • THE FEAST OF THE NATIVITY OF OUR LORD *(98)*
You have given Your Divine Son to take our human nature upon Himself,
   and to be born this day of the Blessed Mother:
Grant that we who have been made Your children through adoption and grace
   may daily be renewed by Your Spirit . . .

JAN • The Feast of St. Timothy and St. Titus *(23)*
You called Timothy and Titus to be evangelists and teachers,
  and made them strong to endure hardship:
Help us, we pray, to stand fast in adversity, and live godly and righteous lives,
  that with sure confidence we may look for our blessed hope . . .

FEB • Porphyry of Gaza : *Monk and Bishop, Gaza, c. 420*
You raised up Your servant Porphyry of Gaza, Almighty God,
  to be a faithful shepherd of Your people:
Grant Your Spirit, we pray, to all bishops, priests, ministers, and leaders,
  that they also may serve You as true stewards of Your divine mysteries . . .

MAR • Oscar Romero : *Bishop and Martyr of South America, 1980*
By Your grace and power, Your holy martyr Oscar Romero
  triumphed over suffering and was faithful unto death:
Strengthen us, we pray, that we may endure reproach and persecution,
  and faithfully bear witness to Your name . . .

APR • Stephen of Perm : *Missionary Bishop, Russia, 1396*
Almighty God, You raised up Your servant Stephen of Perm
  to be a shining light in this world: Shine in our hearts, we pray,
that we also in our generation may show forth Your praise,
  because You have called us out of darkness into Your marvelous light . . .

MAY • Augustine of Canterbury : *First Archbishop of the English Nation, 605*
We bless Your Holy Name for Your servant Augustine,
  whose labors in propagating Your Church we recall this day:
Grant that all whom You call and send may do Your will,
  and bide Your time, and see Your glory . . .

JUN • John and Paul : *Early Christian Martyrs, Rome, c. 362*
By Your grace and power, Almighty God, Your holy martyrs John and Paul
  triumphed over suffering and were faithful unto death:
Grant that we, remembering them with thanksgiving,
  may be so faithful in our witness, that we too may receive the crown of life . . .

JUL • The Feast of the Parents of the Blessed Mother of Our Lord *(85)*
In thanksgiving we remember this day Your servants Joachim and Anne,
    the parents of the Blessed Mother Mary:
Grant, we pray, that we all may be made one
    in the heavenly family of Your Divine Son . . .

AUG • Elizabeth Bichier des Anges : *Foundress, Sisters of St. Andrew, 1838*
By Your grace, Elizabeth Bichier, kindled with the flame of Your love,
    became a burning and shining light among Your people:
Grant that we also may be aflame with a spirit of love and discipline,
    and walk before You as children of light . . .

SEP • Cosmas and Damian : *Early Christian Martyrs, Syria, c. 303*
In every age, Almighty God, You send those who give their lives for Your sake:
    Inspire us, we pray, with the memory of Your holy martyrs Cosmas and
            Damian
whose faithfulness led them in the way of the Cross,
    and give us courage to bear witness to Your love with our lives . . .

OCT • Philipp Nicolai : *Hymn Writer, 1608*
You are ever present, Almighty God, with artists like Philipp Nicolai,
    and all those who seek through their art to perfect the praises of Your people:
Grant to them even now glimpses of Your beauty,
    and make us worthy at last to behold it unveiled for evermore . . .

NOV • Leonard of Port Maurice : *Franciscan Friar and Missioner, Italy, 1751*
Almighty God, You raised up Your servant Leonard of Port Maurice
    to be a shining light in this world: Shine in our hearts, we pray,
that we also in our generation may show forth Your praise,
    because You have called us out of darkness into Your marvelous light . . .

DEC • The Feast of St. Stephen *(31)*
We give You thanks for the example of Your servant Stephen,
    who looked up to heaven and prayed for his persecutors:
Grant us grace that in all our sufferings for the Truth we also
    may look to Him Who was crucified, and pray for those who persecute us . . .

JAN • **JOHN OF CHRYSOSTOM** : *Bishop of Constantinople, 407*
You gave Your servant John the grace to eloquently proclaim Your Name,
    and to fearlessly bear reproach for its honor:
Grant to all bishops and ministers such faithfulness in the ministry of Your Word,
    that we may partake with them of the glory that shall be revealed . . .

FEB • **GEORGE HERBERT** : *Priest and Writer, England, 1633*
You are ever present, Almighty God, with artists like George Herbert,
    and all those who seek through their art to perfect the praises of Your people:
Grant to them even now glimpses of Your beauty,
    and make us worthy at last to behold it unveiled for evermore . . .

MAR • **JOHN THE EGYPTIAN** : *Hermit, 394*
Your blessed Son became poor that through His poverty we might become rich:
    Deliver us, we pray, from an inordinate love of this world, that we, inspired by
Your servant John the Egyptian, may serve You with singleness of heart,
    and attain to the riches of the age to come . . .

APR • **ZITA** : *Domestic Servant, Italy, 1278*
You have graciously surrounded us with a great cloud of witnesses:
    Grant that we, encouraged by the good example of Your servant Zita
may persevere in running the race that is set before us,
    until we too at last attain to Your eternal joy . . .

MAY • **JOHN CALVIN** : *Renewer of the Church, 1564*
We praise You for those You have sent to call the Church to its tasks
    and renew its life, such as Your servant John Calvin:
Raise up in our own day teachers and prophets inspired by Your Spirit,
    whose voices will proclaim the reality of Your kingdom . . .

JUN • **CYRIL OF ALEXANDRIA** : *Theologian and Doctor of the Church, 444*
You gave Your servant Cyril of Alexandria
    the gift of grace to understand and to teach the truth as it is:
Grant that by such teaching we may come to know You as You are,
    and to come to serve the One Whom You sent . . .

JUL • **CHRISTOPHER** : *Martyr and Patron of Travelers, Asia Minor, 3rd century*
Your presence is to be found wherever we go:
    Preserve all those who must travel,
surround them with Your loving care, protect them from every danger,
    and bring them in safety to their journey's end . . .

AUG • **CAESARIUS OF ARLES** : *Monk and Bishop, Gaul, 542*
You raised up Your servant Caesarius of Arles, Almighty God,
    to be a faithful shepherd of Your people:
Grant Your Spirit, we pray, to all bishops, priests, ministers, and leaders,
    that they also may serve You as true stewards of Your divine mysteries . . .

SEP • **VINCENT DE PAUL** : *Co-Founder of the Sisters of Charity, France, 1660*
We thank You for the life of Your servant Vincent
    and for his ministry of preaching and caring for the poor:
Help us to follow his example and, by Your word and action,
    to make known Your love to others in their need . . .

OCT • **FRUMENTIUS** : *Bishop and Evangelizer of Ethiopia, c. 380*
We thank You for Your servant Frumentius,
    whom You called to preach the Gospel to the peoples of Ethiopia:
Raise up, we pray, in this and every land, heralds of Your kingdom,
    that Your people may proclaim the unsearchable riches of Your ways . . .

NOV • **GREGORY OF SINAI** : *Mystic, Mount Athos and Bulgaria, 1346*
You built Your Church through the love and devotion of Your saints,
    and we give You thanks this day for Your servant Gregory of Sinai:
Inspire us to follow his example
    that we in our generation may rejoice with his in the vision of Your glory . . .

DEC • **THE FEAST OF ST. JOHN THE EVANGELIST** *(92)*
Shed the brightness of Your Light upon us:
    Grant that we, being illuminated by the teaching of Your apostle John,
may so walk in the light of Your Truth,
    that at length we may obtain to the fullness of eternal life . . .

JAN • **THOMAS AQUINAS** : *Priest and Theologian, Italy, 1274*
You enriched Your Church with the singular learning of Your servant Thomas:
    Enlighten us more and more, we pray,
by the disciplined thinking and teaching of Christian scholars,
    and deepen our devotion by the example of saintly lives . . .

FEB • **OSWALD OF WORCESTER** : *Bishop and Monastic Reformer, England, 992*
We praise You, Almighty God, for those like Your servant Oswald of Worcester,
    whom You have sent to call the Church to its true work and to renew its life:
Raise up in our day, we pray, men and women whose voices will
    give strength to Your people and proclaim the reality of Your ways . . .

MAR • **BERTHOLD AND BROCARD** : *Forerunners of Carmelite Friars, Palestine, 1198, 1231*
You call Your witnesses from every land, to reveal Your glory in the world:
    We give You thanks this day, for the example and the devotion of
Berthold and Brocard, and all those of the Carmelite Order;
    strengthen us by their fellowship, that we too may be faithful in Your
                service . . .

APR • **LOUIS GRIGNION DE MONTFORT** : *Founder, Missionaries of the Company of Mary, 1716*
By Your grace, Louis Grignion, kindled with the flame of Your love,
    became a burning and shining light among Your people:
Grant that we also may be aflame with a spirit of love and discipline,
    and walk before You as children of light . . .

MAY • **BERNARD OF MONTJOUX** : *Priest, Italy, 1081*
By Your Spirit You give to some the word of wisdom,
    to others the word of knowledge, and to others the word of faith:
We praise You for the gifts manifested in Your servant Bernard of Montjoux,
    and pray that Your people may never be destitute of such gifts . . .

JUN • **IRENAEUS** : *Bishop of Lyons, c. 202*
You upheld Your servant Irenaeus with strength
    to maintain the truth against every blast of vain doctrine:
Keep us, we pray, steadfast in true religion, that in constancy and peace
    we may walk in the way that leads to life eternal . . .

JUL • **JOHANN S. BACH AND GEORGE F. HANDEL** : *Musicians, 1750, 1758*
Your saints and angels delight to worship You in heaven: Be ever present
  with Your servants who seek through art to perfect the praises of Your people,
and grant to them even now glimpses of Your beauty,
  and make them worthy at length to behold it unveiled for evermore . . .

AUG • **AUGUSTINE OF HIPPO** : *Bishop and Theologian, North Africa, 430*
You are the light of the minds that know You, the life of the souls that love You,
  and the strength of the hearts that serve You:
Help us, following the example of Augustine, so to know You that we
  may truly love You, and so look to You that we may fully serve You . . .

SEP • **LIOBA** : *Abbess and Missionary to Germany, 780*
We thank You for Your servant Lioba,
  whom You called to preach the Gospel to the peoples of Germany:
Raise up, we pray, in this and every land, heralds of Your kingdom,
  that Your people may proclaim the unsearchable riches of Your ways . . .

OCT • **THE FEAST OF ST. SIMON AND ST. JUDE** *(119, Lamedeh)*
We thank You for the glorious company of Your apostles,
  and especially on this day, we remember Simon and Jude:
Grant, we pray, that as they were faithful and zealous in their mission for You,
  so may we, with ardent devotion, make known Your love and mercy . . .

NOV • **CATHERINE LABOURÉ** : *Visionary, Paris, 1876*
You built Your Church through the love and devotion of Your saints,
  and we give thanks for Your servant Catherine Labouré this day:
Inspire us to follow her example
  that we in our generation may rejoice with her in the vision of Your glory . . .

DEC • **THE FEAST OF THE HOLY INNOCENTS** *(124)*
We remember on this day the slaughter of the holy innocents:
  Receive, we pray, into the arms of Your mercy all innocent victims,
and by Your might frustrate the designs of all tyrants,
  and establish Your rule of justice, love, and peace . . .

JAN • **GILDAS THE WISE** : *Monk and Historian, Brittany, c. 570*
By Your grace Your servant Gildas the Wise, kindled with the flame of Your love,
   became a burning and shining light among Your people:
Grant that we also may be aflame with a spirit of love and discipline,
   and walk before You as children of light . . .

MAR • **JOHN KEBLE** : *Priest, Poet, and Reformer of the Church, England, 1866*
Grant that in times of testing we may be obedient to Your will:
   And that, as did Your servant John Keble, we may with courage
do the work that You have given us to do,
   and with integrity endure what we have been given to bear . . .

APR • **CATHERINE OF SIENA** : *Dominican Nun and Mystic, Italy, 1380*
You so kindled the flame of holy love in the heart of blessed Catherine of Siena,
   as she meditated on the passion of Your Son,
that she devoted her life to the poor, and to the unity of the Church:
   Grant that we may also wholly rejoice in the revelation of His glory . . .

MAY • **JOAN OF ARC** : *Martyr, France, 1431*
By Your grace and power, Your holy martyr Joan
   triumphed over suffering and was faithful unto death:
Strengthen us, we pray, that we may endure reproach and persecution,
   and faithfully bear witness to Your Name . . .

JUN • **THE FEAST OF ST. PETER AND ST. PAUL** *(87)*
You were glorified by the martyrdom of the blessed Peter and Paul:
   Grant that we, instructed by their teaching and example,
and knit together in unity by Your Spirit,
   may ever stand firm upon the foundation of Jesus Christ our Lord . . .

JUL • MARY AND MARTHA AND LAZARUS, *Companions of Our Lord*
Your Divine Son enjoyed rest and refreshment
   in the home of Mary and Martha of Bethany:
Give us, we pray, the will to love You and to open our hearts to hear You;
   and strengthen our hands to serve You in others for Your sake . . .

AUG • THE BEHEADING OF JOHN THE BAPTIST
You called Your servant John the Baptist
   to be the forerunner of Your Son in birth and in death:
Grant us strength, we pray, that as he suffered for the truth,
   so may we also resist corruption and vice and receive the crown of glory . . .

SEP • THE FEAST OF ST. MICHAEL AND ALL ANGELS *(103)*
You have ordained in wonderful order the work of mortals and angels:
   Mercifully grant that, as Your holy angels
always serve and worship You in heaven, so by Your appointment
   may they help and defend us here on earth . . .

OCT • JAMES HANNINGTON AND COMPANIONS : *Bishop and Martyr, Africa, 1885*
The death of Your saints, Almighty God, is precious in Your sight,
   and their faithful witness has its great reward,
as was true of Your blessed martyrs James Hannington and his friends:
   We give You thanks for them, and pray we may also obtain Your reward . . .

NOV • DAY OF PRAYER FOR ALL MISSIONS AND MISSIONARIES
We thank You for all Your servants
   whom You have called to preach the Gospel to the peoples of the world:
Raise up in this and every land, we pray,
   men and women who will be heralds of Your kingdom . . .

DEC • MARCELLUS THE RIGHTEOUS : *Monk and Abbot, Constantinople, c. 485*
We thank You for Your servant Marcellus the Righteous,
   who was faithful in the care and nurture of Your flock:
Grant, we pray, that following this example of such a holy life,
   we may grow in Your grace and into the fullness of life in Christ . . .

30 JAN • CHARLES STUART : *Martyr, England, 1649*
By Your grace and power, Almighty God, Your holy martyr Charles Stuart
    triumphed over suffering and was faithful unto death:
Grant that we, remembering him with thanksgiving,
    may be so faithful in our witness, that we too may receive the crown of life . . .

31 JAN • JOHN BOSCO : *Founder of the Daughters of Mary Turin, Italy, 1888*
You call Your witnesses from every land, to reveal Your glory in the world:
    We give You thanks this day, for the example and the devotion of
John Bosco and The Daughters of Mary;
    strengthen us by their fellowship, that we too may be faithful in Your
        service . . .

30 MAR • JOHN CLIMACUS : *Monk and Abbot of Mount Sinai, c. 649*
Shepherd of Your people, we thank You for Your servant John Climacus,
    who was faithful in the care and nurture of Your flock:
Grant, we pray, that following this example of such a holy life,
    we may grow in Your grace and into the fullness of life in Christ . . .

30 APR • MARIAN AND JAMES : *Martyred in Africa, 259*
Almighty God, You gave to Your servants Marian and James the boldness
    to confess Christ in this world, and courage to die for this faith:
Grant that we may always be ready to give a reason for the hope that is in us,
    and to suffer gladly for the sake of our Lord Jesus Christ . . .

31 MAY • THE FEAST OF THE VISITATION OF THE BLESSED MOTHER *(113)*
By Your grace, the Blessed Mother was blessed in bearing Him,
    but still more blessed in keeping Your word:
Grant us who honor the exaltation of her lowliness
    to follow the example of her devotion to Your will . . .

30 JUN • MARTIAL OF LIMOGES: *Missionary Bishop, Gaul, 3rd century*
You raised up Your servant Martial, Almighty God,
    to be a faithful shepherd of Your people:
Grant Your Spirit, we pray, to all bishops, priests, ministers, and leaders,
    that they also may serve You as true stewards of Your divine mysteries . . .

31 JUL • IGNATIUS OF LOYOLA : *Priest and Founder of the Society of Jesus, Spain, 1556*
You called Ignatius of Loyola to the service of Your Divine Majesty:
    Grant that we, inspired and strengthened by his example,
may labor without counting the cost
    and seek no reward other than knowing that we do Your will . . .

30 AUG • AIDAN : *Monk and Bishop of Lindisfarne, 651*
You called Aidan from the cloister to re-establish a mission in northern England,
    and endowed him with gentleness, simplicity and strength: Grant that we,
following his example, may use what You give us for the relief of human need,
    and to persevere in commending the Gospel of Christ . . .

30 SEP • JEROME : *Priest and Monk of Bethlehem, 420*
We give You thanks for Jerome and all of those
    who have labored to render the Holy Scriptures in the language of the people:
Grant, we pray, that Your Spirit will overshadow us as we read the written Word,
    and that Christ, the living Word, will transform us . . .

31 OCT • THE SAINTS AND MARTYRS OF THE REFORMATION *(33)*
You call Your witnesses from every nation to reveal Your glory in their lives:
    Keep us, we pray, ever constant in faith and zealous in witness,
after the example of the saints and martyrs of the Reformation,
    that we, like them, may be faithful in the service of Your kingdom . . .

30 NOV • THE FEAST OF ST. ANDREW THE APOSTLE *(19)*
You gave such grace to Your apostle Andrew that he readily obeyed
    the call of Your Divine Son and brought his brother with him:
Give us, who are called by Your Word, the grace to follow without delay,
    and to bring those who are near to us into Your gracious presence . . .

31 DEC • THE VIGIL FOR THE FEAST OF THE HOLY NAME OF OUR LORD *(8)*
You gave to Your Divine Son the name of Jesus to be the sign of our salvation:
    Grant that the remembrance of this holy day to which we are drawing nigh,
may both deepen our devotion and set forward our salvation,
    and make us ever more prepared to come into Your presence . . .

Notes for Saying the Canticles

This section includes *Canticles*—hymns and songs of praise taken from the Scriptures—as well as the *Nicene Creed*, the *Te Deum*, and a *Litany of Penitence*. They are ancient statements of the tenets of the faith, and have been said by the faithful for centuries. Saying them in a thirty-day cycle allows their words, and the faith and hope and wisdom that are held in them, to shape and inform one's prayer and devotion.

The order in which they appear moves in a roughly chronological order from the most ancient hymns from the Hebrew Scriptures through texts from the Gospels, the Letters of the New Testament, and so forth. The last of them, the Litany of Penitence, ends the cycle with confession, clearing the heart, so to speak, to present it fresh and clean for praise again.

In many communities, Canticles are used in place of or in addition to the particular Canticle prescribed for each individual Office. In other places, they are read as a song of praise between each of the Scripture readings for the day. Another place in the Office where one might use one of them is following the *Our Father*, just before the *Blessing* is pronounced.

When you read them, read them as praise and worship, with joy and clarity, remembering that "God inhabits the praises of His people," as the psalmist wrote.

Finally, when shared with others in prayer, they are generally read in unison. The first lines, in caps and small caps, are to be used as an antiphon. The mark [A] at the end of the Canticle is there as a reminder to repeat the antiphon.

THE CANTICLES

O Lord, open our lips;
    and our mouths shall proclaim Your praise.
       —FROM THE PSALMS

We give You thanks, Almighty God,
    for all Your servants who, through art and music,
have sought to perfect the praises of Your people:
    Grant that we, who join our voices with all who praise Your name,
may even now have glimpses of Your beauty,
    and ever rejoice to sing Your praise. *Amen.*
       —A COLLECT FOR ARTISTS AND MUSICIANS

Never fear to precede the dawn
    to praise and bless and sing Christ your Lord.
       —FROM THE RULE OF TAIZÉ

O ALL YOU WORKS OF GOD, BLESS THE LORD:
PRAISE AND MAGNIFY GOD FOR EVER.

O you heavens, and you waters that be above the firmament,
and all you mighty powers, bless the Lord:
    Praise and magnify God for ever.

O sun and moon, and stars of heaven,
and showers and dew, bless the Lord:
    Praise and magnify God for ever.

O winds of God, and fire and heat,
and winter and summer, bless the Lord:
    Praise and magnify God for ever.

O dews and frosts, and frost and cold,
and ice and snow, bless the Lord:
    Praise and magnify God for ever.

O nights and days, and light and darkness,
and lightning and clouds, bless the Lord:
    Praise and magnify God for ever. [A]

BENEDICTE, OMNIA OPERA DOMINI
A Song of the Cosmic Order from *the Song of the Three Young Men*

O ALL YOU WORKS OF GOD, BLESS THE LORD:
PRAISE AND MAGNIFY GOD FOR EVER.

O let the earth bless the Lord in mountains and hills,
and all green things upon the earth, bless the Lord:
   Praise and magnify God forever.

O wells, bless the Lord, and seas and floods,
and whales, and all that move in the waters, bless the Lord:
   Praise and magnify God forever.

O birds of the air, bless the Lord, and beasts and cattle,
and all the children of the world, bless the Lord:
   Praise and magnify God forever.

O you angels, bless the Lord, and people of God,
and priests and servants, bless the Lord:
   Praise and magnify God for ever.

O you spirits, bless the Lord, and you souls of the righteous,
and holy and humble of heart, bless the Lord.
   Bless the Creator, the Redeemer, and the Giver of Life:
Praise and magnify God for ever. [A]

BENEDICTE, OMNIA OPERA DOMINI
A Song of the Earth and All Its Creatures from *the Song of the Three Young Men*

BLESSED ARE YOU—CREATOR, REDEEMER, AND GIVER OF LIFE:
PRAISED AND EXALTED ABOVE ALL FOR EVER.

Blessed are You, O God of our fathers and mothers,
praised and exalted above all for ever.
Blessed are You for the Name of Your majesty,
praised and exalted above all for ever.
Blessed are You in the temple of Your holiness,
praised and exalted above all for ever.
Blessed are You that beholds the depths,
praised and exalted above all for ever.
Blessed are You on Your glorious throne,
praised and exalted above all for ever.
Blessed are You in the highest of heavens,
praised and exalted above all for ever. [A]

BENEDICTUS ES, DOMINE
A Song of Praise from *the Song of the Three Young Men*

WE WILL SING TO YOUR NAME,
FOR YOU ARE LOFTY AND UPLIFTED.
YOU ARE OUR STRENGTH AND OUR REFUGE.

You have become our Saviour.
You are our God, and we will praise You;
the God of our people and we will exalt You.
Your right hand is glorious in might;
Your right hand has overthrown the enemy.

Who can be compared with You, among all gods?
Who is like You, glorious in holiness,
awesome in renown, and worker of wonders?

With Your constant love, You led the ones You redeemed;
and with Your might, You brought us to safety.
You will bring us to your holy dwelling, the place You have made for Yourself,
the sanctuary Your hand has established.
And there You shall reign for ever and ever. [A]

CANTEMUS DOMINO
A Song of Moses from *the Book of Exodus*

GOD OF OUR FATHERS, MERCIFUL LORD, GRANT US WISDOM:
DO NOT REFUSE US A PLACE AS YOUR SERVANTS.

You made all things by Your Word,
and in Your wisdom fashioned us to rule over creation,
    to be the stewards of the world in holiness and righteousness,
and to administer justice with an upright heart.
    We are weak, and with but a short time to live,
too feeble to understand Your justice and law.
    Let no one claim to be perfect in the eyes of their fellows,
for if the wisdom You give is found wanting,
    all their knowledge will be of no account.

    With You is the Spirit of Wisdom, familiar with all Your works,
and present with You when You created the world,
    the One Who knows what is acceptable to You,
and is in keeping with Your commandments.
    Send her forth from Your holy heavens,
bid her come down and labor by our side,
    that we may learn what is pleasing to You.
For she knows and understands all things;
    she will guide us in all that we do, and guard us in all her glory. [A]

DEUS PATRUM MEORUM
A Song of the Knowledge of Wisdom from *the Book of Wisdom*

WE PRAYED AND UNDERSTANDING WAS GIVEN TO US;
WE CALLED TO YOU AND WERE GIVEN THE SPIRIT OF WISDOM.

We preferred her to wealth and to power,
compared to her, all our riches were nothing.
We counted no precious stone as her equal,
before her gold is but a handful of dust, and silver no more than the clay.
We loved her more than health and beauty,
and preferred her to the light of the day,
for her light never sleeps.

All good things that came to us came because she was with us,
and countless riches they were, they cannot all be told.
Everything was ours to enjoy,
for all is brought forth by her wisdom,
though we did not know then, that she is their source.

We learned about her simply and slowly, in quiet,
and pass on what we know without holding back,
and we will not hide the riches she brings.
To us, she has become unfailing treasure,
and those who receive it are commended to You by the gift of her ways. [A]

PROPTER HOC OCTAVI
A Song of the Spirit of Wisdom from *the Book of Wisdom*

WHEN WE WERE YOUNG,
WE ASKED IN OUR PRAYERS FOR YOUR WISDOM.

In Your sanctuary, before we set out on our travels,
we laid claim to her, and we shall seek her to the end.
From the first blossom of spring to the reaping of the harvest,
she has been the delight of our heart.
From our youth
our steps have followed her without swerving.

We had hardly begun to listen when we were rewarded,
and we gained for ourselves much instruction.
We made much progress in our studies—
all glory to You Who has granted us wisdom.
We set our hearts on finding her,
and by keeping ourselves pure, we found her.
With her we gained understanding from the first,
therefore we will never be at a loss.
Because we passionately yearned to discover her, a noble possession was ours.
As our reward we were given eloquence,
and with it, we shall praise You. [A]

CUM ADHUC JUNIOR ESSEM
A Song of Pilgrimage from *the Book of Ecclesiasticus*

You are the Lord,
and this is Your holy word.

"Stop dwelling on things long past,
and brooding over days gone by.
   Behold, I am about to do something new;
it is unfolding right before you.
   Can you not yet see it?"

Even through the wilderness, You shall make a way for us,
and a path for us even in the wasteland.
   Rivers shall spring forth in the desert,
where Your children shall drink,
   so that we might proclaim Your praise. [A]

Ego Dominus
A Song of the New Creation from *the Book of Isaiah*

LET THE WILDERNESS AND THE DRY LAND BE GLAD;
let the desert rejoice and burst into flower.
LET THE WHOLE EARTH SING AND SHOUT FOR JOY.

Strengthen all the weary hands,
make steady the knees that tremble,
and say to those who are anxious, "Be strong and be not afraid."
The eyes of the blind will be opened,
and the ears of the deaf will be cleared.
Then the lame shall leap like the deer,
and the tongues of the speechless shall sing for joy.

For waters will spring up in the wilderness,
and there will be streams in the desert.
And those whom You have set free will return crowned with joy.
Their rejoicing will be everlasting,
and their sorrow and weariness shall then take flight. [A]

LAETABITUR DESERTA
A Song of the Wilderness from *the Book of Isaiah*

SEEK THE LORD WHILE THE LORD MAY BE FOUND;
CALL OUT THE NAME WHILE GOD IS YET NEAR.

Let the wicked forsake their unrighteous ways,
and the unrighteous their wicked thoughts.
Let us return to You that You might have mercy,
to You Who does always forgive.

For Your thoughts are not our thoughts,
and Your ways are not our ways.
As far as the heavens are above the earth,
so are Your ways above our ways,
and Your thoughts above our thoughts.

As the rain and the snow come down from the sky,
not to return until they water the earth, so it is with Your word.
It will not return to You empty,
without accomplishing its purpose,
the thing for which You have sent it. [A]

QUAERITE DOMINUM
A Song of the Word of the Lord from *the Book of Isaiah*

WE THAT HAVE WALKED IN DARKNESS HAVE SEEN A GREAT LIGHT;
ON ALL THOSE WHO LIVED IN A LAND AS DARK AS DEATH, A LIGHT HAS DAWNED.

You have increased our joy and given us great gladness,
we rejoice in Your presence as those who rejoice at the harvest.
You have broken the yoke that has burdened us,
the rod that was laid on our shoulders.
For a Child will be born unto us, unto us a Son will be given.
To bear the symbol of dominion on His shoulder,
to be called, Wonderful, Counselor,
Almighty God, Eternal One, The Prince of Peace.
And wide will be the dominion, and boundless will be the peace
that will be bestowed upon His kingdom,
to establish and support it with righteousness, now and for evermore.

On him will Your Spirit rest:
the spirit of Wisdom and understanding, the spirit of counsel and power,
the spirit of knowledge and the fear of the Lord,
and the fear of the Lord shall be his delight.
He will not judge by appearance or hearsay,
but will judge with equity and defend the humble.
He will wear the belt of justice, and truth will be his girdle.

Then the lion will lie down with the lamb,
and the wolf will lie with the kid,
and the calf and the young lion will feed together,
with a little child to tend to them.
There will be neither hurt nor harm in all Your holy mountain,
for the land will be filled with the knowledge of You,
as the waters still cover the sea. [A]

POPULUS, QUI AMBULABAT
A Song of the Messiah from *the Book of Isaiah*

Surely it is God Who saves us;
we will trust in you and not be afraid.

For You are our stronghold, and our sure defense,
and You will be our saviour.
We shall draw water with rejoicing,
from the springs of Your salvation.
And we shall give our thanks to You, and call upon Your Name.
We shall make your deeds known among all people;
and see that they remember that Your Name is exalted.
We shall sing praises to You, for You have done great things,
and this shall be known in all the world.
All Your children shall cry aloud, and sing out their joy,
for the Holy One is in our midst. [A]

Ecce, Deus
The First Song of Isaiah from *the Book of Isaiah*

ARISE, SHINE, FOR OUR LIGHT HAS COME,
AND THE GLORY OF GOD HAS DAWNED UPON US.

Behold, darkness covers the land, and deep gloom enshrouds all people.
But over us the Lord will rise, and glory will appear upon us.
Nations will stream to the light, and kings to the brightness of the dawning.
Our gates will always be open, by day or by night they will never be shut.
Violence will no more be heard in our land,
nor ruin or destruction within our borders.
We shall call our walls Salvation, and all our portals Praise.
The sun will no more be our light by day;
by night we will not need the brightness of the moon.
The Lord will be our everlasting light,
and our God will be our glory. [A]

SURGE, ILLUMINARE
The Third Song from *the Book of Isaiah*

COME, LET US RETURN TO THE LORD;
COME, LET US RETURN TO GOD.

You have struck us, but You will heal us.
You have wounded us, but You will bind our wounds.
You will revive us after two days,
and on the third day You will raise us up,
that we may live in Your presence.

Let us press on to know You,
Whose coming is as sure as the sun,
and as certain as showers of spring.
Our love in return is like morning mist,
like the dew that fades away.

You have shaped us by the words of the prophets,
Your judgment goes forth as clearly as light.
Our steadfast love is what You desire of us, not just our sacrifice;
our knowledge of You,
and not just our offerings. [A]

VENITE ET REVERTAMUR
A Song of Humility from *the Book of Hosea*

O LORD AND RULER OF THE HOSTS OF HEAVEN,
YOU MADE THE HEAVENS AND THE EARTH, WITH ALL THEIR VAST ARRAY.

All things quake with fear at Your presence;
they tremble because of Your power.
But Your merciful promise is beyond all measure;
it surpasses all that our minds can fathom.
O Lord, You are full of compassion, long-suffering, and abounding in mercy.
You hold back your hand; You do not punish as we deserve.
In Your great goodness, Lord, You have promised forgiveness to sinners,
that we may repent of our sin and be saved.

And now, O Lord, we bend the knee of our hearts,
and make our appeal, sure of Your gracious goodness.
We have sinned, O Lord, we have sinned,
and we know our wickedness only too well.
Therefore we make this prayer to You: Forgive us, Lord, forgive us.
Do not let us perish in our sin,
nor condemn us to the depths of the earth.

For You, O Lord, are the God of those who repent,
and in us You will show forth your goodness.
Unworthy as we are, You will save us,
in accordance with Your great mercy,
and we will praise You without ceasing all the days of our life.
For all the powers of heaven sing Your praises,
and Yours is the glory to ages of ages. [A]

DOMINE OMNIPOTENS
A Song of Penitence from *the Prayer of Manasseh*

A NEW SONG WILL WE SING TO YOU,
FOR YOU ARE GREAT AND GLORIOUS AND MARVELOUS IN STRENGTH.

May Your every creature serve You,
for You spoke and all things were made.
You sent Your Spirit and all was created,
there is no thing that can resist Your voice.
Should the mountains be shaken to their foundations,
should the rocks melt before Your holy face,
You would still show your mercy to all things,
and You would still have compassion
    for those who fear You.
For every sacrifice is but a small thing indeed,
    but whoever fears You is great for ever. [A]

HYMNUM CANTEMUS
A Song of God's Mercy from *the Book of Judith*

BLESSED ARE THE POOR AMONG US,
AND HAPPY ARE THEY.

Blessed are the ones who are poor,
they will be shown the kingdom of God.
Blessed are the ones who are poor in spirit,
they too will be given the kingdom.
Blessed are the ones who weep and mourn,
they shall find comfort
and be filled with laughter.

Blessed are the humble and the meek,
the whole world will be theirs.
Blessed are the ones who show mercy,
mercy will be shown to them.
Blessed are the ones who hunger for righteousness,
they shall be filled indeed.
Blessed are those whose hearts are pure,
they will see the very face of God.
Blessed are the ones who make peace,
they will be called God's own.
Blessed are the ones who are persecuted in their hearts;
they are the ones who will truly know God.

Blessed are the ones
who have worked hard to find life,
and have found it.
Blessed are the ones who hear the word of the Lord,
and truly keep it.
Blessed are the ones who have not seen Me,
and yet have still believed. [A]

BEATI PAUPERES
A Song of the Blessed from *the Gospel According to Matthew*

IN THE BEGINNING WAS THE WORD,
AND THE WORD WAS WITH GOD, AND THE WORD WAS GOD.

It was through the Word that all things came to be.
Nothing was created without it,
    all that has come to be is alive with its life.

The Word became flesh and dwelt among us,
full of grace and full of truth.
    The Light Absolute was then in the world,
the Light to enlighten all people.
    But when the Light came into the world,
the world did not recognize him,
    even though it owed its very being to him.
Even those to whom the Light was given
    did not know who he was.

But to all who would receive him, he gave the power
to become the children of Light,
    the very daughters and sons of God.
That Light is the light of the world and it still shines in the darkness,
    and the darkness will never overcome it. [A]

IN PRINCIPIO
A Song of Emmanuel from *the Gospel According to John*

BLESSED BE GOD, WHO HAS GIVEN TO US
EVERY SPIRITUAL BLESSING IN THE HEAVENLY REALMS.

Before the foundation of the world,
You chose us in Christ for Your children,
   to be without blemish in Your sight, to be full of love.
And You ordained that we would be adopted
   as Your children through Jesus, Your Son.
This was Your will and Your pleasure,
   in order that the glory of Your gracious gift,
so graciously conferred upon us in Your beloved One,
   might redound to Your praise.

Our release has been secured and our sins forgiven.
In the richness of Your grace,
   You lavished on us all wisdom and insight.
You made known to us Your purpose,
   in accordance with the plan You ordained in Christ,
to be put into effect when the time was ready:
   Namely, that the whole universe,
everything in heaven and in earth,
   might be brought into unity with Christ. [A]

BENEDICTUS DEUS
A Song of God's Grace from *the Letter of Paul to the Ephesians*

CHRIST OUR PASSOVER HAS BEEN SACRIFICED FOR US;
THEREFORE LET US KEEP THE FEAST.

And let us keep it not with the old leaven,
the leaven of malice and evil,
but with the unleavened bread of sincerity and truth.

Christ being raised from the dead
will never die again;
death no longer has dominion over him.
The death that he died, he died to sin, once for all;
but the life that he lives, he lives to God.
So consider yourselves dead unto sin,
and alive unto God in Christ our Lord.

Christ has been raised from the dead,
the first fruits of those who have fallen asleep.
For since by a man came death,
by a man has come also the resurrection of the dead.
For as in Adam all die, so also in Christ shall all be alive. [A]

PASCHA NOSTRUM
Christ Our Passover from *the First Letter of Paul to the Corinthians*

YOU HAVE RESCUED US FROM THE DARKNESS,
AND BROUGHT US TO THE KINGDOM OF YOUR SON.

Through Your Son our release is secured, and our sins are forgiven.
He is the image of You, the invisible God,
    and He is primary over all creation.
In Him, all in heaven and earth was created,
    all things visible, and all things yet unseen.

The whole universe has been created through Him and for Him.
He exists before all things, and all things are held together in Him.
    He is the head of the body of all faithful people;
He is the origin of the Church, and the first to return from the dead,
    to become in all things supreme.

For in Him You chose to dwell in Your fullness,
and through Him to reconcile all to Yourself,
    all things, whether on earth or in heaven,
making peace through the shedding
    of blood on the cross. [A]

PATER ERIPUIT
A Song of Redemption from *the Letter of Paul to the Colossians*

FAITH AND HOPE AND LOVE LAST FOR EVER,
AND THE GREATEST OF THESE IS LOVE.

Love is patient and kind.
Love never envies, never boasts, is never conceited, never rude.
Love is never selfish, never quick to take offense.
Love keeps no score of wrongs,
    and takes no pleasure in the sins of others,
but always delights in the truth.
There is nothing that love cannot face;
there is no limit to its faith, its hope, its endurance.
Love will not ever come to an end.

Prophecies will cease; tongues of joy will fall silent;
and all of our knowledge will vanish.
For our knowledge and prophecy are partial,
and the partial will vanish when the whole is revealed.
When we were children, we spoke as children,
and thought as children, and reasoned as children.
But when we grew older, we finished with childish things.
At present we see as through a glass darkly;
    one day we shall see things clearly.
Our knowledge for now is partial, but one day it will be whole,
    as is Your knowledge of us. [A]

CARITAS PATIENS EST
A Song of Divine Love from *the First Letter of Paul to the Corinthians*

THE LIFE-GIVING LAW OF THE SPIRIT
SETS US FREE FROM THE LAW OF SIN AND DEATH.

All who are led by the Spirit are the children of God.
The Spirit affirms to our spirits that indeed we are Your own,
    and if children, then heirs—fellow-heirs with Christ.
But we must share in His sufferings if we would share in His glory.

The suffering we now endure
bears no comparison with the glory in store.
    And the whole world waits in hope for the children of God to be seen. [A]

LEX ENIM SPIRITUS VITAE
A Song of God's Children from *the Letter of Paul to the Romans*

HERE IS THE MESSAGE THAT WE NOW HAVE HEARD:
GOD IS LIGHT, AND THERE IS NO DARKNESS IN GOD.

If we claim to be sharing in Your life
while we go on living in darkness,
  our words and our lives are a lie.

But if we live in the light, as You are the light,
then we share a common life,
  and the blood of Your Son cleanses us from all sin.

If we claim to be sinless,
we are deceiving ourselves,
  and the truth does not live within us.

If we confess our sins,
You may be trusted to forgive them,
  and to cleanse us from every wrongdoing.

If we say we have committed no sin,
we make You out to be a liar,
  and Your Word has no place within us. [A]

HAEC EST ANNUNTIATIO
A Song of Repentance from *the First Letter of John*

LET US LOVE ONE ANOTHER,
BECAUSE GOD IS THE SOURCE OF ALL LOVE.

Every one who loves is Your child and knows You,
but the unloving know nothing, for You are love.
    This is the way that love was shown among us:
The Divine One was sent into the world
    that we might have Your life through Him.

This is what love really is:
Not that we have loved You,
    but that You have loved us,
and sent a sacrifice to atone for our sins.
    If You thus have loved us, then we must also love one another.

You have never been seen by anyone,
but if we love one another, then You dwell in us,
    and Your love is brought to perfection within us. [A]

CARISSIMI, DILIGAMUS NOS INVICEM
A Song of God's Love from *the First Letter of John*

O RULER OF THE UNIVERSE, LORD GOD,
GREAT DEEDS ARE THEY THAT YOU HAVE DONE.

Your great deeds surpass all our understanding.
Your ways are the ways of righteousness and truth,
    O God of all the ages.

Who can fail to do you homage,
and to sing the praises of Your Name?
    For You only are the Holy One.
All nations will draw near and bow down before You,
    because Your just and holy works have been revealed. [A]

MAGNA ET MIRABILIA
A Song of the Redeemed from *the Book of Revelation*

SPLENDOR AND HONOR AND KINGLY POWER
ARE YOURS BY RIGHT, O LORD OUR GOD.

For you created everything that is,
and by Your will they were created
   and have their being.

And Yours by right,
O Lamb that was slain,
   for with Your blood You have redeemed for God,
from every family, language, people, and nation,
   a kingdom of priests to serve our God.

And so to him who sits upon the throne,
and to Christ the Lamb,
   be worship and praise, dominion and splendor,
for ever and for evermore. [A]

DIGNUS ES
A Song to the Lamb from *the Book of Revelation*

We believe in one God,
the Father, the Almighty, maker of heaven and earth,
of all that is, seen and unseen.

We believe in one Lord, Jesus Christ,
the only Son of God,
eternally begotten of the Father,
God from God, Light from Light,
true God from true God,
begotten, not made,
of one Being with the Father.
Through Him all things were made.

For us and for our salvation
He came down from heaven:
By the power of the Holy Spirit
He became incarnate from the Virgin Mary,
and was made man.
For our sake He was crucified under Pontius Pilate;
He suffered death and was buried.
On the third day He rose again
in accordance with the Scriptures;
He ascended into heaven
and is seated at the right hand of the Father.
He will come again in glory to judge the living and the dead,
and His kingdom will have no end.

We believe in the Holy Spirit,
the Lord, the giver of life,
who proceeds from the Father and the Son.
With the Father and the Son He is worshiped and glorified.
He has spoken through the Prophets.

We believe in one holy, catholic, and apostolic Church.
We acknowledge one baptism for the forgiveness of sins.
[†] We look for the resurrection of the dead,
and the life of the world to come.
Amen.

The Nicene Creed

YOU ARE GOD: WE PRAISE YOU.
YOU ARE THE LORD: WE ACCLAIM YOU.

You are the eternal One: And all creation worships You.
To You all angels, all powers of heaven,
 Cherubim and Seraphim, sing in endless praise:

Holy, holy, holy Lord, God of power and might,
heaven and earth are full of Your glory.
 The glorious company of apostles praise You,
the noble fellowship of prophets praise You,
 the white-robed army of martyrs praise You.
Throughout the world the holy Church acclaims You:
 Father, of majesty unbounded;
Your true and only Son, worthy of all worship;
 and Holy Spirit, advocate and guide.

You, Christ, are the king of glory, the eternal Son of the Father.
When You became man to set us free,
 You did not shun the Virgin's womb.
You overcame the sting of death,
 and opened the kingdom of heaven to all believers.
You are seated at God's right hand in glory.
 We believe that You will come and be our judge.

Come then, Lord, and help Your people,
bought with the price of Your own blood,
 and bring us with Your saints, to glory everlasting. [A]

TE DEUM LAUDAMUS

MOST HOLY AND MERCIFUL GOD:

We confess to You and to the whole communion of saints in heaven and earth,
    that we have sinned by our own fault.
We have been deaf to Your call to serve, as Christ served us.
We have not been true to the mind of Christ, and have grieved your Holy Spirit.
    Have mercy on us, O Lord.

We confess to you all our past unfaithfulness:
Our pride, hypocrisy, and the impatience of our lives;
    We confess to You, O Lord.
Our self-indulgent appetites and ways, and our exploitation of others;
    We confess to You, O Lord.
Our anger at our own frustration, and our envy at those more fortunate;
    We confess to You, O Lord.
Our intemperate love of worldly goods and comforts,
    and our dishonesty in daily life and work;
    We confess to You, O Lord.
Our negligence in prayer and worship,
    and our failure to commend the faith that is in us;
    We confess to You, O Lord.

Accept our repentance for the wrongs we have done:
For our blindness to human need and suffering,
    and our indifference to injustice and cruelty;
    Accept our repentance, O Lord.
For all false judgments, for uncharitable thoughts toward our neighbors,
    and for our prejudice and contempt toward those who differ from us;
    Accept our repentance, O Lord.
For our waste and pollution of your creation,
    and our lack of concern for those who come after us;
    Accept our repentance, O Lord.

Almighty God, have mercy on us:
[†] Forgive us our sins through Jesus Christ, and strengthen us in all goodness,
    and by the power of the Holy Spirit keep us in eternal life.
    Hear us, O Lord.

Restore us, good Lord, and let your anger depart from us:
Favorably hear us, for your mercy is great.
    Accomplish in us Your salvation, that we may show forth Your glory.
And by the cross and the passion of Your Son,
    bring us with all Your saints to the joy of His Resurrection. *Amen.*

A LITANY OF PENITENCE

Notes for Saying the Psalter

Say the Psalms aloud whenever possible, reading them slowly and carefully, allowing the words to dwell within you.

The title of the Psalm, the lines in caps and small caps, can be used as an antiphon, said before and after the Psalm, and, in the case of longer Psalms, between sections of the Psalm. The mark [A] is a reminder and a guide to repeat that line.

When you share the prayers with someone else, the Psalms are best read responsively, two lines at a time. When you pray alone, a pause between each pair of lines is helpful in allowing the words to sink in.

In many communities where the Psalter is prayed regularly, each Psalm is followed by the Gloria and by a minute or two of silence.

You may choose to say all of the day's Psalms at one of the Offices or separate them into morning or evening readings, or in some other way that works best for you.

Be aware that this paraphrase has been deliberately made in a way that invites you to address God in the second person, and some of your favorite phrases may well have been changed a bit. Do not hesitate to use the words that are familiar to you if it adds to your prayer. But also, do not shy away from using new words, for some meaning that is new and fresh and rich may well await you.

Finally, remember that the Psalms have been prayed by the faithful in just such a pattern for thousands of years. The Psalms reflect and speak to and of all of life, all of its joy and its pain, all of its mystery and its wonder. Listen deeply to the words of these ancient prayers, and listen for the prayer of God that rises in your heart.

THE PSALTER

Create in us a clean heart, and renew a right spirit within us.
Grant us the joy of Your saving help, and sustain us with Your Spirit.
—FROM THE PSALMS

We praise You with joy, Almighty God,
for Your grace is better than life itself:
Hear our prayers, and listen to our cries.
Keep us as the apple of Your eye,
hide us in the shelter of Your arms.
In the shadow of Your wings, we sing for joy. *Amen.*
—A PSALM PRAYER

In your life of prayer and meditation,
seek the command that God addresses to you
and put it into practice without delay.
—FROM THE RULE OF TAIZÉ

1. HAPPY ARE THEY WHO DO NOT WALK IN THE WAY OF SINNERS.
Their delight is in Your way; they meditate on it day and night.
    They are like trees planted beside the waters, bearing fruit in due season.
It is not so with the wicked; they are as chaff, taken away in the wind.
    You know the way of the righteous; the way of the wicked is doomed. [A]

2. WHY ARE THE PEOPLE IN AN UPROAR AND MUTTER EMPTY THREATS?
Why do kings of the earth rise up in revolt against You?
    The One Who has made us is laughing, holding them in derision.
This is Your decree: "I myself have set my anointed on the holy hill.
    This is my Son; this day have I begotten him.
When he asks, I will give him the nations and the ends of the earth."
    Be warned, you rulers; be wise, you kings of the earth.
Submit to the Almighty with fear, and with trembling bow down before God.
    Happy are they who take their refuge in You. [A]

3. HOW MANY THERE ARE AGAINST US; HOW STRONG IS OUR ADVERSARY.
You are a shield about us; You are the One Who lifts up our heads.
    We call aloud upon You, and You answer from Your holy hill.
We lie down and we go to sleep; we wake again because You sustain us.
    We do not fear those that have set themselves against us.
Rise up, O God, and set us free, for deliverance belongs to You,
    and may Your blessing be upon Your children. [A]

4. ANSWER US WHEN WE CALL, O DEFENDER OF OUR CAUSE.
You set us free when we are hard-pressed; have mercy and hear our prayer.
    We know that You do wonders for the faithful, that when we call, You hear us.
We tremble then, and shall not sin; we shall speak to our hearts in silence.
    We shall offer the appointed sacrifices and put our trust in You.
Many are saying, "O that we would see better times!"
    Lift up the light of Your countenance upon us, we pray.
You have put gladness in our hearts, more than when our wealth increases.
    We shall lie down at peace, for You make us to dwell in safety. [A]

5. GIVE EAR TO OUR WORDS, WE PRAY, CONSIDER OUR MEDITATION.
Hearken to our cries for help, for we make our prayers to You.
In the morning, You hear our voice; early we begin our watch for You.
In Your mercy, we will go into Your house, and bow down before You.
Lead us in Your righteousness; make Your ways straight before us.
All who take refuge in You will be glad and sing out their joy for ever.
You will shelter them, so that those who love Your Name may exalt in You.
For You will bless the righteous and defend them with Your favor. [A]

6. DO NOT REBUKE US IN YOUR ANGER NOR PUNISH US IN YOUR WRATH.
Have pity on us and heal us, for we are weak; our spirits shake with terror.
How long, we ask, how long?
Turn to us, O God, and deliver us; save us, for Your mercy's sake.
We grow weary of our groaning, our beds are drenched with tears.
Our eyes are wasted away with grief, and are worn away because of our enemies.
Depart from us all evil, for the Almighty has heard our weeping.
You have heard our supplication, and You accept our prayer.
Our enemies shall be confounded and shall turn away from us in fear. [A]

7. WE TAKE OUR REFUGE IN YOU; SAVE US AND DELIVER US.
Stand up, O God; rise up against the fury of our enemy.
Awake, O God, and decree Your justice; let Your people gather round You.
Be seated on Your lofty throne, O Most High, and judge us all.
Give judgment for us, O God, according to Your righteousness.
Establish the righteous, for You test the mind and the heart.
You are our defense, the saviour of the true in heart.
We will bear witness that You are the Righteous One,
and we will praise the Name of the Most High. [A]

8. HOW EXALTED IS YOUR NAME IN ALL THE EARTH.
When we consider Your heavens, and the works of Your hands,
the moon and stars that You have set in their courses,
what are we that You should be mindful of us?
Who are we that You should seek us out?
You have made us but a little lower than angels, and adorned us with honor.
You have given us mastery over the works of Your hands:
the beasts of the fields, the birds of the air, the fish of the sea,
and whatsoever walks upon the paths of the earth. [A]

9. WE WILL GIVE THANKS TO YOU WITH OUR WHOLE HEART.
We will be glad and rejoice in You, and tell of Your marvelous works;
     For You have maintained our cause, and are enthroned for ever.
You are the One Who rules in righteousness, and judges the people with equity.
     You are the refuge for the oppressed, a refuge in the time of trouble.
Those who know Your Name will seek You, and they will never be forsaken.
     We will sing our praise to You, and proclaim what You have done for us.
Have pity on us, we pray; You alone can lift us from the gates of death,
     so that we might rejoice in Your salvation and tell out all Your praise.
The needy will not always be forgotten, and the hope of the poor will not perish. [A]

10. WHY DO YOU STAND SO FAR OFF, AND HIDE YOURSELF IN TIME OF TROUBLE?
The innocent are broken and humbled and helpless.
     They say You have forgotten them, that You hide Your face and never notice.
Rise up, O God, and lift Your mighty hand; do not forget the afflicted.
     Surely You behold their trouble and misery; see it and take it into Your hands.
The helpless commit themselves to You, for You are the helper of the abandoned.
     Break the power of wickedness, search it out until You find none.
The Almighty will hear the desire of the humble and strengthen their hearts,
     to give justice to the oppressed, so that mortals may strike terror no more. [A]

11. IN YOU HAVE WE TAKEN REFUGE.
See how the wicked bend their bow to ambush the true of heart.
     When the foundations are being destroyed, what can the righteous do?
You are in Your holy temple; Your throne is in Your heaven.
     Your eyes behold the inhabited world; Your eyes will weigh our worth.
You judge the righteous and the wicked, and hate the ones who do violence.
     For You delight in righteous deeds, and the just shall see Your face. [A]

12. HELP US , O GOD, FOR THE FAITHFUL HAVE VANISHED AMONG US.
Wickedness prowls on every side, that which is worthless is prized.
　　Everyone speaks falsely with their neighbor,
with smooth tongues, from a double heart.
　　O that You would silence such talk.
"I will rise up," You have said, "because the needy are oppressed,
　　and the poor cry out in misery, and I will give them the help they long for."
Your words are pure, O God, like silver refined in the fire.
　　Watch over us, we pray, and save us from ourselves for ever. [A]

13. WILL YOU FORGET US FOR EVER? HOW LONG WILL YOU HIDE YOUR FACE?
How long will we have confusion in our minds and our hearts?
　　How long will our enemy triumph? How long will You hide Your face?
Look upon us and answer us; give light to our eyes, lest we sleep in death.
　　Lest our enemies claim that they have prevailed, rejoicing that we have fallen.
We put our trust in Your mercy; we are joyful because of Your saving help.
　　We will sing and praise Your Name, for You have dealt with us richly.
We will praise the Name of the One Most High. [A]

14. IT IS A FOOL WHO SAYS IN THEIR HEART THAT THERE IS NO GOD.
You look down from heaven upon us all, to see if there are any who are wise,
　　to see if there is even one of us who seeks You.
And every one of us proves faithless; there is not one of us, not one.
　　Have we no knowledge, we who do not call upon Your Name?
See how we tremble with fear,
　　for well we know that the Almighty keeps company with the righteous.
O that Your deliverance would come, O God.
　　When You have restored our fortunes, we will rejoice and be glad. [A]

15. WHO MAY DWELL IN YOUR HOUSE? OR ABIDE UPON YOUR HOLY HILL?
Whoever leads a blameless life, does what is right, and speaks the truth.
  Those who have no guile, those who do no evil,
and those who do not hold their neighbor in contempt.
  Those who honor those who fear You, and reject the things of the wicked.
Those who swear to do no wrong, and do not take back their word.
  Those who do not give away money in the hope of gain,
and those who do not take advantage of the weak.
  Whoever does these things shall not be overthrown. [A]

16. PROTECT US, O GOD, FOR WE TAKE OUR REFUGE IN YOU.
You are our God, our good above all other.
  You are our portion and our cup, You are the One Who upholds us.
Our boundaries enclose a pleasant land, and we have a goodly heritage.
  We bless You, for You give us counsel in our hearts night after night.
We have set You always before us, with You at our side, we shall not fall.
  Our hearts are glad and our spirits rejoice; we shall rest in hope.
For You will not abandon us to the grave, You will show us the path of life.
  In Your presence, there is fullness of joy. [A]

17. HEAR OUR PLEA OF INNOCENCE, AND GIVE HEED TO OUR CRY.
Listen to our prayer, which does not come from lying lips.
  Let Your eyes be fixed on justice, let our vindication come from You.
Summon us by night and weigh our hearts; melt them and find no impurity.
  We have heeded Your words and give no offense with our lips.
Our footsteps hold fast to Your ways; in Your paths, we will not stumble.
  We call upon You and You will answer; incline Your ear and hear us.
O Saviour of those who take refuge in You, show us Your loving kindness.
  Keep us as the apple of Your eye, and hide us in the shadow of Your wings.
When we wake we shall see You, and be satisfied to behold Your likeness. [A]

18. WE LOVE YOU, O GOD, FOR YOU ARE OUR STRENGTH.
You are our rock, in Whom we trust; You alone are worthy of our praise.
   We will call upon You and so shall we be saved.
The breakers of death rolled over us, the torrents of oblivion made us afraid.
   The cords of hell entangled us; the snares of death were set for us.
We called upon Your Name, crying out to you in our distress.
   You heard our voice in Your heavenly dwelling, our cry came unto Your ears.
You reached down from on high and drew us out of the waters.
   You delivered us from the enemy too strong for us.
The enemy confronted us in the day of disaster, but You were our support. [A]
   You rescued us and brought us out because You delight in us.
With the faithful, You show Yourself to be faithful;
   With the forthright, You show Yourself to be forthright;
With the pure, You show Yourself to be pure, and You will save a humble people.
   You are our lamp; You make our darkness bright.
With Your help we can break through any wall.
   Your ways are perfect; Your word has been tried by fire. [A]
You are a shield to all who trust in You.
   For who are You, but the God of all?
And who is the Rock, except the Almighty?
   You are the One Who gives us strength and makes our way secure.
You make us sure-footed, and able to stand upon the heights.
   Your right hand sustains us, and Your loving care.
Blessed are You, the Rock of our salvation.
   We will extol Your Name to all people, and sing Your praise for ever. [A]

19. THE HEAVENS THEMSELVES DECLARE THE GLORY OF GOD.
All the earth shows the work of Your hands.
One day tells its tale to another; one night imparts wisdom to the next.
Though they use no language, and their voices cannot be heard,
The message goes to the ends of the earth, and the sound goes on for ever.
In the deep is set a pavilion for the sun; and it comes forth like a bridegroom.
Like a champion it rises to run its course; nothing can hide from its heat. [A]
Your law is perfect; and it revives the soul.
Your testimony is sure; and it gives wisdom to the innocent.
Your statutes are just; and they rejoice the heart.
Your commandments are clear; and they give light to the eyes.
Your judgments are true; and they are righteous altogether.
More to be desired than gold are they; and sweeter far than honey.
By them are Your servants enlightened;
In keeping them, there is great reward. [A]
Who can tell how they offend You? Cleanse us from our secret faults.
Keep us from presumptuous sins; let them not hold dominion over us.
Then we shall be sound and whole and innocent of great offense.
Let the words of our mouths, and the meditations of our hearts,
be acceptable in Your sight, O God, our strength and our redeemer. [A]

20. ANSWER US IN THE DAY OF TROUBLE; DEFEND US BY YOUR HOLY NAME.
Send us help and strength from Your holy place.
Remember our offerings and accept our sacrifices.
Grant to us our heart's desire and prosper all our plans.
Grant us our requests, and may we shout for joy in Your name.
We know that You will give victory to Your children.
We know that You will answer from Your holy place.
We will call upon Your Name; we will arise and stand upright.
Give victory to your children, we pray, and answer when we call. [A]

21. YOUR CHOSEN ONE REJOICES, HOW GREATLY HE REJOICES.
You have given Him His heart's desire; and have not denied His requests.
He asked for life and You gave it to Him, for ever and for ever.
His honor is great; splendor and majesty are bestowed upon Him.
You will give him everlasting bliss, and make Him glad in Your presence.
He trusts in You; because of Your loving kindness, he will not fall.
Be exalted, God, in Your might; and we will sing and praise Your power. [A]

22. WHY HAVE YOU FORSAKEN US? WHY ARE YOU SO FAR FROM US?
We cry aloud to You in the daytime, but You do not answer;
    By night as well, but we find no rest.
Yet You are the Holy One, enthroned upon our praises.
    Our fathers and mothers trusted in You and You delivered them.
You are the One Who took us from our mother's womb and kept us safe.
    We have been entrusted to You since before we were even born. [A]
Be not far from us, for trouble is near and there is no one to help.
    We are poured out like water, our spirits faint within us.
Our mouths are dry, and we are laid in the dust of the grave.
    Be not far away, we pray; You are our strength, hasten now to help us.
Save us and we will praise You, declaring Your Name to all. [A]
    We praise You, standing in awe and giving You glory.
You do not despise the poor, nor hide Your face from them.
    You hear us when we cry out.
Our praise shall always be of You;
    we will perform our vows in the presence of Your people.
The poor shall be satisfied, and all those who seek You shall praise You.
    To You alone do all who sleep in the earth bow down in worship;
And all who go down to the dust shall bow before You.
    Our souls shall live for You; our descendants shall serve You.
They shall be known as Your children for ever;
    And they make You known to all people. [A]

23. YOU ARE OUR SHEPHERD AND WE SHALL NOT WANT.
You make us to lie down in green pastures; You lead us beside still waters.
    You restore our souls; and You guide us along the paths of righteousness.
Though we travel the valley of the shadow of death, we will fear no evil;
    For You are with us; Your rod and Your staff will comfort us.
You have spread a table before us in the presence of our enemies.
    You anoint us with Your blessing, and our cup is running over.
Surely goodness and mercy will follow us for all of our days;
    And we will dwell in Your house for ever. [A]

24. THE EARTH IS YOURS AND ALL THAT IS IN IT.
Who can ascend Your holy hill; who can stand in Your holy place?
    Those who have clean hands and a pure heart;
Those who have not pledged themselves to falsehood.
    They shall receive a blessing from the Lord,
and a just reward from the God of salvation.
    Such is the generation of those who seek your face. [A]
Lift up your heads, O you gates, and the King of glory shall come in to you.
    Lift them high, O doors, and the King of glory shall enter.
And who is this King of glory? It is the Lord, strong and mighty.
    It is You, the Lord of hosts Who is the King of glory. [A]

25. TO YOU WE LIFT UP OUR SOULS; AND WE PUT OUR TRUST IN YOU.
Show us Your ways, and teach us Your paths.
    Lead us in Your truth; in You have we put our trust.
Remember Your compassion and love, for they are from everlasting.
    Remember not the sins of our youth; remember us according to Your love. [A]
Gracious You are, and upright; therefore You teach sinners in Your ways.
    You guide the humble in doing what is right and teach Your ways to the lowly.
All of Your paths are love and faithfulness to those who keep Your ways.
    To those who fear You will You teach the way that they should choose.
You are a friend to them, and You will show them Your covenant. [A]
    Our eyes will ever look to You, for You shall pluck our feet from the net.
For Your Name's sake, we pray, deliver us from out of all of our troubles.
    Turn to us and have pity, for we are alone and in misery.
The sorrows of our hearts have increased; bring us out of trouble.
    Look upon our misery and forgive us all our sin.
Protect us and deliver us, for we have trusted in You.
    Let integrity and uprightness preserve us, for our hope has been in You. [A]

26. SPEAK FOR US, FOR WE HAVE TRUSTED IN YOU AND HAVE NOT FALTERED.
Test us, and try us; examine our hearts and minds.
    For Your love is ever before us, and we have walked faithfully with You.
We will wash our hands in innocence, that we may come before You,
    Singing songs of thanksgiving, recounting Your wonderful deeds.
We love the place where You dwell, the place where Your glory abides.
    Redeem us, we pray, and have pity upon us; do not sweep us away. [A]

27. YOU ARE OUR LIGHT AND OUR SALVATION, WHOM THEN SHALL WE FEAR?
You are the strength of our life, of whom shall we be afraid?

Though war should come and an army stand against us, we shall not fear.
One thing we have asked of You, one thing do we seek:

That we may dwell in Your house all the days of our lives,
That we might behold Your beauty, and seek You in Your temple. [A]

In the day of our trouble, You keep us safe, hiding us in Your shelter.
So we offer our oblations with gladness; we will sing and make music to You.

Hear our voices when we call; have mercy on us and answer us.
Hide not Your face from us, nor turn away from us in displeasure.

You have been our helper, cast us not aside; do not forsake us now.
Though even our mothers and fathers forsake us, You will sustain us.

Show us Your ways; lead us on a level path. [A]
What if we had not believed

that we would see Your greatness in the land of the living?
We shall tarry, and wait patiently for You.

We shall be strong, for You shall comfort us. [A]

28. WE CALL TO YOU; BE NOT DEAF TO OUR CRY.
Hear the voice of our prayer when we lift our hands and cry to You.

Do not abandon us to those who speak peace while strife is in their hearts;
Or leave us at the mercy of those who have no understanding of Your ways.

Blessed are You, for You have heard the voice of our supplication.
You are our strength and our shield; and our spirits trust only in You.

Therefore our hearts dance for joy, and we shall praise You with our songs.
You are the strength of Your children, a safe refuge for all Your people.

Save us, and bless Your inheritance; shepherd us, and carry us for ever. [A]

29. WE SHALL ASCRIBE TO YOU ALL GLORY AND HONOR.
We ascribe to You the honor due Your Name.

We shall worship You in the beauty of holiness.
Your voice is upon the waters; Your glory thunders all around us.

Your voice is a powerful voice; Your voice is the voice of splendor.
You are enthroned above the tumult; enthroned above for evermore.

You shall give strength to Your children, shall grant us the blessing of peace.
And in Your temple all will be crying, "Glory to the Name of the Lord." [A]

30. WE WILL EXALT YOU BECAUSE YOU HAVE LIFTED US UP.
We cried out to You, and You restored us to health.
    You brought us up from the dead as we were going down to the grave.
We sing to You, and give You thanks for the remembrance of Your holiness.
    Your wrath endures but the twinkling of an eye; Your favor for a lifetime.
Weeping may be ours for a night, but true joy comes in the morning. [A]
    While we felt secure, we thought we could never be disturbed,
As though Your favor had made us as strong as the mountains.
    Then You hid Your face from us, and we were filled with fear.
"What profit is there if we go down to the Pit?" we cried;
    "Will the dust praise You or declare Your faithfulness?
Hear us, and have mercy upon us; be our helper again," we prayed.
    And You have turned our wailing into dancing and clothed us with joy.
Therefore our hearts sing to You without ceasing;
    and we will give You our thanks for ever. [A]

31. IN YOU HAVE WE TAKEN REFUGE, DELIVER US IN YOUR RIGHTEOUSNESS.
Incline Your ear to us; make haste to help us and deliver us.
    Be our strong rock, a castle to keep us safe; guide us for the sake of Your Name.
Save us from the net that is secretly set for us, for You are our strength.
    Into Your hands we commit our spirits; for You have redeemed us. [A]
We will rejoice and be glad because of Your mercy, for You know our distress.
    You have not shut us away in the power of the enemy;
You have set our feet in open places.
    Have mercy on us, for we are in trouble; we are consumed with sorrows.
Our life is wasted away with grief and our years with sighing;
    And our strength has failed us.
We are forgotten, like the dead; we are useless.
    We can hear the whispering that is all around us, we have seen the fear.
But we have trusted in You, and our times are in Your hands.
    Make Your face to shine upon Your servants; save us in Your loving kindness.
Let us not be ashamed for having called upon You. [A]
    How great is Your goodness to those who fear You,
How great are the things You have done in our sight.
    We shall love You, O God, and worship You;
We shall be strong, and let our hearts take courage. [A]

32. HAPPY ARE THEY WHOSE SINS ARE FORGIVEN.
Happy are we when You impute no guilt to us;
  when our spirits have held no guile.
While we held our tongues, we withered away because of our own groaning.
  Then we acknowledged our sin to You, and did not conceal our guilt.
We confessed our sins, and You forgave our transgressions.
  Therefore we will make our prayers to You in times of trouble. [A]
You are our hiding place; You preserve us from our troubles.
  You instruct us and teach us in the ways that we should go.
Great are the tribulations of wickedness,
  But mercy embraces all those who trust You.
We shall be glad, and rejoice in Your name;
  We shall shout for joy, with all who are true of heart. [A]

33. IT IS GOOD FOR THE JUST TO SING PRAISES.
We shall praise You with the harp; we shall sing songs to Your Name.
  We shall sing for You a new song; and sound a fanfare with all our skill.
For Your Word is right, and all Your works are sure.
  You love righteousness and justice; Your loving kindness fills the earth.
By Your word were the heavens made and all the heavenly hosts.
  Let the whole earth fear You; let all who dwell within it stand in awe. [A]
For You spoke and it came to be; You commanded and it stood strong.
  Your will stands fast for ever, the designs of Your heart from age to age.
You look down from heaven and behold all people.
  You have fashioned the hearts of all of us, and You understand our works.
No one is delivered by their own strength, not even the strongest among us.
  Your eye is upon those who fear You, upon those who wait for Your love.
Our souls wait for You; You are our help and our shield.
  Our hearts rejoice in You, for in Your Name have we put our trust. [A]

34. WE WILL BLESS YOU AT ALL TIMES; PRAISE SHALL ALWAYS BE ON OUR LIPS.
We will glory in Your Name; let the humble hear and rejoice.
 We will proclaim Your greatness, and exalt Your Holy Name.
We sought You and You answered us, and delivered us from our terror.
 We look upon You and You are radiant; let not our faces be ashamed.
We called in our affliction and You heard us, saving us from trouble.
 Your angels surround those who fear You, and You will deliver them.
We can taste and see that You are good, that happy are they that trust in You.
 May all Your saints fear You, for those who do lack nothing. [A]
Who among us desires life? Then they must learn the fear of the Lord:
 To keep their lips from lying, and their tongues from spreading evil.
We shall turn from evil and do good; we shall seek peace and pursue it.
 Your face is against all evil, to root its remembrance from the earth. [A]
Your eyes are upon the righteous, Your ears are open to their cries.
 The righteous cry and You hear them, and deliver them from their trouble.
You are near to the brokenhearted, and save those whose spirits are crushed.
 Many are the troubles of the righteous, but You will deliver them.
You will ransom the lives of Your servants; and none of them will be punished. [A]

35. FIGHT THOSE WHO FIGHT AGAINST US.
Take up Your shield and armor and rise up to help us.
 Bar the way against our enemy, and be our salvation.
Let our enemy be as the chaff before the wind; let Your angels drive them away.
 For they have secretly set a net for us, and without a cause.
You have seen all this, do not be silent; do not remain so far away.
 How long will You simply look on? Do not let them triumph over us. [A]
Awake, and arise to our cause; come quickly to our defense.
 Grant us justice according to Your righteousness.
We will glory in Your victory, and be joyful in Your Name.
 We will offer our thanks in the great congregation;
And our tongues will tell of Your righteousness all the day long. [A]

36. YOUR LOVE AND YOUR FAITHFULNESS REACH TO THE HEAVENS.
Your righteousness is strong like the mountains;
    Your justice is like the great deep.
You save both man and beast; how priceless is Your love to us.
    We seek our shelter in the shadow of Your wings.
We feast in Your abundance, and drink from the river of Your delights.
    For with You is the well of life, and in Your light, we see light.
Continue Your loving kindness to those who know You,
    And Your favor to those who are true of heart. [A]

37. WE WILL PUT OUR TRUST IN YOU AND DO GOOD.
If we take our delight in You, we shall receive our heart's desire.
    If we commit our ways unto You, then it shall come to pass.
Your righteousness will be as clear as the light;
    And Your dealings will become as bright as noonday. [A]
We shall be still before You and wait patiently, refraining from anger;
    Leaving rage alone; without worry, for worry only leads to evil.
For You care for the lives of the godly; their inheritance will last for ever.
    You direct their steps, and strengthen those in whom You delight.
If they stumble they do not fall, for You uphold them by Your hand.
    We have been young and now we are old;
And we have never seen the righteous forsaken. [A]
    Your righteous ones are generous, and their children shall be a blessing.
For You love justice, and You do not forsake the faithful.
    We shall turn from all evil and do good, and dwell in Your land for ever.
We shall wait upon You and keep to Your ways.
    We shall mark the honest and observe the upright. [A]
There is a future for those who are peaceable.
    The mouth of the righteous utters wisdom; they speak what is right.
Your laws are in their hearts; their footsteps shall not falter.
    Our deliverance comes only from You, our strength in time of trouble.
You will rescue us and help us, because we seek our refuge in You. [A]

38. DO NOT REBUKE US IN YOUR ANGER, WE PRAY.

There is no health in us because of our sin and of Your indignation.

Our iniquities overwhelm us, like a burden too much for us to bear.

We are utterly bowed down; we go about as in mourning all the day long.

We are numb and crushed; and wail from the groaning of our hearts.

Our hearts are pounding and our strength fails; our eyes are growing dark.

Our friends draw back from our affliction and stand away from us.

We are like the deaf who cannot hear; from whose lips can come no defense. [A]

You know our desires, O God; our sighing is not hidden from You.

In You have we fixed our hope, and we know that You will answer.

Truly we are on the verge of falling, and our pain is always with us.

We will confess our sin and be sorry for our iniquities.

Do not forsake us; be not far from us; make haste to help us. [A]

39. WE WILL KEEP WATCH ON OUR WAYS SO THAT WE DO NOT OFFEND.

Let us recall the number of our days, that we may see how short life is.

You have given us a mere handful; our lifetime is as nothing in Your sight.

We walk about like shadows, and in vain we are in turmoil.

We heap up riches and cannot tell who will gather them. [A]

And now where is our hope? Only in You; deliver us from our transgressions.

Take Your affliction from us; we are worn down by what we have suffered.

Hear our prayer, and give ear to our cry; hold not Your peace at our tears.

For we are but sojourners in this land, as were our mothers and fathers.

Turn Your gaze from us that we may be glad again; before we are no more. [A]

40. WE WAITED PATIENTLY FOR YOU; AND YOU STOOPED AND HEARD OUR CRY.

You lifted us out of the mire and put a new song of praise on our lips.

Great things have You done; how great are Your wonders and designs.

There is none to compare with You; and happy are they who trust in You.

Oh, that we could tell of Your works; but they are more than we can say. [A]

You take no pleasure in sacrifice; You have required no burnt offerings from us.

So we simply say, "Behold, we come to You."

In Your Book, it is written of us,

that we love to do Your will, that Your law is in us.

You know that we have not held back from proclaiming Your Name.

We have not concealed Your righteousness or Your love.

We have spoken of Your faithfulness; do not withhold Your compassion. [A]

Trouble is upon us; our sins have overtaken us; and our hearts will surely fail.

Be pleased, we pray, to deliver us; let all who seek You rejoice and be glad.

Let those who love You continually bless Your Name.

Though we are poor and afflicted, You will hold us in Your regard.

Do not tarry, for You only are our help and our deliverance. [A]

41. HAPPY ARE THEY WHO REMEMBER THE POOR, YOU WILL DELIVER THEM.
You preserve them and keep them alive, and do not give them over to the enemy.
     You sustain them and minister to them in their illness.
"Be merciful," we cry; "heal us for we have sinned."
     You will be merciful and lift us up.
By this shall we know that You are pleased with us:
     that our enemy does not triumph.
You hold us fast; and set us before Your face for ever. [A]

42. AS A DEER LONGS FOR THE WATERBROOK, SO OUR SOULS LONG FOR YOU.
Our souls are athirst for the living God, when shall we come into Your presence?
     Our tears have been our food both night and day; where now is our God?
We pour out our souls when we think of how we led others to Your house,
     With the voice of praise and thanksgiving, with all who keep the holy days.
Why are our souls so heavy now? Why are they so disquiet within us?
     We will trust in You; and give thanks to the One Who is our help. [A]
Our souls are heavy within us,
     therefore we remember You from the land we call home.
One deep calls to another; all Your rapids and floods have gone over us.
     You grant us Your loving kindness in the day; at night Your song is with us. [A]
Why have You forgotten us? Why now when we are oppressed?
     When our bones are broken and our enemy mocks us?
Why are our souls so heavy? Why are they so disquiet within us?
     Give judgment in our behalf, we pray; and defend our cause.
Deliver us from deceit, for You only are our strength.
     Why have You put us so far from You? Why do we go so heavily now? [A]
Send out Your light and Your truth that they may lead us,
     That they may bring us to Your holy hill and dwelling,
That we may go into the altar of gladness and give our thanks.
     We shall put our trust in You,
and we will yet give thanks to the One Who is our help. [A]

In some texts, Psalms 42 and 43 are considered one Psalm.

44. WE KNOW OF THE DEEDS YOU DID FOR OUR FATHERS AND MOTHERS.
Surely it was You Who gave us our victories too, and every day we gloried in You.
　　Nevertheless, we have been humbled; and are led like sheep to the slaughter.
We are the scorn of our neighbors, a mockery to those around us.
　　Our humiliation is daily before us, and shame has covered our faces.
All this has come upon us, yet we have not forgotten Your covenant.
　　Our hearts have not turned back, nor have our steps strayed from Your paths.
Even though we are thrust down in misery and covered in darkness. [A]
　　If we forget Your name, or stretch out our hands to another god,
Will You not find it out? For You have made the secrets of our heart.
　　Awake, O God, why are You sleeping? Arise and do not reject us for ever.
Why have You hidden Your face and forgotten our affliction?
　　We sink down to the dust, our bodies cling to the earth.
Rise up for us and help us; and save us for the sake of Your steadfast love. [A]

45. OUR HEARTS ARE STIRRING WITH A NOBLE SONG.
We will recite what we have fashioned for Your Chosen One:
　　You are the fairest of us all; grace flows from Your lips;
God has blessed You for ever.
　　Ride out and conquer in the cause of truth and for the sake of justice.
Your own right hand will show You marvelous things;
　　And your enemies shall lose heart.
Your throne will endure for ever;
　　And You will be anointed with the oil of gladness.
Your Name will be remembered for all generations;
　　And we will praise You for ever. [A]

46. THE GOD OF HOSTS IS WITH US.
You are our refuge and our strength, a very present help in time of trouble.
　　Therefore, we will not fear, though the mountains tremble and the seas rage.
There is a river whose streams make glad the City of God.
　　You are in her midst, she will not be overthrown.
You are the One Who makes war to cease,
　　Who breaks the bow and shatters the spear.
We come now to see Your works, the things You have done here on earth.
　　We will be still and know that You are God;
And You will be exalted in all the earth. [A]

47. WE WILL CLAP OUR HANDS AND SHOUT TO YOU WITH A CRY OF JOY.
For You are the Most High, the great God over all the earth.
　　You have gone up with a shout and we will sing our praises to You.
For You are the God of all the earth;
　　and we will sing our praises with all our skill.
You reign over all the nations; You sit upon Your holy throne.
　　The rulers of all the earth belong to You, and You are highly exalted. [A]

48. GREAT IS THE ALMIGHTY ONE AND GREATLY TO BE PRAISED.
Beautiful and lofty, the joy of all the earth, is the City of God.
　　You are present in her citadels, You are known to be her sure refuge.
As we have heard, so have we seen: You have established her for ever.
　　We have waited in silence in the midst of Your temple.
Your praise, like Your Name, reaches to the ends of the earth.
　　Your right hand is full of justice.
Let the mountains be glad and the cities rejoice because of Your judgments.
　　You are our God for ever and ever, our guide for evermore. [A]

49. OUR MOUTHS SHALL SPEAK OF WISDOM, OUR HEARTS OF UNDERSTANDING.
Why should we be afraid in evil days, when wickedness surrounds us,
　　the wickedness of those who put their trust in their great riches?
We can never ransom ourselves or deliver to You the price of our life.
　　For the cost is too great that we should ever have enough to repay it,
Though we might live for ever and ever and never see the grave. [A]
　　We can see that the wise die also; they too perish, leaving their wealth.
Even though they are honored, they cannot live for ever.
　　Such is the way of those who trust in themselves,
And those who delight in their own words.
　　Death is their shepherd, like a flock they are destined to die. [A]
But You will ransom our life, and save us from the grasp of death.
　　We shall not become envious when some become rich,
for they will carry nothing with them.
　　Though they thought highly of themselves, and were praised by many,
They shall join the company of those who will never see the light again.
　　Those who are honored, but have no understanding, shall perish. [A]

50. THE GOD OF GODS HAS SPOKEN.
You have called the earth from the rising of the sun to its setting.
 You reveal Your glory from out of Your City, perfect in its beauty.
You will come and You will not keep silence.
 You will call the heavens and the earth to bear witness to Your judgment.
Let the heavens and the earth declare the righteousness of Your cause. [A]
 Let us gather before You those who are loyal to the covenant You have made.
You are our God and You will bear witness against us.
 You do not accuse us because of the offerings that are always before You.
We shall offer our sacrifice of thanksgiving and make good our vows.
 We shall call upon You in the day of our trouble,
You will deliver us and we will honor You. [A]
 Why do we take Your covenant and ignore Your words?
We refuse discipline, loose our lips for evil, and harness our tongues to a lie.
 We speak evil against our brothers and sisters.
These things have we done and You kept still
 and we thought that You were like us.
You have made Your accusation and put Your case before us.
 We should consider it well, we who forget You,
lest there be no one to deliver us.
 Whoever offers the sacrifice of thanksgiving honors You;
But to those who keep Your ways will You show Your salvation. [A]

51. HAVE MERCY UPON US, O GOD, HAVE MERCY.
According to Your loving kindness and compassion, blot out our offenses.
 Wash us from wickedness and cleanse us from our sin.
For well we know our transgressions, and our sins are ever before us.
 Against You have we sinned and done what is evil in Your sight.
You are justified when You speak against us, and upright in Your judgments.
 For we have been wicked since the beginning, sinners from the very start.
Purge us from our sin and we shall be pure; wash us and we will be clean.
 Hide Your face from our sins and blot out our iniquities. [A]
Look for the truth within us, and make us to understand Your wisdom.
 Make us to hear of joy and gladness;
So that the body You have broken may rejoice.
 Create in us a clean heart, and renew a right spirit within us.
Grant us the joy of Your saving help again, and sustain us with Your Spirit.
 We shall teach Your ways to others, that sinners might return to You.
Deliver us, and we shall sing of Your righteousness;
 Open our lips and we shall proclaim Your praise.
For the sacrifice of God is a troubled spirit;
 And a broken and contrite heart, You do not despise. [A]

52. HOW CAN WE BOAST OF WICKEDNESS ALL THE DAY LONG?
Our tongues are like razors; we plot ruin and deception.
　We love evil more than good, and lying more than speaking truth.
We love words that hurt; please take us from the land of the living.
　The righteous see us and laugh at us, and say that we do not truly trust in You.
O that we might be like a green tree in Your house, trusting in You for ever.
　O that we might give thanks and declare the goodness of Your Name. [A]

54. SAVE US, O GOD, BY YOUR NAME; IN YOUR MIGHT, DEFEND OUR CAUSE.
Hear our prayer; and give ear to the words of our mouths.
　For those who have no regard for You have risen up against us.
You are our helper; You are the One Who sustains us.
　We will offer You our sacrifice, and praise Your Name, for it is good.
For You have rescued us from every trouble, and shown us the ruin of our enemy. [A]

55. HEAR OUR PRAYER, AND DO NOT HIDE YOURSELF FROM OUR PETITIONS.
We have no peace because of our cares; listen to us and answer us.
　We are shaken by the noise of the enemy, and the pressure of wickedness.
Our hearts quake within us, and the terrors of death have fallen upon us;
　Fear and trembling and horror have come over us.
O that we had wings like a dove; we would fly away and be at rest.
　We would flee to a far-off place, and make our home in the wilderness.
We would hasten to escape from the storm and the tempest. [A]
　We have seen violence and strife; trouble and misery are in our midst.
There is corruption within us; we are never free of oppression and deceit.
　Had it been an enemy set against us, we could have borne it;
But it was one after our own hearts, a companion, our own familiar friend,
　One with whom we took sweet counsel, and walked beside in Your house.
We will call upon You, and You will deliver us.
　In the morning, at noon, at evening, we will lament and You will hear.
Our companions set themselves against us; they have broken their covenant.
　We will cast our burdens upon You, and You will sustain us. [A]

Psalm 14 and Psalm 53 are virtually the same, and so Psalm 53 has been omitted.

56. HAVE MERCY ON US, FOR OUR ENEMY IS HOUNDING US.
All day long the enemy assaults us and oppresses us.
    But whenever we are afraid, we shall put our trust in You.
In You, Whose Word we praise, in You we trust and will not be afraid.
    You have noted our lamentations, and collected our tears in Your bottle.
Are they not recorded in Your book?
    Whenever we call upon You, our enemy will be put to flight.
This we know, for You are by our side.
    We are bound by the vows we have made; and make our offerings to You.
For You have rescued our souls from death, and our feet from stumbling;
    That we may walk before You in the land of the living. [A]

57. BE MERCIFUL TO US, FOR WE HAVE TAKEN REFUGE IN YOU.
In the shadow of Your wings, we take refuge until the time of trouble is past.
    We will call upon You, the One Who upholds our cause.
For You will send forth from heaven and save us,
    sending forth Your love and faithfulness.
Exalt Yourself above the heavens, and Your glory over all the earth.
    Our hearts are firmly fixed on You, our hearts are firmly fixed.
We shall sing and make melody to You;
    We ourselves shall waken the dawn with our praises.
We will confess Your name among all people,
    For Your compassion is greater than the heavens,
and Your faithfulness reaches to the clouds. [A]

58. SURELY THERE IS A REWARD FOR THE RIGHTEOUS.
Do our rulers indeed decree righteousness, or judge the people with equity?
    Or do they devise evil in their hearts, and deal out violence in the land?
Let those who do evil vanish like water that runs off;
    Let them wither like the grass trodden underfoot.
Let them be swept away like a brier, before they bear fruit.
    The righteous will be glad and say, "There is a God that rules the earth." [A]

59. RESCUE US FROM OUR ENEMY, O GOD.

Protect us from those that rise up against us, for You are our God.

Rouse Yourself, and come quickly to our side.

Our eyes are fixed on You, our strength; You only are our stronghold.

You mercifully rise up to meet us;

We will look with triumph on our enemy.

Let everyone know that You rule the world to the ends of the earth.

We will sing of Your strength and celebrate Your love each morning.

For You have become our stronghold, our refuge in the day of trouble.

To You will we sing, for You are merciful to us. [A]

60. YOU HAVE CAST US OFF AND BROKEN US; TAKE US BACK TO YOURSELF.

You have been angry; You have shaken the earth and split it open.

Repair the cracks in it, for it totters on the brink.

You have made us to know hardship, and given us drink to make us stagger.

You have set a banner for those who fear You, to be a refuge for us all.

Save us by Your right hand, that those who are dear to You may be delivered.

Have You cast us off? Do You no longer stand with us?

Grant us Your help against our enemy, for vain is the help of all others.

With You we will do valiant deeds; our enemy shall be tread underfoot. [A]

61. HEAR OUR PRAYER, AND LISTEN TO OUR CRY.

We call upon You from the ends of the earth, with heaviness in our hearts.

Set us upon the rock that is high above us.

For You have been our refuge, a strong tower against the enemy.

We will dwell in Your house for ever,

and take our refuge in the shadow of Your wings.

For You have heard our vows, and joined us with those who fear You.

So that we shall always sing Your praise, and fulfill our vows day by day. [A]

62. FOR YOU ALONE OUR SOULS IN SILENCE WAIT.
You alone are our rock and our salvation, so that we shall not be shaken.
　　In You alone is our safety and our honor and our refuge.
We shall put our trust in You always, and pour out our hearts before You.
　　Though our wealth increases, we will not set our hearts upon it.
You have spoken, and we have heard You, that all power belongs to You.
　　Steadfast love is Yours; and you will repay us according to our deeds. [A]

63. YOU ARE OUR GOD, AND EAGERLY WE SEEK YOU.
Our souls thirst for You, as in a dry land where there is no water.
　　Therefore we gaze upon You in Your holy places, to behold Your glory.
Your loving kindness is better than life itself; our lips shall give You praise.
　　We will bless You as long as we live, and lift our hands in Your Name.
When we remember You on our beds, and meditate on You in the night,
　　Then our souls are content, and we praise You with joyful lips.
You have been our helper, and in the shadow of Your wings, we rejoice.
　　Our souls cling to You, and Your right hand holds us fast. [A]

64. HEAR OUR VOICE WHEN WE COMPLAIN, O GOD.
Our human hearts and minds are a mystery,
　　You can loose an arrow at them and suddenly they will be wounded.
Hear us, we pray, and protect us from the fear of our enemy.
　　Everyone will stand in awe of You,
recognizing Your works and declaring Your deeds.
　　The righteous will rejoice and put their trust in You,
And all who are true of heart will glory in Your Name. [A]

65. YOU ARE TO BE PRAISED AMONG YOUR PEOPLE.
To You that hears prayer shall people come because of their transgressions.
    Our sins are stronger than we are, but You will blot them out.
Happy are they whom you have chosen and drawn into Your courts.
    They will be satisfied by the beauty and holiness of Your house. [A]
Mighty things will You show us, in Your righteousness.
    You are the hope of the ends of the earth and of the seas far away.
You make fast the mountains and still the raging waters.
    You make the dawn and the dusk to sing for joy.
You visit the earth and water it with rain, and bless it with Your increase.
    You crown the year with Your goodness; Your paths overflow with plenty.
May the fields and the hills of the wilderness be clothed with joy.
    May the meadows and valleys be plentiful; let them shout for joy and sing. [A]

66. WE WILL BE JOYFUL, AND SING ALOUD THE GLORY OF YOUR NAME.
All the earth bows down before You, and sings out Your Name:
    "Come and see the works of God, how wonderful is God to all people."
You turned the sea into dry land, and therefore we rejoice in You.
    In might You rule for ever; and Your eyes keep watch over all. [A]
We shall bless the Lord, and make the voice of praise to be heard in the land.
    For You have tested us and tried us and proved us.
You have brought us into the snare, and laid a heavy burden upon us.
    We went through the fire and water,
but You brought us to a place of refreshment.
    We will enter Your house and pay the vows that we have promised.
We shall speak out, and tell all who will listen what You have done.
    We called out to You, and You attended the voice of our prayer.
Blessed be the One Who has not rejected us;
    Blessed be the One Who has not withheld Your love. [A]

67. BE MERCIFUL TO US AND BLESS US; SHOW THE LIGHT OF YOUR FACE.
May Your ways be known in all the earth, and Your saving help among us.
    May all nations be glad and sing for joy, for You will judge us with equity.
The earth has brought forth her increase; May You grant to us Your blessing.
    May all people praise You; may the ends of the earth stand in awe of You. [A]

68. LET THE RIGHTEOUS BE GLAD AND REJOICE BEFORE YOU.
We sing praises to You, to exalt the One Who rides upon the heavens.
    We call out Your Name, and will be merry and joyful before You.
You give the solitary a home, and bring prisoners to freedom.
    You send the gracious rain upon Your inheritance, refreshing the weary land.
Your people find a home in the wilderness;
    And in Your goodness You make provision for the poor. [A]
Blessed be Your Name; day by day the God of salvation bears our burdens.
    You are our God, the One by Whom we escape death.
Send forth Your strength, establish what You have made for us.
    Ride forth in Your ancient heavens, and send forth Your mighty voice.
We sing our praise to You; we ascribe to You all power and majesty.
    How wonderful are all Your holy places; Your strength is in the skies.
Blessed be Your Name! Blessed be Your Name! [A]

69. SAVE US, FOR THE WATERS ARE RISING OVER US.
We are sinking, there is no firm ground for our feet.
  We have come into deep waters and the torrent washes over us.
We grow weary with our weeping, and our eyes fail from seeking You.
  You know well our foolishness, our faults are not hidden from You.
Let not those who hope in You be put to shame because of us.
  Let not those who seek You be disgraced on our account. [A]
For Your sake we have suffered reproach and shame has covered our face.
  We have become as strangers, even to our own kindred.
In Your great mercy, answer us with Your unfailing help.
  Save us, we pray, do not let us sink; let us be rescued.
Let not the torrents wash over us, nor let the deep swallow us up.
  Answer us, for Your love is kind; in Your compassion turn to us.
Hide not Your face; be swift to answer, for we are in distress.
  Reproach has broken our spirits, and they cannot be healed. [A]
We have looked for sympathy and comfort, but there is none.
  We are afflicted and in pain, and only Your help can lift us up.
We will praise Your name, and proclaim Your greatness in song.
  The afflicted shall see and be glad; those who seek You shall live.
For You listen to the needy; Your prisoners You do not despise.
  Let the heavens and the earth praise You, for only the Almighty can save us. [A]

70. BE PLEASED TO DELIVER US; O GOD, MAKE HASTE TO HELP US.
Let all who seek You rejoice and be glad in You.
  Let all who love Your salvation for ever proclaim Your greatness.
As for us, we are poor and needy; come to us quickly, we pray.
  You are our help and our deliverer; do not tarry, we pray. [A]

71. IN YOU HAVE WE TAKEN REFUGE; LET US NEVER BE ASHAMED.
In Your righteousness, set us free; incline Your ear to us and save us.
   Be our strong rock, and a castle to keep us safe.
For You are our hope, our confidence since we were young.
   We have been sustained by You since our birth; our song is always of You.
   Let our mouths be full of Your praise and Your glory all the day long. [A]
Do not cast us off in our old age; forsake us not when our strength fails.
   Be not far from us, we pray; come quickly to help us.
We shall always wait in patience, and we shall praise You more and more.
   We shall recount Your saving acts though we do not know them all.
We shall recall Your mighty works and Your righteousness, and Yours alone.
   You have taught us since we were young, and to this day we speak of You.
Now that we are old, do not forsake us,
   Until we tell Your story to all who are to come. [A]
Who is like You? Your righteousness reaches to the heavens.
   You have shown us great troubles and adversities;
But You will restore our life, and bring us up from the deep.
   You strengthen us more and more; You enfold and comfort us.
Therefore, we will praise You, O Holy One.
   Our lips will sing with joy, and so will the souls You have redeemed.
Our tongues shall proclaim Your greatness all the day long. [A]

72. GRANT YOUR JUSTICE AND RIGHTEOUSNESS TO YOUR CHOSEN ONE.
May the One You have chosen rule Your people in righteousness and justice.
   May He defend the needy, rescue the poor, and preserve the oppressed;
And live as long as the sun and the moon, from one generation to another.
   May He come down like showers that water the earth.
May there be an abundance of peace in His time.
   And may He rule from sea to sea, and may His foes bow down before him. [A]
For He will deliver those who cry out distress, the oppressed who have no helper.
   He shall have pity on the lowly and the poor; preserving the lives of the needy.
Long may He live! and may prayer be made for Him always.
   May His name remain for ever, established as long as the sun endures.
Blessed be Your Name, for You alone do such wondrous deeds.
   Blessed be Your Name for ever; may the earth be filled with Your glory. [A]

73. TRULY YOU ARE GOOD TO THOSE WHO ARE PURE OF HEART.
As for us, our feet had slipped, and we had nearly fallen;
    Because we envied the proud, and took note of the prosperity of others.
In vain, it seemed, we had sought to keep our hearts clean and innocent.
    When we tried to understand such things, it was too much for us.
Until we entered Your sanctuary, and saw the end of the wicked.
    Like a dream when one awakens, You made their image vanish.
When our minds became embittered, we were sorely wounded in our hearts.
    We were stupid and had no understanding, like brute beasts before You. [A]
Yet we were always with You; You hold us by Your right hand.
    You will guide us by Your counsel, and afterwards receive us with glory.
Whom have we in heaven but You? Having You, we desire nothing on earth.
    Though our flesh and our heart should waste away,
You are our strength and our portion for ever.
    It is good for us to be near You; we have made You our God and refuge. [A]

74. WHY HAVE YOU CAST AWAY THE SHEEP OF YOUR PASTURE?
Do You not remember the people that You redeemed for Your very own?
    Turn Your steps to the endless ruins; the enemy has destroyed everything.
Your adversaries roar in Your holy places; they have set fire to Your temples.
    They have defiled Your dwellings, seeking to destroy them all together.
There are no signs left to see; no prophet remains; no one can say how long.
    How long will the enemy blaspheme Your Holy Name? [A]
Why do You hold back Your hand, and keep hidden Your mighty arm?
    You have been our God from ancient times, victorious in all the earth.
Yours is the day and the night; You established the sun and the moon.
    You fixed the boundaries of the earth; You set the summer and winter.
Do not hand the dove over to the wild beasts; do not forget Your poor.
    Do not turn away the oppressed; let the poor and the needy praise You.
Arise, we pray; look upon Your covenant and maintain Your cause. [A]

75. WE GIVE YOU THANKS, O GOD, WE GIVE YOU THANKS.
We give You thanks, calling Your name, and declaring Your deeds.
    You will appoint a time when You will judge us with equity.
Though all the earth trembles, You will keep its foundations fast.
    Judgment comes neither from the east or from the west;
Nor is it from the mountains or the wilderness.
    You are the One Who judges, who puts one down and lifts another.
We will rejoice for ever, singing praise to the God of our fathers and mothers. [A]

76. HOW GLORIOUS YOU ARE, MORE SPLENDID THAN THE MOUNTAINS.
What terror You inspire! Who can stand before You when You are angry?
    Who can stand when You rise up to judgment and rise to save the oppressed?
When You pronounce Your judgment, the whole earth is afraid and still.
    We will make our vows to You, and we shall keep them.
Let all who gather around You bring gifts to You,
    For You are the One Who is worthy to be feared. [A]

77. WE WILL CRY ALOUD TO YOU, AND YOU WILL HEAR US.
In the day of our trouble, we seek You, and refuse to be comforted.
    We think only of You; we are restless and our spirits faint.
Our eyes will not close so that we can rest; we are troubled and cannot speak.
    We consider the days gone by; we remember the years long past.
We listen to our hearts in the night; we ponder and search our minds. [A]
    Will You cast us off for ever? Will You no more show Your favor?
Have You forgotten to be gracious? Do You withhold Your compassion in anger?
    Has Your right hand lost its power? [A]
We will remember Your works, and call to mind Your wonders of old.
    We will meditate on all Your acts, and ponder Your mighty deeds.
Your way is holy; who is so great a God as You?
    You are the One Who works wonders; and Your strength has redeemed us.
By the hand of Your servants, You have led us like a flock. [A]

78. WE WILL DECLARE THE MYSTERIES OF TIMES GONE BY.
We will not hide from what our fathers and mothers have taught us.

We will recount Your wonderful works for generations to come;
How You gave Your decrees, and established a law for Your children,

That generations to come might know and teach their children,
Teaching them to put their trust in You, and keep Your commandments.

Our hearts were not always steadfast, our spirits not always faithful.
We refused to keep our covenant, and refused to walk in Your ways.

We forgot what You had done, and the wonders You have shown us. [A]
We went on sinning against You, rebelling against the Most High.

We tested You in our hearts, demanding more and more.
When You heard us, You were full of wrath, and Your anger mounted.

For we had no faith, nor did we trust in Your saving power.
You cared for us anyway, and fed us from on high.

We were well filled but it did not stop our craving.
So Your anger rose against us, and still we had no faith. [A]

Whenever we were afflicted, we would seek You and repent.
We would remember that You are our redeemer.

But we would only flatter You, and our hearts were not steadfast.
In Your mercy, You forgave us, holding back Your anger.

You know that we are only flesh, a fleeting breath that does not return. [A]
Again and again, we provoked You.

We did not remember Your power, and how You had rescued us,
How You had been with us in the wilderness and led us to safety,

How You brought us to a holy place, and granted us our inheritance.
Still we tested and defied You, and did not keep Your ways.

We were undependable and disloyal, provoking Your anger with our idols.
Then we awoke as from a deep sleep, and built for ourselves a new sanctuary.

You chose One to be our shepherd, to lead us with a true and faithful heart. [A]

79. THE WICKED HAVE COME INTO YOUR INHERITANCE, O GOD.
Your holy temple has been profaned; Your holy city is in ruins.
  Your people are a reproach to their neighbors, objects of scorn and derision.
How long will You be angry? Will Your fury blaze like fire for ever?
  Remember not our past sins; let Your compassion be swift to meet us.
Help us, for the glory of Your Name; deliver us, and forgive us our sins.
  Hear the sighing of the sorrowful and spare us, for we are Your people.
We will give You thanks for ever, and we will praise You from age to age. [A]

80. SHINE FORTH, YOU THAT ARE ENTHRONED WITH ANGELS.
How long will You be angry, despite the prayers of Your people?
  You have fed us with the bread of tears, and with bowls of tears to drink.
We have become the derision of our neighbors; our enemies laugh us to scorn.
  Turn now, we pray, look down upon us from heaven.
Behold and tend this vine; preserve what Your right hand has planted.
  Let Your hand be on the One You have made so strong for Yourself.
And so that we will never turn away, give us life, that we may call on Your Name.
  Restore us, we pray; show us the light of Your face, and we shall be saved. [A]

81. WE SING WITH JOY, AND SHOUT TO YOU ON HIGH.
We raise a song and sound the timbrel; we play the harp and play the strings.
  We blow the horn at the new moon, and again on the day of the feast.
For this is a statute for Your people, a law for Your glory.
  It has been laid upon us as a solemn charge, when You delivered us. [A]
You eased our shoulders from bearing the burden, and set us free.
  We called on You in our trouble, and You saved us.
We tested You and You answered us in secret.
  You are our God, the One Who brought us out of captivity.
And yet we listened to Your voice, and would not obey Your law.
  So we were given over to our stubbornness, left to follow our own devices. [A]
O that we would listen to You; O that we would walk in Your ways.
  You would soon subdue our enemies, turning Your hand against our foes.
You would feed us with the finest wheat, and with honey from the rock. [A]

82. YOU STAND IN THE COUNCIL OF HEAVEN, AND GIVE YOUR JUDGMENT.
How long shall we judge unjustly, and grant our favor to the wicked?
   We must save the weak and the orphan; defend the humble and the needy;
Rescue the poor and the weary; delivering them from the wicked.
   We go about in darkness; we do not see and do not understand.
We are, all of us, children of the Most High, and all of us are mortal.
   Arise, we pray, and rule the earth, and take all people for Your own. [A]

83. DO NOT BE SILENT, WE PRAY; DO NOT KEEP STILL OR HOLD YOUR PEACE.
Your enemies are in tumult, and those who hate You have risen up.
   They plot in secret against Your people, those whom You would protect.
Cover their faces with shame, we pray, that they may seek Your Name.
   Let them be disgraced and terrified; let confusion reign among them.
Let them know that You are God, the One Most High over all the earth. [A]

84. HOW DEAR TO US IS YOUR DWELLING.
Our souls have a longing for Your courts; our hearts rejoice in You.
   Happy are they that dwell in Your house, they will always be praising You.
Happy are they whose strength is in You,
   whose hearts are set in the pilgrim way.
Those who go through the desolate valley will find it a place of springs.
   They will climb from height to height and You will reveal Yourself to them. [A]
Hear our prayers, we pray; look upon the face of Your anointed ones.
   For one day in Your courts is better than a thousand in our own rooms.
You are both sun and shield, giving grace and glory;
   No good thing will You withhold from those who walk with integrity.
Happy are they who put their trust in You. [A]

85. YOU HAVE BEEN GRACIOUS TO US, AND YOU HAVE RESTORED OUR FORTUNES.
You have forgiven our iniquity, and blotted out our sins.
   You have withdrawn all Your fury, and turned away from indignation.
Restore us then, we pray; let Your anger depart from us.
   Will You prolong Your anger for ever, displeased with us from age to age?
Will You not give us life again, that we may rejoice in You? [A]
   Show us Your mercy, we pray, and grant us Your salvation.
We will listen to Your words of peace to those who turn their hearts to You.
   Truly Your salvation is near, that Your glory may dwell with us.
Mercy and truth have met together; righteousness and power have kissed.
   Truth shall spring up from the earth; righteousness shall look upon us.
Righteousness shall go before You, and peace will be the pathway for our feet. [A]

86. BOW DOWN YOUR EAR AND ANSWER, FOR WE ARE POOR AND IN MISERY.
Keep watch over the lives of the faithful; save the servants who trust in You.
Be merciful to us, for You are our God; we call upon You all the day long.
Gladden the souls of Your servants, for to You we lift up our hearts.
You are forgiving, and great is Your love toward all who fear You. [A]
Give ear to our prayer; attend the voice of our supplication.
In the time of trouble we will call upon You, and You will answer.
Among all gods, there is none like You, nor anything like Your works.
For You alone are the Holy One, and You do wondrous things.
Teach us Your way and we will walk in Your Truth; knit our hearts to Yours.
We will thank You with all our heart, and glorify Your holy Name.
For great is Your love toward us; You have delivered us from the grave.
You are gracious and full of compassion, slow to anger and of great kindness.
Turn and have mercy upon us; give Your strength to Your servants.
Show us a sign of Your favor, O God; grant us Your help and comfort. [A]

87. ON THE HOLY MOUNTAIN STANDS YOUR BELOVED CITY.
Glorious things are spoken of Your City.
All are to be counted among her citizens, for in Your city were they born.
Everyone was born of her, and the Most High sustains her.
As we are enrolled, You shall say of all that they too were born in the City.
All our singers and dancers will rejoice, that all their fresh springs are in You. [A]

88. BY DAY AND BY NIGHT WE CRY TO YOU.
Let our prayers enter Your presence; incline Your ear to our lamentations.
For we are full of trouble; our life is at the brink of the grave.
We have become like those lost among the dead, like those with no strength,
Those whom You remember no more, those cut off from Your right hand.
You have laid us in dark places; Your anger weighs heavily upon us.
Our friends are far from us; we are imprisoned and cannot get free.
Our sight has failed us; we stretch out our hands, calling upon You daily. [A]
Do You work Your wonders for the dead? Do they rise up to give You thanks?
Is Your loving kindness declared in the grave, or Your faithfulness in the ruins?
Is Your righteousness to be found in a forgotten land? [A]
As for us, we cry to You for help each morning.
Why have You rejected us? Why have You hidden Your face from us?
Ever since our youth, we have borne Your terrors with a troubled mind.
Your anger has swept over us; our friends have been put away from us;
And the darkness is our only companion. [A]

89. YOUR LOVE FOR EVER WILL WE SING.
From age to age, we will proclaim Your faithfulness.

For we are persuaded that Your love is established for ever,
and Your faithfulness is in the heavens.

The heavens bear witness to Your wonders; Your faithfulness is all around. [A]
Who is like You, O God? Who can be compared to You?

You rule the raging of the sea, and still the singing of the waves.
Yours are the heavens and the earth, and all that is within.

You have a mighty arm; strong and high is Your own right hand.
Righteousness and justice are the foundations of Your throne;

Love and truth go before You always. [A]
Happy are they that know the festal shout; and walk in the light of Your presence.

They rejoice each day in Your Name, and are jubilant in Your righteousness.
You are the glory of their strength, and by Your favor are they exalted.

Truly You are their ruler, the Holy One is their king indeed. [A]
But You have cast off Your anointed and are enraged.

How long will You hide Yourself? Will You hide Yourself for ever?
Remember how short our life is, how frail indeed You have made us.

Who can live and not see death? Who can resist the power of the grave?
Where is Your loving kindness of old that You promised?

Blessed be Your Name for evermore! Amen, we say, so be it. [A]

90. YOU HAVE BEEN OUR REFUGE, FROM ONE GENERATION TO ANOTHER.
Before the mountains stood or the land was born, from age to age, You are God.
    A thousand years in Your sight are like yesterday;
And they pass like a watch in the night.
    We are swept away as in a dream; we fade suddenly like the grass.
In the morning it is green and flourishing, and in the evening, it is gone.
    The sum of our years is but labor and sorrow;
They pass too quickly and we are gone. [A]
    Teach us to number our days, that we may apply our hearts to wisdom.
Be gracious to Your servants; satisfy us in Your loving kindness;
    So shall we rejoice and be glad all of the days of our life.
Make us glad by the measure of our days, days in which we suffer adversity.
    Show Your works to Your servants, and Your splendor to our children.
May Your grace be upon us to prosper the works of our hands. [A]

91. THOSE WHO DWELL WITH YOU, ABIDE IN THE SHADOW OF THE ALMIGHTY.
We shall say that You are our refuge, our God in whom we trust.
    And You will deliver us from the snare of the hunter and from pestilence.
You will cover us with Your wings; Your faithfulness will be our shield.
    We shall not be afraid of terror by night, or of the arrow that flies by day.
We shall not fear plague in the darkness, nor the sickness that lays waste at noon.
    Because we have made You our dwelling, no evil shall come to us. [A]
You will give Your angels charge over us, and keep us in all our ways.
    Angels will bear us up, lest we dash our feet against a stone.
Because we are bound to You in love, You will deliver us.
    We will call upon You and You will answer; You will be with us in our trouble.
With long life will You satisfy us, and show us Your salvation. [A]

92. IT IS GOOD TO GIVE THANKS TO YOU, TO SING PRAISES TO YOUR NAME.
It is good to tell of Your love in the morning,
    and Your faithfulness at the close of the day.
You have made us glad; we shout for joy at the work of Your hands.
    How great are Your works, and how deep are Your thoughts.
You make the faithful to flourish like the palm tree;
    those who are planted in Your house shall flourish in Your courts.
They shall still bear fruit in their old age, that they may show Your love.
    You are our rock, in Whom there is no fault. [A]

93. YOU ARE THE ALMIGHTY, AND HAVE GIRDED YOURSELF WITH STRENGTH.
Ever since the world began, Your throne has been established.
  You are from everlasting, and made the world so it cannot be moved.
The waters have lifted up their voices; they have lifted up their waves.
  But mightier than the sound of many waters is the One Who dwells on high.
Your testimonies are sure, and holiness adorns Your house for ever. [A]

94. RISE UP, O JUDGE OF THE WORLD; RISE UP, AND SHOW YOURSELF.
How long shall the ways of wickedness triumph? How long?
  The ways that murder the orphan and stranger, and crush Your people.
Those who do such things say that You do not see and You do not care.
  You made our eyes and ears, can You not see and hear?
Does the One that has made the whole world have no knowledge? [A]
  You know well our thoughts, how like a puff of wind they are.
Happy are they whom You instruct, those You teach from Your ways.
  You will not abandon or forsake Your own.
Judgment will again be just, and followed by the true of heart.
  If You do not come to our help, we shall soon dwell in a land of silence. [A]
As often as we have said that our feet have slipped, You have upheld us.
  When many cares fill our minds, Your consolations cheer our souls.
Can a corrupt tribunal have any part with You, once they have made evil into law?
  They conspire against the life of the just, and they condemn the innocent.
But You have become our stronghold; You are the rock of our trust. [A]

95. COME, LET US RAISE A JOYFUL SONG.
Let us raise a shout of triumph to the rock of our salvation.
  Let us come into Your presence with thanksgiving, singing songs of triumph.
For You are a great God, a great king over all gods.
  The depths of the earth are in Your hands; mountains belong to You.
The sea is Yours, for You made it, and the dry land Your hands fashioned.
  Let us bow down in worship; let us kneel before the One who made us.
For You are our God, and we are the flock that You shepherd.
  We will know Your power and presence this day,
if we will but listen for Your voice. [A]

96. WE SING TO YOU A NEW SONG; WE SING WITH ALL THE EARTH.
We sing to You and bless Your holy Name;
  we proclaim the news of Your salvation.
We declare Your glory and Your wonders among all people.
  For great You are and greatly to be praised. [A]
Oh, the majesty of Your presence, and the splendor of Your sanctuary.
  We ascribe to You the honor due Your Name;
We bring our offerings and come into Your courts.
  We worship You in the beauty of holiness,
and may the whole earth tremble before You.
  You are God, and You will judge us with equity. [A]
Let the heavens rejoice and the earth be glad.
  Let the seas thunder and the fields rejoice and all that dwell therein.
Let even the trees shout with joy before You. [A]

97. YOU ARE THE MOST HIGH; LET THE WHOLE EARTH BE GLAD.
Though clouds and darkness are roundabout You,
  Your foundations are just and righteous.
The heavens declare Your righteousness, and all people can see Your glory.
  For You are God, the Most High over all the earth.
You love those that hate evil; and You preserve the lives of Your saints.
  Light springs up for the righteous, and gladness for the true of heart.
We rejoice in You, and give our thanks to Your Holy Name. [A]

98. WE SING TO YOU A NEW SONG, YOU HAVE DONE MARVELOUS THINGS.
With Your strong right hand and holy arm, You have won a great victory.
  Your righteousness has been shown in the sight of all peoples.
You have remembered Your mercy and faithfulness, and shown them to all.
  Shout with joy, all you lands; lift up your voice and sing.
Shout before the Lord; sing out with trumpet and harp and the voice of song.
  Let the sea make a noise, and the land, and all that dwells therein.
Let the rivers clap their hands, and let the hills ring for joy.
  For You judge the world with equity, and all people in righteousness. [A]

99. YOU ARE GOD, LET ALL PEOPLE TREMBLE BEFORE YOU.
You are great in Zion, and high above all peoples.
  Let us confess Your Holy Name, for You are the Holy One.
O mighty One, and lover of justice, You have established Your equity.
  We proclaim Your greatness, and we fall down before You.
We have called upon Your Holy Name, and You have answered us.
  We have kept Your decrees and Your testimonies.
You have answered us indeed, You are the One Who forgave us.
  We proclaim Your greatness, and we worship You in the holy places.
For You, our God, are the Holy One. [A]

100. WE SHALL BE JOYFUL IN THE NAME OF THE MOST HIGH.
We shall serve You with gladness, and come into Your presence with a song.
  We know that You are God, the One Who has made us, to Whom we belong,
That we are Your people and the sheep of Your pasture.
  We shall enter Your gates with thanksgiving, and into Your courts with praise.
We shall tell out our thanks, and call upon Your Name.
  For You are good, and Your mercy is everlasting.
And Your faithfulness endures from age to age. [A]

101. WE WILL SING OF MERCY AND JUSTICE; TO YOU WE WILL SING OUR PRAISE.
We will strive to follow a blameless course, to walk with sincerity in our house.
  We shall set no worthless thing before us; the things of evil shall not remain.
A crooked heart shall be far from us; we will not know evil and slander.
  Our eyes will look to the faithful among us, that they may dwell beside us.
Those who lead a blameless life shall be our servants;
  Those who act deceitfully shall not continue in our sight. [A]

102. HEAR OUR PRAYER, O GOD AND LET OUR CRY COME BEFORE YOU.
Hide not Your face in the day of our trouble.

Incline Your ear to us; when we call, make haste to help us.
Our days drift away like smoke, our hearts are withered like the grass.

We lie awake and groan; we are like sparrows on the lonely rooftops.
We have eaten ashes for our bread, and mingled our drink with our tears.

Our days pass away like shadows; we wither and we waste away. [A]
You will build up Your people, and Your glory will appear.

You will look with favor upon the homeless, and not despise their pleas.
Let this be told to a future generation, so that a people unborn may praise You.

For You have looked down from Your heaven and beheld the earth,
That You might hear the captive's groan, and set free those condemned to die. [A]

You will endure for ever, and Your Name from age to age.
In the beginning You laid a foundation for the earth,

And the heavens are the work of Your hands.
They will perish; they shall wear out like a garment.

But You are always the same, and Your years will never end. [A]

103. MAY ALL THAT IS WITHIN US BLESS YOUR HOLY NAME.
May we bless You, and forget not all of Your benefits.

You forgive our sins and heal our infirmities.
You redeem our lives from the grave, and crown us with mercy and kindness.

You satisfy us with good things, and our strength is renewed.
You execute righteousness and justice for all who are oppressed.

You are full of compassion and mercy, slow to anger and of great kindness. [A]
You have not dealt with us according to our sins,

Nor rewarded us according to our wickedness.
As high as the heavens are above the earth, so is Your mercy.

As far as east is from the west, so far have our sins been removed.
As a father cares for his children, so do You care for us.

You know whereof that we are made, and remember that we are but dust.
Your merciful goodness endures for ever, for those who keep Your ways.

All Your works shall bless You, in all times and in all places.
. May our souls always bless You, and all who hearken to Your voice. [A]

104. HOW EXCELLENT IS YOUR GREATNESS, O GOD.
You wrap Yourself with light for a cloak, and spread out the heavens for a curtain.
    You make the winds Your messengers, and the flames of fire Your servants.
You make the clouds for Your chariot, and ride on the wings of the wind.
    You set the earth on its foundations, and it shall not be moved.
You send the springs into the valleys, to flow between Your mountains.
    Beside them birds make their nests and sing among the trees. [A]
You water the mountains from on high, satisfying the earth by Your word.
    You make the grass to grow for the flocks, and plants to serve Your children,
That we may bring forth good from the earth: wine to gladden our hearts,
    Oil to make a cheerful countenance, and bread to strengthen the heart.
You appointed the moon to mark the seasons, the sun knows when to set.
    You made darkness to bring the night, that wild beasts might find their food.
And we go forth to our daily work, and to labor until evening. [A]
    How manifold are Your works, in Your wisdom You made them all.
The earth is full of Your creatures, we look to You for food in due season.
    You give it to us and we gather it; You open Your hands and we are filled.
You hide Your face and we are afraid, You take our breath and we return to dust.
    You send Your spirit, and we are created, and You renew the earth. [A]
May Your glory endure for ever; and may You rejoice in all Your works.
    We will sing songs to You as long as we live;
we will praise You while we have our being.
    We will rejoice in You, and may our words please You. [A]

105. WE GIVE OUR THANKS TO YOU, AND CALL UPON YOUR HOLY NAME.
We will sing praises to You, and make Your deeds known among us.
 We will sing praises to You, and speak of Your marvelous works.
We will glory in Your Holy Name, may the hearts of all who seek You rejoice.
 We will search for You and Your strength, and continually seek Your face.
We will remember the wonders You have done, and Your righteous judgments. [A]
 You are God, Your judgments prevail in all the world.
You have always been mindful of Your covenant,
 The promise You made for a thousand generations,
The covenant You made with Abraham, the oath You swore to Isaac,
 The promise You established as a statute for Your people,
When they were but sojourners in the land.
 You have remembered Your word and Your servants,
And You have led us forth with gladness and shouts of joy,
 That we might keep Your ways and observe Your statutes. [A]

106. WE GIVE YOU THANKS, FOR YOUR MERCY ENDURES FOR EVER.
Who can declare all Your mighty acts, or show forth all Your praise?
 Happy are they who act with justice, and always do what is right.
Remember us, we pray, with Your favor, and visit us with Your saving help,
 That we may be glad with Your people, and glory in Your inheritance. [A]
We have sinned as did our mothers and fathers; we have done wrong.
 But You saved us for Your Name's sake to make Your power known.
You have saved us from the hand of those who hate us,
 And redeemed us from the hand of our enemy.
You have led us through deep waters, as though they were dry land.
 And we believed Your word, and sang Your song of praise. [A]
But we soon forgot Your deeds, and did not wait upon Your counsel.
 Cravings seized us in the wilderness, and we put You to the test.
You gave us what we asked, but sent a leanness to our souls.
 We forgot that You were our Saviour, and the great things You have done.
We refused the pleasant places and did not believe Your promises.
 We exchanged our glory for idols, and forgot Your wonderful deeds.
We sat grumbling in our places and would not receive Your voice. [A]
 Many a time You delivered us, but we have rebelled against Your love.
Nevertheless you have seen our distress, and listened to our cries.
 You remembered Your covenant, and relented according to Your mercy.
Save us again, we pray, and gather us up that we may give You thanks.
 Blessed be Your Name, from everlasting to everlasting. [A]

107. WE GIVE YOU THANKS, FOR YOU ARE GOOD.
Let all whom You have redeemed proclaim that You are their salvation.
   Let us give thanks for Your mercy, the wonders You do for Your children.
Some of us wandered in the desert, and found no place in which to dwell.
   We were hungry and thirsty, and our spirits languished within us.
Then we cried to You in our trouble, and were delivered from our distress.
   Our feet were placed on a path that was straight.
We give You thanks for Your mercy, and the wonders You do for Your children,
   For You satisfy the thirsty and fill the hungry with good things. [A]
Some of us sat in darkness and gloom, bound fast in our misery,
   Because we had rebelled against Your word and despised Your counsel.
Our spirits were humbled, and we stumbled and found no one to help us.
   Then we cried to You in our trouble, and were delivered from our distress.
We were led from the darkness and gloom, and our bonds were broken.
   We give You thanks for Your mercy, and the wonders You do for Your children,
For You break the bonds that hold us, and shatter the bars that confine us. [A]
   Some of us were foolish and took to rebellious ways.
We were afflicted by our sins, and we drew near to the doors of death.
   Then we cried to You in our trouble, and were delivered from our distress.
You sent forth Your word, and healed us, and saved us from the grave.
   We give You thanks for Your mercy, and the wonders You do for Your children,
To You we offer thanksgiving, and tell of Your acts with joy. [A]
   Some of us went down to the sea in ships, to ply our trade in deep waters.
We beheld all Your works and the wonders of the deeps.
   Then the storms arose and tossed high the waves, and our hearts were afraid.
Then we cried to You in our trouble and were delivered from our distress.
   You stilled the storm to a whisper, and brought us into the harbor we sought.
We give You thanks for Your mercy, and the wonders You do for Your children,
   And we exalt You before all people and praise You in the congregation. [A]
We give You thanks for You are good, and Your mercy endures for ever.
   You changed deserts into pools of water, and dry land into water springs.
You blessed us so that we increased greatly, and lifted the poor from their misery.
   Whoever is wise will ponder these things, considering the mercy of God. [A]

108. OUR HEARTS ARE FIRMLY FIXED; WE WILL SING AND MAKE MELODY TO YOU.
We wake our hearts to sing, we ourselves shall waken the dawn.
  We will confess Your name among all peoples.
Your loving kindness is greater than the heavens;
  Your faithfulness reaches the clouds.
Your glory is over all the earth,
  so that those who are dear to You might be saved.
Grant us Your help against our enemy,
  for in vain is the help of all others.
With You we will do valiant deeds;
  and the enemy shall be trampled. [A]

109. HOLD NOT YOUR TONGUE, FOR THE MOUTH OF DECEIT IS AGAINST US.
We are spoken against with lies and hateful words and without cause.
  Despite our love, we are accused; but as for us, we pray for them.
Evil is repaid for good, and hatred for our love.
  Deliver us, we pray, deal with us according to Your Name. [A]
We are poor and needy, and our hearts are wounded within us.
  Our knees are weak from fasting; our flesh is wasted and frail.
We fade away like the shadows when they lengthen.
  We have become a reproach to others; they see us and shake their heads. [A]
Help us, we pray, for Your mercy's sake.
  Let everyone know we are saved by Your hand,
And that You are the One Who has done it.
  And we will give great thanks to You, in the midst of the multitudes.
We shall praise You because You stand on the side of the needy,
  To save those who are condemned. [A]

Psalm 110 has been intentionally omitted.

III. WE WILL GIVE THANKS TO YOU WITH OUR WHOLE HEART.
Great are all Your deeds, and studied by all who delight in them.
  Full of majesty and splendor, Your righteousness endures for ever.
You make Your works that we might remember You,
  And Your grace and Your compassion to us.
You give food to those who fear You;
  You are ever mindful of Your covenant.
You have shown Your people the power of Your works,
  Giving them a land in which to dwell. [A]
The works of Your hands are faithfulness and justice;
  and all Your commandments are sure.
They stand fast for ever, because they are done in truth and equity.
  You sent redemption to Your people, and commanded Your covenant for ever.
To fear You is the beginning of wisdom;
  those who act upon it have a good understanding. [A]

II2. HAPPY ARE THEY WHO FEAR YOU AND DELIGHT IN YOUR COMMANDMENTS.
Light shines in darkness for the upright; they are merciful and full of compassion.
  It is good for them to lend generously, to manage their affairs with justice.
The righteous will never be shaken; they will be kept in everlasting remembrance.
  Their hearts are right; they trust in You; they are not afraid of rumors.
They give freely to the poor; their righteousness stands fast for ever.
  They put their trust in You, and they hold up their heads with honor. [A]

II3. MAY YOUR HOLY NAME BE BLESSED BY YOUR SERVANTS.
From the rising of the sun to its setting, let Your Holy Name be praised.
  You are high above the heavens, Your glory over all the earth.
Who is like You, enthroned on high, and still You stoop to behold us?
  Who but You takes up the weak from out of the dust?
Who but You will lift the poor from out of the ashes? [A]

II4. OUR HOME HAS BECOME YOUR DWELLING-PLACE, O GOD.
When we returned from the land of our bondage,
  from the land where we were strangers
Then our home became Your sanctuary,
  and our own dwelling-place Your dominion.
May the whole earth tremble at Your presence,
  at Your presence with those You have chosen.
You are the One Who has turned the hard rock into a pool of water,
  the One Who has turned stone into a flowing spring. [A]

115. To Your Name we give all glory; not to us but to You.
Why should the heathen ask where is our God?

They keep idols of silver and gold, the work of human hands.
Their gods have mouths, but they cannot speak; eyes, but they cannot see.

Their gods have ears, but they cannot hear; hands, but they cannot feel.
Those who make such idols are like them, and so are they who trust in them.

The dead cannot praise You, nor can those who go down in silence. [A]
We give You glory because of Your love and faithfulness.

You are mindful of us and bless us; You are our help and our shield.
Increase us more and more, we pray, and our children after us.

May we be blessed by the Maker of heaven and earth.
The heaven of heavens belongs to You, but the earth is entrusted to us.

And we will bless You, from this time forth, and for evermore. [A]

116. WE LOVE YOU, BECAUSE YOU HAVE HEARD OUR VOICE.
You have inclined Your ear to us whenever we call upon You.
    The cords of death entangled us; we came to grief and sorrow.
Then we called upon You to save our life,
    And You were gracious and full of compassion.
You watch over the innocent; we were brought low and You helped us.
    Our souls may turn again to their rest, for You have treated us well.
You have rescued us from death;
    You cleansed the tears from our eyes, and kept our feet from stumbling. [A]
How shall we repay You for all the good things You have done for us?
    We shall walk in Your presence in the land of the living.
We shall lift up the cup of salvation, and call upon Your Name.
    We shall fulfill our vows to You, in the presence of Your people.
We shall offer a sacrifice of thanksgiving, in the courts of Your love. [A]

117. MAY ALL THE PEOPLE PRAISE YOU FOR EVER.
May all the nations praise You, O God;
    May all people everywhere give honor to Your Name,
For Your loving kindness toward us is great,
    and Your faithfulness endures for ever. [A]

118. WE SHALL GIVE OUR THANKS TO YOU, FOR YOU ARE GOOD.
We called upon You in our distress; You answered by setting us free.
    You are with us, we shall not fear; what can anyone do to us?
You are at our side to help us; it is better to rely on You than on all others.
    You are our strength and our song, and You have become our salvation. [A]
We shall not die, but live, and declare Your mighty works.
    Open for us the gates of the righteous; and we shall enter and give thanks.
We will give thanks for You have answered us, and become our salvation.
    The same stone that the builders rejected has become the cornerstone;
And it is Your doing, and it is marvelous in our sight.
    This very day You have acted, let us rejoice and be glad. [A]
Blessed is the one who comes in Your Name,
    We bless them from the house of God.
You are our God and we shall thank You;
    You are our God and we shall exalt You. [A]

119. *ALEPH.* HAPPY ARE THEY WHOSE WAY IS BLAMELESS.
Happy are they who observe Your decrees, and seek You with all their heart;
   Who never do anything wrong, but always walk in Your ways.
You laid down Your commandments, that we should fully keep them.
   Oh, that our ways were so direct, that we might keep Your statutes.
Then we should not be put to shame when we regard them.
   When we have learned Your judgments, we will thank You with honest
      hearts.
We will keep to Your statutes; do not utterly forsake us, we pray. [A]

BETH. WE SHALL CLEANSE OUR WAYS BY KEEPING YOUR WORDS.
With our whole hearts we seek You; let us not stray from Your commandments.
   We treasure Your promises within us, that we may not sin against You.
Blessed are You; instruct us in Your ways;
   With our lips, we will recite all Your judgments.
We take greater delight in the way of Your decrees than in all manner of riches.
   We will meditate on Your ways, and only give attention to Your statutes.
We delight in You; we will not forget Your word. [A]

GIMEL. DEAL BOUNTIFULLY WITH US, THAT WE MIGHT KEEP YOUR WORD.
Open our eyes that we might see the wonders of Your law.
   We are but strangers here; do not hide Your ways from us.
Our souls are consumed with longing for Your judgments.
   You have rebuked our insolence; we are accursed when we stray from You.
Turn us from shame and rebuke, for we have kept Your decrees.
   Though the ways of the world conspire against us, we meditate on Your ways.
For Your decrees are our delight, and they are our counselors. [A]

DALETH. OUR SOULS CLING TO THE DUST; GRANT US LIFE BY YOUR WORD.
We have confessed our sins and You answered us; instruct us in Your ways.
   Make us to understand Your decrees, that we may see Your works.
Our souls melt away for sorrow; strengthen us according to Your Word.
   Take us from the ways of lying; let us find grace through Your law.
We have chosen the way of faithfulness, and set Your judgments before us.
   We hold fast to Your decrees; do not let us be put to shame.
We will run the way of Your statutes, for You have set our hearts at liberty. [A]

*Psalm 119 is divided into sections, according to the Hebrew alphabet. Only the
Hebrew word for each letter is used to mark the sections in this book.*

HE. TEACH US YOUR STATUTES; WE SHALL KEEP THEM TO THE END.
Grant us understanding, and we shall keep Your law with all our heart.
   Make us to go in the way of Your commandments, for that is our desire.
Incline our hearts to Your decrees, and not to unjust gain.
   Turn our eyes from wanting what is worthless; grant us life in Your ways.
Fulfill Your promise to Your servants, we pray, to those who fear Your Name.
   Turn away the reproach we dread, because Your judgments are good.
We long for Your commandments; in Your righteousness, preserve our life. [A]

VAU. LET YOUR LOVING KINDNESS COME TO US, AND YOUR SALVATION.
Do not take the word of truth from us, for our hope is in Your judgments.
   We shall continue to keep Your law; we shall keep it for ever and ever.
We shall walk at liberty, because we study Your commandments.
   We shall tell of Your decrees before others, and will not be ashamed.
We delight in Your commandments, which we have always loved.
   We lift our hands to them, and meditate on Your ways. [A]

ZAIN. REMEMBER YOUR WORD TO US, BECAUSE YOU GIVE US HOPE.
This is our comfort in our trouble: that Your promise gives us life.
   When we remember Your judgments of old, we take great comfort.
Your statutes have been like songs to us, wherever we are strangers.
   We remember Your Name in the night, and dwell upon Your law.
This is how it has been with us, because we have kept Your ways. [A]

CHETH. YOU ONLY ARE OUR PORTION, WE PROMISE TO KEEP YOUR WORD.
We entreat You with all our hearts, be merciful according to Your promise.
   We have considered our ways and turned our feet toward Your decrees.
We hasten, and do not tarry, to keep Your commandments.
   Though the cords of wickedness entangle us, we do not forget Your law.
At midnight, we rise to give our thanks, because of Your righteous judgments.
   We are companions of all who fear You, and of those who keep Your ways.
The earth is full of Your love; instruct us in Your Word. [A]

TETH. YOU DEAL GRACIOUSLY WITH US ACCORDING TO YOUR WORD.
Teach us discernment and knowledge, for we believe in Your ways.
   Before we were afflicted we went astray, but now we keep Your Word.
You are good and You bring forth good; instruct us in Your ways.
   Our delight is in Your law; we will keep Your commandments.
It is good for us that have been afflicted, that we might learn Your truth.
   The law of Your mouth is dearer to us than gold and silver. [A]

YOD. GIVE US UNDERSTANDING, THAT WE MAY LEARN YOUR WAYS.
Those who fear You will be glad when they see us, because we trust in You.
We know Your judgments are right, that in faithfulness You afflicted us.
Let Your loving kindness be our comfort, as You have promised.
Let Your compassion come to us that we may live; Your law is our delight.
Let the arrogant be put to shame; we will meditate on Your decrees.
Let those who fear You and know Your laws come to us.
Let our hearts be sound in Your statutes, that we may not be put to shame. [Λ]

CAPH. OUR SOULS LONG FOR YOUR SALVATION; OUR HOPE IS IN YOUR WORD.
Our eyes fail from watching for Your promise; when will You comfort us?
How much longer must we wait? When will Your judgment come?
All Your commandments are true; help us, for we are persecuted by lies.
They have almost made an end of us, but we have not forsaken You.
In Your loving kindness, revive us; that we may keep Your decrees. [A]

LAMED. YOUR WORD IS EVERLASTING; IT STANDS FIRM IN THE HEAVENS.
Your faithfulness remains from generations;
You established the earth and it abides.
By Your decrees it continues to this day, for all things are Your servants.
If we did not delight in Your law, we might have perished in our affliction.
We will never forget Your commandments, because by them You give us life.
We are Yours, for we study Your ways; O that You would save us.
Though wickedness lies in wait for us, we apply our minds to Your decrees.
We see that all things must end, but Your commandments have no bounds. [A]

MEM. O HOW WE LOVE YOUR LAW; ALL DAY LONG, IT IS IN OUR MINDS.
Your truth makes us wiser than the enemy, and it is always with us.
We have understanding as do our teachers, for Your decrees are our study.
We have wisdom as do our elders, because we keep Your commandments.
We restrain our feet from every evil path, that we may keep Your Word.
We do not shrink from Your judgments, because You have taught us.
How sweet are Your words! sweeter than the taste of honey.
Through Your truth, we gain understanding and contempt for every lying way. [A]

NUN. YOUR WORD IS A LANTERN TO OUR FEET, A LIGHT UPON OUR PATH.
We are determined to keep to Your righteous judgments.
 We are deeply troubled; preserve our life according to Your Word.
Accept the willing tribute of our lips, and teach to us Your judgments.
 Our life is always in Your hands, yet we do not forget Your law.
Your decrees are our inheritance; and they are the joy of our hearts.
 We have applied our hearts to fulfilling them, for ever and to the end. [A]

SAMECH. WE HATE THOSE WITH DIVIDED HEARTS, BUT YOUR LAW WE ADORE.
You are our refuge and our shield; our hope is in Your Word.
 Sustain us according to Your promise, let us not be disappointed.
Hold us up and we shall be safe; our delight will be in Your statutes.
 Our flesh trembles with dread of You; we are afraid of Your judgments. [A]

AIN. WE DO WHAT IS JUST AND RIGHT; DO NOT DELIVER US TO OUR ENEMY.
Be surety for Your servants' good; let not our enemy oppress us.
 Our eyes have failed from watching for Your salvation and Your promise.
Deal with Your servants according to Your kindness, and teach us Your ways.
 We are Your servants; grant us understanding of Your truth.
It is time for You to act, for Your laws have been broken.
 Truly we love Your commandments, more than gold and precious stones.
We hold Your commandments to be true; the paths of falsehood we abhor. [A]

PE. YOUR DECREES ARE WONDERFUL; WE OBEY THEM WITH ALL OUR HEARTS.
When Your Word goes forth, it gives light and understanding to the simple.
 Turn to us in mercy, as You always do to those who love Your Name.
Steady our footsteps in Your Word; let no iniquity have dominion over us.
 Rescue us from those who oppress us, and we will keep Your ways.
Let Your countenance shine upon Your servants, and teach us Your decrees.
 Our eyes shed streams of tears, because people do not keep Your law. [A]

TZADDI. YOU ARE RIGHTEOUS AND UPRIGHT ARE YOUR JUDGMENTS.
You have issued Your decrees with justice, and in perfect faithfulness.
 Your Word has been tested to the uttermost; Your servants hold it dear.
We are small and of little account, yet we do not forget Your judgments.
 Your justice is everlasting, and Your law is truth.
Trouble and distress have come upon us; yet Your decrees are our delight.
 The righteousness of them is everlasting; grant us understanding, we pray. [A]

KOPH. WE CALL OUT WITH OUR WHOLE HEART; HELP US KEEP YOUR STATUTES.
We call to You that You would save us; we will keep Your statutes.
 Early in the morning we cry to You, for in Your Word we trust.
Our eyes are open in the night watches, we meditate on Your promise.
 Hear our voice, we pray, according to Your kindness, and grant us life.
You are near to us, and all Your commandments are true.
 Long have we known that You have established Your statutes for ever. [A]

RESH. BEHOLD OUR AFFLICTION AND DELIVER US, WE DO NOT FORGET YOUR LAW.
Plead our cause and deliver us, and redeem our life as You have promised.
 Great is Your compassion; preserve us, we pray, according to Your ways.
See how we love Your commandments! In Your mercy, preserve us.
 The heart of Your Word is truth; Your law endures for evermore. [A]

SCHIN. WE ARE PERSECUTED WITHOUT CAUSE, BUT ARE IN AWE OF YOUR WORD.
We are as glad because of Your promises as those who have won great spoils.
 As for lies, we hate them, but Your law is our love.
Seven times a day do we praise You, because of Your righteous judgments.
 Great peace have they who love Your law, for them there is no stumbling block.
 We have hoped for Your salvation, and fulfilled Your commandments.
We have kept Your decrees, and loved them greatly.
 We have kept Your Word; our ways are open before You. [A]

TAU. LET OUR CRY COME BEFORE YOU; GIVE US UNDERSTANDING.
Let our supplication come before You, and deliver us, we pray.
 Our lips shall pour forth Your praise, when You teach us Your ways.
Our tongues shall sing of Your promise, all Your commandments are righteous.
 Let Your hand be ready to help us, for we have chosen Your ways.
We long for Your salvation, and Your law is our delight.
 Let us live, and we will praise You, and let Your judgments help us.
We have gone astray like sheep that are lost;
 Search for us, Your servants, for we do not forget Your statutes. [A]

120. WHEN WE WERE IN TROUBLE, WE CALLED TO YOU, AND YOU ANSWERED US.
Deliver us, we pray, from lying lips and deceitful tongues.
For too long have we lived among the enemies of peace.
We are on the side of peace, but when we speak of it, they are for war. [A]

121. WE LIFT OUR EYES TO THE HILLS, WHERE DOES OUR HELP COME FROM?
Our help comes only from You, the Maker of heaven and of earth.
You will not let our feet be moved;
You watch over us and never slumber and never sleep.
You keep watch over us; You are the shade at our right hand;
The sun will not strike us by day, nor the moon by night.
You guard us from all evil; You guard us body and soul.
You guard our going out and our coming home, now and for evermore. [A]

122. WE ARE GLAD WHEN IT IS TIME TO GO INTO THE HOUSE OF GOD.
Now we stand in Your gates, where Your children gather to praise You.
And we will pray for the peace of Your children:
May peace be within their walls, and may quiet be within their towns.
For the sake of our brothers and sisters, we pray for their prosperity.
Because of the House of the Most High, we will seek to do them good. [A]

123. WE LIFT UP OUR EYES, TO YOU, ENTHRONED UPON THE HEAVENS.
As the eyes of a servant look to the hand of their master,
So will our eyes look to You, until You show Your mercy.
Have mercy on us, we pray; have mercy on us. [A]

124. WHAT IF THE ALMIGHTY ONE HAD NOT BEEN WITH US?
If You had not been with us, when our enemy rose up against us,
We would have been swallowed up by the rage and anger of our foe.
The waters would have overwhelmed us, and covered us over.
Blessed be Your Name! for You have not given us over; we have escaped.
Our help is in Your Name; our help is in the Maker of heaven and earth. [A]

125. THOSE WHO TRUST IN YOU CANNOT BE MOVED.
They are like Your own holy mountain, which stands fast for ever.
As the hills stand about the city, so do You stand with Your children.
Show Your goodness to those who are good, to those who are true of heart.
And may peace be always among Your people. [A]

126. WHEN YOU RESTORED OUR FORTUNES, WE WERE LIKE THOSE WHO DREAM.
Then were our mouths filled with laughter, our tongues with shouts of joy.
  Then did those all around us say that You have done great things for us.
You have done great things for us, and we are glad indeed.
  Restore us again; let those who sow in tears, reap with songs of joy.
Let those who go out weeping, carrying the seed, return with joy at the harvest. [A]

127. UNLESS THE HOLY ONE BUILDS THE HOUSE, OUR LABOR IS IN VAIN.
Unless You keep watch over us, in vain do we keep our vigil.
  It is in vain that we rise early, and in vain that we go to our rest so late.
It is in vain that we eat the bread of toil, for You only give rest to Your beloved. [A]

128. HAPPY ARE THEY THAT FEAR YOU, AND FOLLOW IN YOUR WAYS.
They shall eat the fruit of their labor; happiness shall be theirs.
  Those who fear You shall be blessed.
May You bless us from Your holy heaven; may we see prosperity in our days.
  May we live to see our children's children; and may peace be upon us all. [A]

130. OUT OF THE DEPTHS HAVE WE CALLED TO YOU.
Hear our voice, we pray; consider well the voice of our supplication.
  If You consider what is done amiss, which of us could stand blameless?
There is forgiveness with You; therefore, You are to be feared.
  We wait only for You; our hope is in Your word.
Our souls wait for You, more than watchmen wait for the morning.
  For with You, there is mercy, and plenteous redemption from all our sins. [A]

131. WE ARE NOT PROUD, WE BEAR NO HAUGHTY LOOKS.
We do not occupy ourselves with great matters,
  Or with things too hard for us to understand.
We still our souls, and make them quiet.
  Like a child upon its mother's breast, our souls are quieted within us.
With all Your children, we wait upon You, from now until for evermore. [A]

Psalm 129 has been intentionally omitted.

132. WE COME INTO YOUR HOUSE; AND WITH THE FAITHFUL SING FOR JOY.
You have chosen a people, and You desire to live among them;
   You have sworn an oath that will not be broken:
A son will You sit upon the throne, if we keep Your covenant,
   And if we remember the testimonies You have given us.
Then shall our children sit upon the throne for evermore;
   And this will be Your resting place for ever, and here will You dwell.
You will bless this place with provisions and satisfy the poor with bread.
   You will clothe Your priests with salvation; and Your faithful will rejoice.
You have prepared a lamp for Your Anointed One,
   And his crown shall shine for ever. [A]

133. HOW GOOD IT IS WHEN WE LIVE TOGETHER IN UNITY.
It is like the fine oil used to bless the priests and the holy ones.
   It is like the sweet dew upon the hills in the morning.
You have ordained such unity with this Your blessing:
   Life, and life for evermore. [A]

134. MAY ALL YOUR SERVANTS PRAISE YOU.
May all who stand watch in Your holy place bless Your Name.
   May they lift up their hands in Your sanctuary and praise You.
And may Almighty God, the One Who made heaven and earth,
   Bless us from on high for ever. [A]

135. MAY ALL WHO STAND IN YOUR COURTS PRAISE YOUR NAME.
May they always praise You, for You are good.
   We sing our praises to Your Name, for it is lovely.
We know that You are great, that You are above all gods. [A]
   Whatever You please, that is what You do,
In heaven and earth, in all the seas and in all the deeps.
   You send Your rain and wind from the ends of the earth,
And signs and wonders into our midst.
   Your Name is everlasting; Your renown endures from age to age.
You give justice to Your people, and show compassion to Your servants. [A]
   The idols of the heathen are but the work of human hands;
They have mouths but cannot speak; eyes but cannot see; ears but cannot hear.
   Those who make them are like them, and so are all who trust in them.
May Your servants bless You;
   May all who fear You, bless Your Holy Name. [A]

136. WE GIVE THANKS TO YOU, YOUR MERCY ENDURES FOR EVER.
We give our thanks to the God of all gods, for You are good.
　We give thanks to the God of heaven, for Your mercy endures for ever.
You alone have done great wonders; by Your wisdom You made the heavens.
　You spread out the earth upon the waters; and You created great lights—
The sun to rule the day, and the moon and the stars to govern the night. [A]
　You are the One Who brings us out of bondage;
You are the One Who leads us through the wilderness.
　You are the One Who remembers our low estate;
You are the One Who grants us our inheritance.
　You are the One Who gives food to all creatures;
You are the One Who delivers us. [A]

137. WE WEPT WHEN WE REMEMBERED,
By the waters of Babylon, we sat down and wept.
　Those who held us captive laughed at us, and asked for a song of the holy City.
How can we sing Your song in an alien land? [A]
　If we forget You ever, let our right hand forget all its skill;
Let our tongues be still in our mouths, if we do not remember You.
　Let us be silent if we do not set Your City above our highest joy. [A]

138. WE GIVE YOU THANKS WITH OUR WHOLE HEART.
Before all gods, we will sing Your praise, and bow down before You.
　We will praise Your Name, because of Your love and faithfulness,
For You have glorified Your Name and Your Word above all things.
　When we called, You answered us; You increased our strength within us. [A]
All upon the earth will praise You, when they have heard Your Word.
　They will sing of Your ways, that great is Your glory;
That though You are high above us, You care for the lowly;
　That though we are walking in the midst of trouble, You will keep us safe.
You stretch forth Your hand against our enemies, Your right hand saves us.
　Your love endures for ever, You will make good Your purpose for us.
Do not abandon the works of Your hands, we pray; do not abandon us. [A]

139. YOU HAVE EXAMINED US AND YOU KNOW US.
You know all that there is to know about us, even our thoughts from afar.
　You know whether we work or rest, when we sit down and when we rise.
You have traced our journeys and our resting places;
　You are familiar with all our paths.
There is not a word on our lips that You do not know.
　You have kept close guard on us, and have spread Your hand over us.
Such knowledge is beyond our understanding;
　It is so high and so deep that we cannot reach it. [A]
Where can we hide from Your spirit? Where can we flee from Your presence?
　If we climb up to heaven, You are there;
If we make our bed in hell, You are beside us.
　If we take the wings of the morning, or dwell at the ends of the earth,
Even there Your hand will lead us; Your right hand will hold us fast.
　If we say that darkness will surely cover us, and the light will turn to dark;
The darkness is not dark to You;
　Night is as bright as day, they are the same to You. [A]
You are the One Who created our inmost being,
　And knit us together in our mothers' womb.
We thank You that we are so marvelously made;
　And that we were not hidden from You,
when we were being made in secret,
　And woven together in the depths of the earth. [A]
Search us, we pray, and know our hearts;
　Test us, and know our restless minds.
Look for any wickedness in us;
　And guide us in the Ancient and everlasting ways. [A]

140. YOU ARE OUR GOD; LISTEN TO OUR SUPPLICATION.
You have covered our heads, in the days of our troubles.
　Deliver us from the snares that have been hidden for us.
We know that You will maintain the cause of the poor and the needy.
　Surely the righteous will give You thanks,
And the upright will continue in Your sight. [A]

141. COME QUICKLY TO US; HEAR OUR VOICE WHEN WE CRY TO YOU.
Let our prayer rise before You as incense;
    May the lifting of our hands be as a sacrifice.
Set a watch before our mouths and a guard upon our lips;
    Let not our hearts incline to evil.
Our eyes are turned to You; in You have we taken refuge.
    Protect us from snares that are laid for us, and from the traps of wickedness. [A]

142. WE CRY ALOUD TO YOU, TO YOU ALONE WE MAKE OUR SUPPLICATION.
We pour out our complaint before You, and tell You all of our trouble.
    Whenever our spirits languish, You know all our paths.
We look to our right hand, and find no one to care for us, no place to flee.
    For You alone are our refuge, our portion in the land of the living.
Listen to our cries for help, for we have been brought very low.
    Save us from those who pursue us, for they are too strong for us.
Bring us out from our prison, that we may give thanks to Your Name.
    The righteous shall gather around us, when You deal bountifully with us. [A]

143. IN YOUR FAITHFULNESS, WE PRAY, ANSWER OUR SUPPLICATION.
Enter not into judgment of us; for in Your sight no one living can be justified.
    Our enemy has sought us and crushed us, making us to live in the dark places.
Our spirits faint within us; our hearts are utterly desolate.
    We remember the times long past, and consider the works of Your hands.
We lift our hands to You; our souls grasp for You as in a thirsty land. [A]
    Make haste to help us, we pray, for our spirits fail us.
Do not hide Your face from us, or we shall be like those who go down to the Pit.
    Let us hear of Your love in the morning, for we trust in You.
Show us the road that we must walk, for we lift our souls to You.
    Deliver us from our enemies, we pray, for we flee to You for refuge.
Teach us to do what pleases You, let Your good Spirit guide us.
    Revive us, for Your Name's sake; bring us out of our trouble.
Of Your goodness, destroy our enemies;
    Bring our foes to naught, for we are Your servants. [A]

144. BLESSED BE YOUR NAME! BLESSED BE OUR ROCK.
You are our help and our fortress; our deliverer and shield in whom we trust.
What are we that You should care for us, or even think of us?
Our lives are like a puff of wind; our days are but a passing shadow.
Stretch out Your hand from on high, rescue and deliver us.
We will sing to You a new song, for You alone have rescued us. [A]
May our children be well nurtured and beautiful;
May our homes and our labor be blessed.
May we not be overcome by war;
May there be no sorrow in our streets.
Happy are the people of whom this is so;
And happy are they whose God is the Almighty. [A]

145. WE WILL EXALT YOU, O GOD, AND BLESS YOUR NAME FOR EVER.
Great You are, and greatly to be praised; there is no end to Your greatness.
Each generation shall praise Your works to the next, declaring Your power.
We will ponder the splendor of Your majesty, and all of Your marvelous works.
We shall speak of Your mighty acts, and tell of all Your greatness.
We shall publish the remembrance of Your goodness, and of Your righteousness. [A]
You are gracious and full of compassion, slow to anger and of great kindness.
You show Your love to us all; Your compassion is seen in all Your works.
All Your works praise You; and all Your faithful servants praise You.
They speak of Your power, and make known the glory of Your kingdom.
Your kingdom is everlasting, Your dominion endures for the ages.
You uphold all those who falter, and lift up all those who are bowed down. [A]
The eyes of all are upon You, and You give them food in due season.
You open wide Your hand, and satisfy the needs of every living thing.
You are righteous in all Your ways, and loving in all Your works.
You are near to those who call upon You, and You come to help them.
You preserve all those who love You; our mouths shall speak Your praise.
Let all flesh bless Your Holy Name, for ever and for ever. [A]

146. WE SHALL PRAISE YOU AS LONG AS WE LIVE.
Happy are they whose help and hope is in the Almighty God:
For You made heaven and earth, and You keep faith for ever.
You give food to the hungry and justice to the oppressed.
You set prisoners free, open eyes that are blind,
And You lift up those who are bowed down.
You love the righteous, care for the stranger, and sustain the lonely.
And You shall reign for ever—Alleluia. [A]

147. HOW GOOD IT IS TO SING PRAISES; HOW PLEASANT TO HONOR YOUR NAME.
You heal the brokenhearted, and bind up all their wounds.
   You count the number of the stars, and call them by their names.
Great You are and mighty, there is no limit to Your wisdom.
   You lift up the lowly among us, and You have blessed our children. [A]
We sing to You with thanksgiving, and make music to Your Name.
   For you cover the heavens with clouds, and send rains upon the earth.
You make grass to grow upon the land, and plants for food for Your creatures.
   You take pleasure in those who fear You, those who await Your gracious favor.
You send out Your commandments to all the earth, and Your word runs swiftly.
   You declare Your word to Your children, and reveal Your ways to them. [A]

148. MAY GOD BE PRAISED FROM THE HIGHEST HEAVENS.
All Your angels praise You; all Your hosts praise You.
   The sun and moon praises You; the shining stars praise Your Name.
The heaven of heavens praises You; they praise the name of the Lord.
   For You commanded and all was created, standing fast for ever and ever.
From all the earth and from all the deeps comes Your praise:
   From fire and hail, and snow and fog, and winds that do Your will;
From mountains and hills, from trees and beasts and winged birds;
   From kings and peoples, men and maidens, the young and the old.
Let all You have made praise You,
   For Your Name is to be exalted above all the earth. [A]

149. WE SHALL SING TO YOU A NEW SONG AMONG THE FAITHFUL.
Let us rejoice in You, our maker; let us be joyful in You, our God.
   Let us praise You in the dark; let us sing out Your praise.
For You take pleasure in Your people, and adorn the poor with victory.
   Let all the faithful rejoice in triumph; let us be joyful in Your Name. [A]

150. WE PRAISE YOU IN YOUR HOLY TEMPLE; WE PRAISE YOU FOR YOUR POWER.
We praise You for Your mighty acts; we praise You for Your greatness.
   We praise You with the horn and the lyre and the harp.
We praise You with the timbrel and with the dance.
   We praise You with the strings and with the pipe.
We praise You with the resounding cymbals.
   Let everything that has life and breath praise the Almighty God. [A]

Notes for Saying the Gospel

The readings for this section are laid out in a series of thirty readings, one reading for each day. The reading can be used at all of the Offices, or it can be done at any one of the Offices, the one you choose to spend the most time with, or the one that allows you the most time for thoughtful reading of and meditation on the text. It breaks into two parts easily, left page and right page, and that may help you to determine how much or how often you read it each day.

The paraphrased text itself is taken from the words of Christ, from both canonical and extra-canonical sources, sort of like a red-letter edition of the Gospel without the black letters at all, and has been arranged by themes. It is very often the case that many of us are so familiar with Gospels as a whole—the stories, the characters, the settings, the events—that over time, what begins to elude us is the word that our Teacher has to offer us. This way of listening to the words of the Teacher may well help those of us who would follow him on this journey.

Whenever possible, the reading should be done aloud, slowly and meditatively. You should listen to it very carefully. Whether the words are familiar to you, or not so familiar, you are reading them, praying them actually, to discover what they are saying to you on this day, in this place, for this time in your journey.

You may want to journal against it, if journaling is part of your practice, concentrating on a sentence or two, or a phrase, that seem to speak to you on a given day. Or you may want to simply spend some time in silence, meditating on the words and the thoughts to which the words and phrases give rise.

In most communities, the reading of the Gospel is followed by either silence or a Canticle or both.

THE GOSPEL

The Word became flesh and dwelt among us,
    full of grace and full of truth.
      —FROM THE GOSPEL ACCORDING TO JOHN

To You all hearts are open and all desires known,
    and from You no secrets are hid:
Cleanse the thoughts of our hearts by the inspiration of Your Spirit,
    that as Your Word is proclaimed,
we may hear with joy, what You say to us today. *Amen.*
      —A COLLECT BEFORE WORSHIP

The Lord waits for us daily
    to translate into action, as we should, his holy teachings.
      —FROM THE RULE OF ST. BENEDICT

WHAT HAVE YOU COME TO THE DESERT TO SEE?
Have you come to see a reed that shakes in the wind?
    Or someone dressed in fine clothes like royalty?
Or a prophet, perhaps?

    You remind me of the children
that shout to each other in the marketplace:
    "We play for you, but you do not dance," they sing;
"We weep for you, but you do not mourn," they cry.
    Will you not believe unless you see signs and wonders?

THIS IS THE NEWS OF THE KINGDOM —
The time has come,
    and the kingdom is upon you.
Repent, then,
    and believe the good news.

    You say to me: "Are you the One?"
And I say to you that I am the hope of the hopeless,
    the helper of those who have no helper,
the treasure of those in need, the physician of the sick,
    and the resurrection of the dead.
And I shall give you what no eye has ever seen,
    what no ear has ever heard,
what no hand has ever touched,
    what has never before arisen in a human heart.

    You say to me:
"Where are you going?"
and "Can we come with you?"
    Come and see, I say to you, come and see.

To welcome me is to welcome the One Who sent me.
To listen to you or to listen to me,
  is not to hear you or me,
it is to hear the One Who sent us.

  Whoever rejects you, rejects me.
Whoever listens to you, listens to me.
  And whoever welcomes me,
welcomes the One Who made us all.

THIS IS THE WAY OF THE KINGDOM—
It is like a person
    who has a treasure buried in their own field,
but they do not even know it.
    They die and leave the field to their children,
who do not know the treasure is there either,
    and so they sell the field.
The new owner begins to work in the field
    and discovers the treasure that is hidden there.
In his joy and excitement,
    he begins to share the treasure with anyone he sees.

    You say to me: "Show us the Father,"
If you have ears, then hear:
    To welcome me is to welcome the One who sent me.

SEE WHAT IS MOVING AMONG YOU.
Are you not wise enough to look at the sky
    and tell whether or not it is going to rain?
Or to look at the trees and know
    that when they begin to bloom the summer is near?
Can you not look around you now
    and see what is moving among you?
Can you not see what is moving within you?

It is not fitting that you are ignorant of your self.
Examine your self that you may understand who you are,
    and in what way you exist, and how you will come to be.
Those who have known themselves
    have already begun to learn about the depth of All.

THIS IS THE WAY OF THE KINGDOM—
A farmer sows seed upon the land.
    Night and day,
while he is asleep and while he is awake,
    the seed is growing.
He does not know how it grows,
    it grows of its own accord.
First the land produces the shoot
    and then the ear, and then the grain.
When the crop is ready, he starts to reap
    because the harvest is come.

    The time is ripe for the harvest now,
and the sickle is ready.
    Do not keep begging for the harvest,
it is large enough.
    What is needed are more workers.
Beg for more workers
    that the harvest might not be lost.

    If you have eyes, then see, I tell you:
Look around you now,
    and see what is moving among you.

YOU MUST BE BORN AGAIN.
You too have come from the kingdom
   and it is to the kingdom that you will return.
But it will not happen
   if you merely sit and watch for it.

   The kingdom is made up of those who are as children.
To enter the kingdom,
   you must become a child.
Blessed are the ones whose hearts are pure, I tell you;
   they are the ones who will see the face of God.

   Flesh can only give birth to flesh,
it is spirit that gives birth to spirit, and spirit alone.
   The words that I give you are both spirit and life.

THIS IS THE WAY OF THE KINGDOM—
Would you patch an old coat with new cloth?
    The patch will tear away
and leave a bigger hole than before.
    Or would you put new wine into old wineskins?
If you do, then the skins will burst
    and the wine will be lost.
New wine must go into new wineskins.

    You say to me:
"What must we do to have life that does not end?
    How can we find the life of the kingdom?"
Truly, I say to you,
    you must be born again.

THE KINGDOM IS ALREADY HERE.
The kingdom does not come at some future time,
    so you cannot say when it will come.
It does not come at some future place,
    so you cannot say where it will come.

    What you are looking for has already come
and you do not know it.
    It is spread out over the whole earth,
and no one sees it.
    It is within you,
and it is without you,
    and it is all around you.

    Many prophets desired to see what you can see
and to hear what you can hear.
    But they could not see it
and they could not hear it.
    Blessed be the One Who has made us,
and Who has hidden these things from the learned
    and reveals them to the simple.
And blessed are the ones who have not seen me
    and yet have still believed.

THIS IS THE WAY OF THE KINGDOM—
It is like a woman on her way home, carrying a jar of grain.
    She did not notice that the jar was cracked
and that the grain trailed behind her as she walked.
    By the time she got home, the jar was empty.

    You say to me:
"When will the kingdom come?"
    and "Where will we find it?"
The kingdom is here among you now, I say to you.
    The kingdom is already here.

KEEP SEEKING UNTIL YOU FIND.
No one who follows me
    will be left to wander in the dark.
They shall be given the light of life.

    So pay attention to what is in front of you
and what is hidden will be revealed.
    For nothing that is hidden will not be made clear,
and nothing that is secret
    will remain secret for ever.

    Let those who would seek
continue seeking until they find.
    When they find, they will become troubled.
When they become troubled, they will be astonished.
    When they are astonished, then all will be theirs.

    Blessed are the ones
who have worked hard to find life
    and have found it.

THIS IS THE WAY OF THE KINGDOM—
There was a woman who,
    no matter what anyone else said of her,
continually confronted a judge
    for vindication in her case.
Time and time again,
    she knocked at his door and pleaded for justice.
The judge cared neither for justice or for the woman,
    but finally he gave in.
Because even though what was right or wrong did not bother him,
    she did.

    Ask and you will receive, I tell you;
seek and you will find;
    knock and the door will open wide before you.
The door will always be open to one who knocks.

    If you have ears, then hear what I say:
Hasten to be saved without being urged;
    be eager for it of your own accord.
And keep seeking until you find.

WHOEVER IS LEAST AMONG YOU WILL BE THE GREATEST.
Who do you think is greater:
    The one who is seated at the head of the table
or the one who serves?
    You have been taught that it is the one
who is seated at the head of the table,
    but I am here among you as one who serves.

    For some, rulers are rulers
and commanders are commanders.
    But for us, rulers are slaves
and commanders are servants.
    Those who would lead
must become the ones who serve.

    Whoever would become great among you
must become the least among you.
    Whoever exalts themselves will be humbled,
whoever humbles themselves will be exalted.

    Blessed are the humble and the meek;
the whole world will be theirs.

THIS IS THE WAY OF THE KINGDOM—
A man set out at daybreak
     to go into the market to hire laborers to work in the vineyard.
He arranged a fair wage with them
     and sent them off to work.
At noon he came again to the marketplace
     and hired more workers,
promising them a fair wage as well.
     The same thing happened again in mid-afternoon
and again as the sun was going down.
     When the day's work was done,
he called them together to pay them,
     paying all of the workers the same wage.
Those who had worked the longest were angry
     because they expected to be paid more.
The master said to them,
     "What does it matter to you if I am generous?"

     You ask me: "Who will be the greatest in the kingdom?"
You have heard it said that no one in history
     is greater than John the Baptizer, and it is true.
But in the future, anyone in the kingdom
     will be greater than he.

     The first will be last,
and the last will be first, I tell you.
     And whoever is least among you will be the greatest.

THIS LIGHT WILL SHINE IN THE DARKNESS.
You do not put a lamp under a basket
   but up on a stand.
You do not put it down in the cellar
   but out in the doorway so that it can be seen.
When you build a fire
   you want it to burn.

   What you have heard only in whispers,
you must shout aloud from rooftops.
   What has only been talked about in darkness,
you must speak abroad in daylight.

THIS IS THE WAY OF THE KINGDOM—
A man sent his servant
   to invite his friends to dinner on short notice.
At each house, the servant said:
   "My master wants you to come to dinner this evening."
The first friend replied:
   "Please give your master my regrets.
I must see some people who owe me money."
   The second friend replied:
"Please excuse me, I am busy this evening.
   I am planning a party for someone else."
The third friend said:
   "I cannot be there, I must collect the rent
from a new property that I own."
   When the servant returned and told his master
that all of his friends had refused the invitation,
   the master was angry.
"Then go out into the streets," he said,
   "and invite anyone that you happen to see."

   If you have ears, then hear this:
If my friends are silent,
   then the stones themselves will begin to shout.
For this light will shine in the darkness.

I CAME TO CALL SINNERS TO REPENTANCE.
To all of you whose load is heavy,
    whose burden is hard to bear,
I say, "Come with me,
    and I will give you rest."
The load that I offer you is light
    and it is good to bear.
Learn from me
    and your souls will find relief.

    In the end, it is only the destitute
who will be found innocent.
    Only the wretched will be guiltless,
only the despised will be blameless.
    Those who are well,
and those who claim they are well,
    have no need of a physician.
Blessed are the poor in spirit;
    they will be given the kingdom.

THIS IS THE WAY OF THE KINGDOM—
It is as though a fisherman throws a net into the sea
    and it is full of all kinds of fish.
When the net is filled
    he brings it ashore,
and the good ones are collected into baskets.

    You ask me:
"Why do you spend your time with
    the publicans and the sinners?"
I say to you truly,
    I came to save that which is lost.
I came to call sinners to repentance.

CONSIDER WHETHER THERE IS DARKNESS OR LIGHT IN YOU.
Your own eye is the lamp of your body.
    If it is healthy, then you are full of light.
But if it is not, then you are filled with darkness.
    It is in the light
that light truly exists.

    If you are whole,
then you will be filled with light.
    But if your heart is divided,
then you will be filled with darkness.
    If the only light that you have within is darkness,
then your darkness is doubly dark.
    And those who travel in darkness
cannot see where they are going.

    You are to be the light of the world
and to set an example for all the world to see
    so that others might see the good that you do
and give glory to the One Who made us.

THIS IS THE WAY OF THE KINGDOM—
The Light has come into the world
    but even yet some prefer the darkness.
Those who are honest will come to the light,
    so that everyone can see that God is in all that they do.

    Within a person of light, there is light.
And it will shine on the whole world.
    If there is no light that shines from within,
then there is only darkness.

    If you have eyes, then see, I tell you:
And consider whether there is darkness or light
    in you.

THE FIRST COMMANDMENT IS TO LOVE GOD.
Do not think that I have come
  to abolish the Law of God,
I have come to fulfill it.
  And I tell you truly
that all of the Law and all of the prophets
  are fulfilled in two commandments.

  The first one is this:
Love God with all of your heart,
  and with all of your soul,
and with all of your mind,
  and with all of your strength.
Pay homage to the One Who made us
  and to Him alone.

THIS IS THE WAY OF THE KINGDOM—
There was a merchant
   who was searching for fine pearls.
When she finds the one that is the most precious,
   she sells everything that she has
in order to buy the one
   that is of the most value.

   God is spirit
and those who would worship God
   must do so in spirit and in truth.

   If you have ears to hear, then hear:
The first commandment is to love God.

THE SECOND COMMANDMENT IS TO LOVE YOUR NEIGHBOR.
Love your neighbor like you love your own soul.
    Take care of your neighbor
the way you would care for your own eyes.
    Whoever gives even as much as a cup of cold water
to the least of their neighbors
    can expect to receive the reward of the faithful.

    Anyone who nurses anger against a brother or sister
must be brought to account for it.
    Those who abuse others must answer for that as well.

THIS IS THE WAY OF THE KINGDOM—
There was a man traveling a road
   and he was attacked by bandits.
He was beaten and robbed and left by the road to die.
   Not long after, a priest passed by,
and when he saw the man beside the road,
   he crossed over to the other side and went on his way.
An official of the nearby town came by.
   But he too passed by on the other side.
A third man came along, a foreigner,
   and when he saw the man, he stopped to help.
He cleaned and bound the man's wounds
   and put him up on his horse
to take him to a nearby inn.
   He gave some money to the innkeeper
and left instructions to do whatever needed to be done,
   promising to pay the balance on his return.
Who was a neighbor to that man, I ask you?
   And who is your neighbor?

   I tell you truly
that all of the Law and all of the prophets
   are fulfilled in two commandments:
Love God
   and love your neighbor.

LOVE ONE ANOTHER AS I HAVE LOVED YOU.
Do not be proud of yourselves simply because
   you have seen the Light that illumines all,
but be to each other as I am to you.
   Be all goodness as the One Who made us in all goodness.

   If you seek only to protect your own life,
then you will lose it.
   But if you would lose your own life,
then you will save it indeed.
   There is no greater love
than to lay down your life for another.
   And if there is such love in you,
then others will know that you are my follower.

THIS IS THE WAY OF THE KINGDOM—
If you hold a kernel of wheat in your hand,
    then there will be no harvest.
Unless it falls to the ground and dies,
    it remains a single seed.
But if the kernel dies,
    then there will be a rich harvest.
Is this not the way that it is?

    This is what I say to you that you must do:
Love one another as I have loved you.

YOU CANNOT SERVE TWO MASTERS.
One cannot ride two horses at the same time,
　　or bend two bows at the same time.
And one cannot be the servant of two masters
　　at the same time.
You will love the one and hate the other,
　　or you will hate the one and love the other.

A kingdom divided is a kingdom defeated,
　　A household divided is a household destroyed,
A heart divided is a heart in darkness.

THIS IS THE WAY OF THE KINGDOM—
The kingdom can divide the household even:
　　three against two and two against three,
mother against daughter
　　and father against son.
To accept the kingdom
　　is to reject your mother and father
and to reject your brother and sister.
　　No one who cares more for their family
than they do for me
　　is worthy of the kingdom.
But those who would give up their family
　　for the sake of the kingdom
will not be denied the reward of the faithful.
　　If you have ears, then hear:
You cannot serve two masters at the same time.

YOUR HEART IS WHERE YOUR TREASURE IS.
Would it profit you to gain the whole world
   and lose yourself in the bargain?

   Men and women do not live by bread alone.
And life does not consist of the abundance of possessions.
   Work for the things that will last,
the things of the life that does not end,
   rather than for the things that perish.

   Be on your guard against all kinds of greed.
Seek treasure that is unfailing,
   treasure that will endure,
treasure that cannot be lost—
   not to moths, not to thieves,
not to death itself.

THIS IS THE WAY OF THE KINGDOM—
A rich man was making long-term plans
    and said to himself:
"I will plant and sow and reap and gather
    until my storerooms and my barns are full.
Then I will have all that I will ever need."
    That night he died in his sleep.

    I tell you truly
that it is easier for a camel to go through the eye of a needle
    than it is for a person with riches to enter the kingdom.

    If you have ears, then hear what I tell you:
Your heart is where your treasure is.

MUCH IS REQUIRED OF THOSE TO WHOM MUCH IS GIVEN.
Those who are dishonest in a little
   will prove to be dishonest in much.
And if one cannot be trusted
   with what belongs to someone else,
then who will give them something of their own?
   If one cannot even be trusted with
the wealth of this world,
    how can they be trusted with the things that are real?

THIS IS THE WAY OF THE KINGDOM—
There was a master who was going away
    to a far country for a time.
He called for his three stewards
    and gave them money to be used while he was away.
To the first, he gave three measures,
    to the second he gave two,
and to the third he gave one.
    Upon his return, he called the stewards
for an accounting of their activities.
    The first steward reported he had doubled the money.
The master was pleased with him
    and doubled his authority.
The second steward reported that he too
    had doubled the money.
And the master doubled his authority as well.
    The third steward reported that he had buried the money
so as not to lose it,
    because he was afraid.
The master was angry with him
    and took away everything the steward had.

    Those who are found faithful in a little
will be found faithful in much.
    But when they have carried out their orders,
they should say to themselves
    that they have only fulfilled their duty,
for I tell you truly:
    Much is required of those to whom much is given.

THE MEASURE YOU GIVE IS THE MEASURE YOU WILL RECEIVE.
You must do for others
   as you would have them do for you.
What you do not want done to you,
   then do that to no one else.

Be just in your judgments,
and do not judge superficially.
   If you do not judge others,
then you will not be judged.
   If you do not condemn others,
you will not be condemned.
   By your own words will you be justified,
and by your own words will you be condemned.

Use what you have been given to win friends,
so that when what you have been given is gone,
   you will be received into the life of the kingdom.

THIS IS THE WAY OF THE KINGDOM—
There was a man
   who was about to fire his steward for fraud.
He told the steward to prepare the accounts.
   The steward said to himself:
"I am too old and weak to dig,
   and I am too proud to beg.
Where will my friends come from in the future?"
   So he called his master's debtors together,
and said to them:
   "I am leaving here and the accounts must be settled.
If you owe my master a hundred measures of oil,
   then pay fifty, and the debt will be cleared.
If you owe a hundred measures of grain,
   then pay eighty, and the debt will be forgiven."
The debtors were well pleased with the steward,
   and even the master had to smile
at the steward's wisdom.

   If you have ears then hear what I tell you:
The measure that you give
   is the measure that you will receive.

BEAR FRUIT THAT IS WORTHY OF YOUR REPENTANCE.
It is by the fruit of the tree
    that you know a good tree from a bad tree.
A good tree does not produce bad fruit
    and a bad tree does not produce good fruit.
Grapes cannot be picked from briars,
    or figs from thistles.

    Good people produce good out of
the abundance of their hearts,
    just as bad people produce bad
out of the abundance of their hearts.
    The mouth always speaks
out of the abundance of the heart,
    and how can anyone's words be good,
if their heart is evil?

THIS IS THE WAY OF THE KINGDOM—
A farmer planted wheat in his fields.
    In the night, an enemy came
and planted weeds among the wheat.
    When the wheat began to grow,
the workers saw the weeds and went to tell their master.
    They offered to go through the fields
and pull up the weeds,
        but the master said not to bother.
He knew that when the harvest came
    the workers would know the good from the bad.
Then the bad could be thrown away
    and the good could be gathered into the barn.

    I am appointing you to bear good fruit,
fruit that will last.
    Those who dwell in me
as I dwell in them
    will bear much good fruit.

    The glory of the One Who made us is this:
That you bear fruit that is worthy
    of your repentance.

THE ONE WHO MADE US IS MERCIFUL, WE MUST BE MERCIFUL, TOO.
Blessed are the ones who show mercy,
    mercy will be shown to them.

    You have heard this saying:
"I desire mercy, not sacrifice."
    And if you knew what this saying means,
then you would not condemn anyone.

    I did not come to destroy lives
but to save them.
    I have been sent to heal the brokenhearted,
to proclaim liberty to captives and
    recovery of sight to the blind;
to set at liberty those who are oppressed and
    to proclaim the coming of the kingdom.

THIS IS THE WAY OF THE KINGDOM—
There was a man who had two sons.
    The younger one went to his father
and asked for his inheritance.
    His father gave it to him and the son left home
to seek his fortune in a far country.
    But he wasted all of the money on reckless living
and when a famine fell upon the land,
    he found himself tending swine just to stay alive.
Finally he said to himself,
    "Even the swine have more than I do.
I am going home and beg for my father's mercy."
    When he was still a long way off,
his father saw him and ran to meet him.
    "Father, forgive me," said the son.
"I am no longer worthy even to be called your son.
    Let me live here as one of your servants."
But the father threw his arms around his son and kissed him,
    and called to his servants for clean clothes and shoes
and gave his own ring for his son's finger.
    Rejoicing, he told the servants to prepare a feast
and to invite all of his friends.
    "My son who was lost has come home," he cried.
The elder son, returning from the fields,
    heard the noise from the feast as he drew near the house.
When he learned what had happened
    he was so angry that he would not go in.
His father came out to him and the elder son said angrily,
    "I am faithful to you and always have been,
while my brother has done nothing but bring you disgrace.
    Yet you have never thrown a feast for me."
"My dear son," the father said, "You are always with me,
    and everything I have is yours and always will be.
Come into the house, this is the time for rejoicing.
    Your brother who was dead has come back to life."

    Truly I say to you:
The One Who made us is merciful,
    we must be merciful, too.

YOU MUST FORGIVE OTHERS IF YOU WANT TO BE FORGIVEN.
Whenever you stand with your gift before the altar
    and recall a grievance that stands between
you and your neighbor,
    you must leave your gift at the altar,
and first go and offer peace to your neighbor.
    Then you may offer your gift to God.

    Whenever two make peace with each other,
then the two become one,
    and they will be able to move mountains together.
Blessed are the ones who make peace,
    they will be called God's own children.

    If you forgive others the wrongs they have done,
then God will forgive you.
    But unless you forgive others from the heart,
then you will not be forgiven.
    Because where little has been forgiven,
then little love has been shown.

THIS IS THE WAY OF THE KINGDOM—
There was a master who decided
    to settle his accounts with his debtors.
A man was brought to him,
    a man who owed the master a huge sum of money.
When he told the master that he could not pay the debt,
    the master ordered him to be sold into slavery,
along with his wife and his children,
    so that the master could get some of his money back.
The debtor fell on his face and begged for mercy,
    telling the master that he would repay every cent
if the master would but show some mercy.
    The master was compassionate
and let him go and canceled the debt.
    As soon as the debtor had been freed
he ran into a slave who owed him a small amount of money,
    and he grabbed the slave around the neck
and demanded to be paid.
    The slave begged for mercy
but the man would not hear of it
    and had him thrown into prison.
When the master heard the story,
    he sent for the debtor again.
"Would it not be only fair to show mercy
    the way that mercy was shown to you?"
And the master was so angry
    that he had the man returned to the authorities
until the entire large debt was repaid.

    You have been taught that you should
forgive one another seven times.
    But I say to you truly,
forgive one another not seven times,
    but seventy times seven.
Forgive the debt that is owed you by another
    as God forgives the debt that you owe.
You must forgive others
    if you want to be forgiven.

LOVE YOUR ENEMIES.
You have been taught
   that you should love your friends
and hate your enemies,
   that you should take an eye for an eye
and a tooth for a tooth.

God's sun rises every day on the evil and the good.
The rain falls every day on the just and the unjust.

   It is no credit to you
if you love only those who love you,
   or if you embrace only your brothers and sisters.
Anyone, everyone does that.
   How is that more than others do?

THIS IS THE WAY OF THE KINGDOM—
If someone strikes your left cheek,
      then offer your right cheek as well.
If someone takes your coat,
      then offer them your shirt.
If someone forces you to go one mile for them,
      then offer to go another.

      You must do good to those who hate you,
bless those who curse you and pray for those who abuse you.
      Love your enemies.

GIVE TO EVERYONE WHO BEGS OF YOU.
Every fox has a den
    and every bird has a nest.
It is only the sons and daughters of humankind
    that have nowhere to lay their heads.

    The rich get more and more of everything
and the poor lose even what little they have.
    And the poor will always be with you.
Blessed are the poor;
    they will be shown the kingdom of God.

    Do not give only to those
who will repay you with interest.
    Rather give to those who will not repay you at all.
Give alms from what you have
    and everything will be made clean for you.
When you give a feast,
    do not invite only your friends,
but invite the poor, those who cannot repay you.
    There is where you will find joy.

THIS IS THE WAY OF THE KINGDOM—
At midnight a friend comes to your door
        and calls from outside:
"A traveler has arrived at my house in the night
        and I have no food for him to eat
and no place for him to sleep.
        Can you help me?"
But you call back from behind the door:
        "The hour is late and we are all in bed.
Leave us alone."

Can you not judge for yourselves what is right?
If you have ears, then hear what I say:
        Give to everyone who begs of you.

PAY ATTENTION TO HOW YOU LISTEN TO ME.
For this I was born,
    and for this I have come:
to bear witness to the Truth.
    This is the work that God requires:
Believe in the one that God sent.
    I tell you truly that heaven and earth will pass away
but the things that I say will not.
    Whoever discovers the meaning of them
will not know the taste of death.

Anyone who listens to what I say
and puts their trust in the One Who sent me
    has hold of the life of the kingdom,
the life that does not end.
    They will not come up for judgment
but have already passed from death into life.

Live in the things that I have come to show you
and you will indeed be my friends.
    You will know the truth
and the truth will set you free.
    Blessed are the ones who hear the Word and truly keep it.

THIS IS THE WAY OF THE KINGDOM—
Two men went to build a house.
   The first built his house
with the foundation upon a rock,
   so that when the storms came
the house stood fast.
   The second man built his house upon the sand
with no foundation at all.
   When the storms came
the house was washed away.
   That is what happens to those
who come to me and hear my words
   but do not obey them.

   Do not call me Master
and then not do what I say.
   Do what I tell you, without delay,
without reserve.
   Serve in the straight and narrow and direct way.
Pay attention, I say to you.
   Pay attention to how you listen to me.

DO NOT MAKE A SHOW OF YOUR RELIGION.
It is true that if you do not fast from the world,
    you will not find the kingdom.
If you do not observe the sabbath,
    then you will not find God.

    But when you fast, do not act like the hypocrites
who make a big show of being gloomy.
    Wash your face and comb your hair,
so that no one will know that you are fasting.

    Do not do your acts of charity to win admiration.
Do not even let your left hand know
    what your right hand is doing.

    Do not tithe your goods and money
only to neglect justice and the love of God.
    You ought to do those things without
neglecting justice and the love of God.

    Do not say your prayers
so that everyone can see and hear you.
    Rather, go into your closet and pray in secret.
The One Who sees you in secret,
    will hear you in secret as well.
And do not babble on and on,
    imagining that the more you say,
the more likely it is that your prayer will be heard.
    The One Who made us knows what you need
before you even ask.

THIS IS THE WAY OF THE KINGDOM—
Two men went to the temple to pray.
    One of them, a teacher of the Law, prayed:
"I thank you, God, that I am not a sinner
    because I keep your Law.
I am grateful that I am not a sinner like others,
    especially this man here beside me."
The other man was a tax collector.
    He would not even lift his eyes to heaven.
"Lord, have mercy on me, a sinner," he prayed.
    Which of the two went home justified, do you think?

    Do not be so busy
checking the speck in your brother's eye
    that you fail to notice the stick that is in your own.
And do not make a show of your religion.

THE BLIND CANNOT LEAD THE BLIND.
Do not become like those
    who love to be greeted in the marketplace by everyone,
and be seated first in the congregation
    and be served before everyone else at the feast.
They are the ones who load everyone else with burdens
    and do not lift a finger to help.

    They are the ones who take away the keys of knowledge,
but do not enter the door themselves.
    Then they hinder those who seek to open the door.
Occasions for sin are bound to come for us all.
    But it would be better for you to be thrown into the sea
than for you to be one who causes another to stumble.

    Do not follow their practice,
for they say one thing and then do another.
    They pay lip service to God but their heart is far away
and their worship is in vain.
    It is not what goes into the mouth
that makes for purity or impurity.
    Purity or impurity is defined by what comes out.

    They neglect the commandments of God,
forsaking them for the traditions of men.
    It makes God's word null and void.
They overlook the weightier demands of the Law—
    justice and mercy and peace.
They strain at a gnat and then swallow a camel.

THIS IS THE WAY OF THE KINGDOM—
Can a blind man lead another blind man?
    Will they not both fall into the ditch?

    If they knew they were blind, I tell you,
then they would not be guilty.
    But because they think that they can see,
their guilt remains.
    Unless you show yourselves to be far better than they,
you cannot enter the kingdom.
    The blind cannot lead the blind.

You cannot turn back.
The road that leads to life is a narrow road
    and there are few who find it.
The other road is wide and many travel upon it.
    Take the narrow gate, I tell you.

    The road is hard.
If you would serve me,
    then you must follow me.
For where I am is where my friends must be also.
    They are the ones who love me.

    To follow me, you must deny yourself
and take up your cross every day.
    Pupils do not rank above their teachers,
or servants above their masters.
    A pupil must be content to share in the teacher's lot,
and a servant in their master's.

    Blessed are the ones who are persecuted in their hearts,
for the sake of the kingdom,
    they are the ones who will truly know God.

THIS IS THE WAY OF THE KINGDOM—
You say to me that my family has come
    and is outside looking for me.
But I say to you that my family is here with me,
    looking for God.
These are the ones who are my brothers and sisters.

    You say to me: "I will follow You,
but first let me go and bury my father," or
    "First, let me go and say goodbye to my family."
I say to you: Let the dead bury the dead.
    If you have ears, then hear:
Once you have grasped a plow,
    once you have reached for the kingdom,
you cannot turn back.

I WILL ALWAYS BE WITH YOU.
In the world you will find trouble,
   because you are a stranger to the world as I am.
But do not be afraid of the things that you will suffer.
   Have courage, for the Word has been given to you.
Though you will be plunged into grief,
   your grief will be turned to joy.
Blessed are the ones who weep and mourn;
   they will be comforted and filled with laughter.

   You did not choose me, I chose you.
So have confidence and be of good courage.
   Know that your faith has saved you
and that your faith will save you.
   That if you bring forth what is already in you,
it is enough to save your very soul.

   You are no longer my disciples,
you are my friends.
   And I have told you all of these things
so that you might have my joy in you,
   and so that your joy might be complete.
And so that you might have peace.
   My peace is my gift to you.

THIS IS THE WAY OF THE KINGDOM—
If you were to ask your mother for bread,
    would you get a stone?
If you were to ask your father for a fish,
    would you get a snake?
If your earthly parents know how to care for you,
    then how much more can you trust
your heavenly Father?
    Whatever you ask for my sake,
will be given you for my sake.

    Trust always in God, I say to you,
and trust also in me.
    Split open the wood and I am there.
Lift the stone and I am among you.
    Wherever two or three of you gather,
I will be there with you
    and our hearts will rejoice,
and no one will take that joy from you.

    If you have ears to hear, then hear:
I will always be with you.

DO NOT WORRY ABOUT TOMORROW.
Why should you worry about your life
    all day and all night?
About what you will eat and what you will wear?
    With all of your worrying,
could you add even a single hour to your life?
    If you cannot do a simple thing like that,
why should you worry about all the rest, then?

    You are worried and distracted by many things,
but there is only one thing that matters:
    Be sure you find the kingdom.
Be sure of God's rule over you
    and the other things that you need
will be added to you as well.
    When you can leave behind
those things that will not be able to follow you,
    then you will be able to put yourselves at rest.

This is the way of the kingdom—
Look at the flowers in the fields,
 they do not spin or weave.
Yet Solomon in all of his glory
 shone less brightly than they.
Look at the sparrows.
 They do not plant or sow,
they do not reap or save.
 Yet every day God gives them food to eat.
God counts the sparrows, to be sure,
 but God counts even the hairs on your head.
Surely you must know that you are worth more than sparrows.

 Take care lest your hearts be weighed down
with the cares of this life.
 This day will have enough trouble
and tomorrow will bring trouble of its own.
 Seek the kingdom first,
everything else will come in due season.

 If you have ears, then hear what I say:
Do not worry about tomorrow.

Do not be afraid.
It is the Father's good pleasure
    to give you the kingdom.
And I am well pleased to be with you,
    and to be joint heirs with you.

It is true that whoever is not with us
is against us.
    Whoever does not gather with me, scatters.
But do not be afraid for your body,
    be afraid of losing your soul.
Watch, therefore, and pray always.

To fight against the house of the powerful,
one must be ready to defeat the arms that protect it.
    So be on your guard,
for the trouble that you expect will surely come.
    Build your city upon a hill
and fortify it well.
    Then it cannot be hidden and it cannot be taken.

Keep your lamps lit
like those who wait for the master to return
    from the wedding feast,
the ones who are waiting to open the door
    as soon as he returns with his bride.

THIS IS THE WAY OF THE KINGDOM—
It is like a builder
   who is planning to build a tower.
First, he counts the cost.
   It is like a ruler planning a battle.
First, he counts the size of both armies.
   It is like an assassin practicing against the side of a house.
When he is ready,
   then he goes in search of the enemy.
And it is like a shepherd who leaves the flock,
   to go in search of the one that has gone astray.

   Set your troubled hearts at rest
and let go of your fears.
   You are my friends
and I will send you power from above,
   the gift that has been promised,
the spirit of truth that will guide you into all Truth.

   Be watchful, then,
and strengthen the things that remain.
   Remember what you have seen and heard,
and hold fast.

   Do not be afraid, I say to you,
Do not be afraid, be ready.

GO AND LET YOUR LIGHT SHINE.
The kingdom must be proclaimed.
    It is what I was sent to do.
While there is light,
    we must carry on the work of the One Who sent us.

As I have been sent, now I am sending you.
Go on your way while there is light,
    so that the darkness does not overtake you.
Trust the light while it is with you,
    that you may become its children.

You are being sent as lambs to the wolves.
Be as shrewd as snakes, and as innocent as doves.
    Remember that prophets are without honor in their own country,
and that doctors are often ignored in their own homes.
    Remember that we always live in the shadow of the cross.

Be as passersby, unseen and unnoticed.
Take no protection for the journey,
    no shoes for your feet, no pack for your back.
Take the same clothes for winter and summer,
    for day and for night.
Travel in peace, without useless chatter.
    Let your Yes mean yes and your No mean no.
Do not tell lies
    and do not do what you hate,
for all things are plain in the sight of heaven.

Give Caesar what belongs to Caesar,
give God what belongs to God.
    Remember that the Father's house is a house of prayer,
And do not make it into a den of thieves.

THIS IS THE WAY OF THE KINGDOM—
The sower goes out to spread the seed,
    and some of the seed falls upon the path
where the birds can see it and it is gone.
    Some of the seed falls on rocky soil
and it withers for lack of water.
    Some of the seed falls in among the weeds
and the weeds choke it out.
    But some of the seed falls on good soil
and it grows to yield a rich harvest.

    You are the beloved
and you will be the cause of life in many;
    rejoice and be glad of it.

    Enter any place that welcomes you,
tend to their sick, share their meal,
    and there is where you will find the kingdom.
When they ask you where you have come from,
    say to them that you have come from the Light,
and that you are its children.

    Tell them the things that you have seen and heard:
That the blind can see and the lame can walk;
    that the deaf can hear and the lepers are cleansed;
that the poor have heard the good news;
    that the dead have come back to life.

    Now go.
Go in peace.
    Go and let your Light shine.

APPENDIX

LITURGICAL CALENDAR

TEMPORALE : SEASONS

⊗

ADVENT
Advent Sunday
Winter Ember Days

CHRISTMASTIDE
Christmas Eve
Nativity
Holy Family

EPIPHANY
Epiphany
Baptism of Our Lord

LENT
Ash Wednesday
Spring Ember Days

EASTERTIDE
Palm Sunday
Holy Week
Maundy Thursday
Good Friday
Easter Eve
Easter Day
Easter Week
Rogation Days

ASCENSIONTIDE
Ascension of Our Lord

PENTECOST
Whitsunday
Summer Ember Days

Trinity Sunday
Corpus Christi
Divine Compassion

ORDINARY TIME
Autumn Ember Days

KINGDOMTIDE
All Saints' Day
All Souls' Day

SANCTORALE : HOLY DAYS

⊗

JANUARY
1 Holy Name
2 Macarius
3 Genevieve
4 Elizabeth Seton
5 Twelfth Night
6 Epiphany
7 Lucian
8 Abo
9 Adrian
10 William Laud
11 Theodosius
12 Aelred
13 Hilary
14 George Fox
15 Ita
16 Berard &
   Companions
17 Antony

18 Peter's Confession
19 Wulfstan
20 Fabian
21 Agnes
22 Vincent
23 John the Almsgiver
24 Francis de Sales
25 Paul's Conversion
26 Timothy & Titus
27 John Chrysostom
28 Thomas Aquinas
29 Gildas
30 Charles Stuart
31 John Bosco

FEBRUARY
1 Vigil for Candlemas
2 Candlemas

3 Anskar
4 Cornelius
5 Agatha
6 Dorothy
7 Saints and Martyrs of
   Europe
8 John of Matha
9 Apollonia
10 Scholastica
11 Benedict
12 Marina
13 Catherine dei
   Ricci
14 Cyril &
   Methodius
15 Sigfrid
16 Elias & Friends
17 Seven Founders
18 Martin Luther

19 Thomas Ken
20 Shahdost
21 Saints and Martyrs of
    Africa
22 Margaret of Cortona
23 Polycarp
24 Montanus and Lucius
25 Walburga
26 Porphyry
27 George Herbert
28 Oswald of Worcester

MARCH
 1 David
 2 Chad
 3 The Wesleys
 4 Casimir
 5 John Donne
 6 Colette
 7 Perpetua & Friends
 8 John of God
 9 Gregory of Nyssa
10 Forty Martyrs
11 Sophronius
12 Gregory the Great
13 Euphrasia
14 Matilda
15 Louise de Marillac
16 Julian of Antioch
17 Patrick
18 Cyril of Jerusalem
19 Saint Joseph
20 Cuthbert
21 Nicholas von Flüe
22 Jonathan Edwards
23 Gregory the
    Illuminator
24 Gabriel
25 Annunciation
26 Oscar Romero
27 John the Egyptian
28 Berthold & Brocard
29 John Keble
30 John Climacus

APRIL
 1 Hugh of Grenoble
 2 Francis of Paola
 3 Richard
 4 M. L. King, Jr.
 5 Vincent Ferrer
 6 Michelangelo
 7 John Baptist de la Salle
 8 Saints & Martyrs of the
    Americas
 9 Dietrich Bonhoeffer
10 Teilhard de Chardin
11 George Selwyn
12 Teresa of the Andes
13 Martin the First
14 Tiburtius
15 Stephen Harding
16 Bernadette
17 Robert
18 Leo IX
19 Alphege
20 Agnes
21 Anselm
22 Theodore of
    Sykeon
23 George
24 Egbert
25 Mark
26 Stephen of Perm
27 Zita
28 Louis Grignion
29 Catherine of Siena
30 Marian & James

MAY
 1 Philip & James
 2 Athanasius
 3 Theodosius of the
    Caves
 4 Monica
 5 Hilary of Arles
 6 Florian
 7 John of Beverley
 8 Julian of Norwich
 9 Gregory Nazianus

10 Isidore
11 Francis de Girolamo
12 Simon of Cyrene
13 Andrew Fournet
14 Matthias
15 Hallvard
16 Brendan
17 Robert Bellarmine
18 Eric
19 Dunstan
20 Alcuin
21 Godric
22 Rita
23 Euphrosyne
24 Jackson Kemper
25 Bede
26 Augustine of
    Canterbury
27 John Calvin
28 Bernard of Montjoux
29 Joan
31 Visitation

JUNE
 1 Justin Martyr
 2 Martyrs of Lyons
 3 John XXIII
 4 Petroc
 5 Boniface
 6 Jarlath
 7 Chief Seattle
 8 Melania
 9 Columba
10 Ephrem
11 Barnabas
12 Eskil
13 Anthony of Padua
14 Basil
15 Evelyn Underhill
16 – 21 For Church Unity
22 Alban
23 Joseph Cafasso
24 Nativity of John the
    Baptist
25 Augsburg Confession

26 John & Paul
27 Cyril of Alexandria
28 Irenaeus
29 Peter & Paul
30 Martial of
   Limoges

JULY

1 Oliver Plunket
2 Simeon Salus
3 Thomas
4 Independence Day
5 Athanasius the
   Athonite
6 More & Fisher
7 Thomas Becket
8 Elizabeth of Portugal
9 Veronica Giuliani
10 Seven Brothers
11 Benedict
12 John the Iberian
13 Silas
14 Nicodemus of the
   Holy Mountain
15 Vladimir
16 Osmund
17 Alexis
18 Arnulf
19 Macrina
20 Sojourner Truth
21 Elijah
22 Mary Magdalene
23 Bridget
24 Thomas à Kempis
25 James the Apostle
26 Joachim & Anne
27 Christopher
28 Bach & Handel
29 Mary and Martha
31 Ignatius Loyola

AUGUST

1 Joseph of Arimethea
2 Alphonsus Liguori

3 Peter Eymard
4 John Baptist Vianney
5 Vigil for
   Transfiguration
6 Transfiguration
7 John Mason Neale
8 Dominic
9 Oswald of
   Northumbria
10 Lawrence
11 Clare
12 Hippolytus
13 Florence Nightingale
14 Maximilian
   Kolbe
15 Mary
16 Stephen of Hungary
17 Hyacinth
18 Helen
19 John Eudes
20 Bernard of Clairvaux
21 Abraham
22 Symphorian
23 Rose
24 Bartholomew
25 Louis IX
26 Elizabeth Bichier
27 Caesarius
28 Augustine of Hippo
29 Beheading of John
   the Baptist
30 Aidan

SEPTEMBER

1 Giles
2 Martyrs of New
   Guinea
3 Cuthburga
4 Albert Schweitzer
5 Lawrence Giustiniani
6 Simone Weil
7 Cloud of Nogent
8 Nativity of Mary
9 Constance & Friends

10 Alexander of
   Crummell
11 Protus &
   Hyacinth
12 Cyprian
13 Vigil for Holy Cross
14 Holy Cross
15 Seven Sorrows
16 Ninian
17 Hildegard
18 Dag Hammarskjöld
19 Theodore of Tarsus
20 Saints & Martyrs of
   the Pacific
21 Matthew
22 Martyrs of Agaunum
23 Adamnan
24 Gerard
25 Sergius
26 Cosmas & Damian
27 Vincent de Paul
28 Lioba
29 Michael & All Angels
30 Jerome

OCTOBER

1 Theresa of
   Lisieux
2 Guardian Angels
3 George K. Bell
4 Francis of Assisi
5 Placid
6 William Tyndale
7 Henry Muhlenberg
8 Sergius & Bacchus
9 Denis of Paris
10 Paulinus
11 Bruno
12 Wilfred
13 Edward
14 Justus
15 Teresa of Avila
16 Thomas Cranmer
17 Ignatius
18 Luke

19 Frideswide
20 Bertilla Boscardin
21 Hilarion
22 Philip of Heraclea
23 James, the Brother of
    Our Lord
24 Antony Mary Claret
25 Crispin
26 Philipp Nicolai
27 Frumentius
28 Simon & Jude
29 Hannington &
    Friends
31 Saints and Martyrs of
    the Reformation

NOVEMBER
1 All Saints'
2 All Souls'
3 Saints & Martyrs of
    Asia
4 Charles Borromeo
5 Elizabeth &
    Zechariah
6 Leonard
7 Willibrord
8 Saints & Martyrs of
    the British Isles
9 Nectarius Kephalas

10 Leo the Great
11 Martin of Tours
12 Charles Simeon
13 Saints of the
    Order of St.
    Benedict
14 Gregory Palamas
15 Albert
16 Margaret
17 Hugh of Lincoln
18 Hilda
19 Elizabeth
20 Edmund
21 Gelasius
22 Cecilia
23 Clement
24 Martyrs of Vietnam
25 Isaac Watts
26 Leonard of Port
    Maurice
27 Gregory of Sinai
28 Catherine Labouré
29 For Missionaries
30 Andrew

DECEMBER
1 Charles de Foucald
2 Nicholas Ferrar
3 Francis Xavier

4 John of Damascus
5 Clement of
    Alexandria
6 Nicholas of Myra
7 Ambrose
8 Conception of Mary
9 Hipparchus &
    Friends
10 Thomas Merton
11 Daniel the Stylite
12 Jane de Chantal
13 Lucy
14 John of the Cross
15 Mary di Rosa
16 Adelaide
17 – 23 O Sapienta
24 Christmas Eve
25 The Nativity
26 Stephen
27 John
28 Holy Innocents
29 Marcellus
31 Vigil for Holy Name

GLOSSARY

ADVENT: The first season of the liturgical year, a season of four weeks or slightly less duration that begins with Advent Sunday and ends on Christmas Eve. It is the season of waiting for the coming of the Light of the World.

ALL SAINTS': One of the principal feasts of the Church, commemorating the communion of saints that have gone before us. The feast is celebrated on November 1, and also on the Sunday following.

ANTIPHON: A verse of Scripture, most often from the Psalm or Canticle that is being sung or said, that is used to begin and end the reading.

APPOINTED, PSALM OR CANTICLE: The appointed readings in this book are designated by the number of the day of the month upon which they fall. For example, Psalms 90–94 are "appointed" for Day 18 of each month.

ASCENSION, FEAST OF THE: The feast that commemorates the ascension of Christ into heaven. It is celebrated on the fortieth day of Eastertide.

ASCENSIONTIDE: The season that follows the Ascension. It is a season of preparation for the coming of the Holy Spirit at Pentecost.

ASH WEDNESDAY: The first day of the Lenten season, marked by a solemn service of penitence. The name refers to the custom of marking the forehead with ashes as a sign of our mortality and penitence.

BENEDICTUS (BLESSED BE): The word refers to the Canticle known as the Song of Zechariah (drawn from Luke 1: 68–79). It is most often associated with morning prayer. The term also refers to the anthem (Blessed is he that comes . . .) that is sung after the Sanctus in the Eucharist.

BLESSED MOTHER, FEASTS OF THE: The Church honors the Blessed Mother with many feasts and devotions. The most notable ones include the Immaculate Conception (December 8), the Nativity of Mary (September 8), the Annunciation (March 25), the Purification (February 2), and the Assumption (August 15).

BREVIARY: A book that contains the psalms, hymns, canticles, lessons, and prayers needed to recite the hours of the Divine Office.

CANDLEMAS: A popular name for the feast of the Presentation of Our Lord in the Temple. It is observed on February 2.

CANONICAL HOURS: See Daily Office.

CANTICLE: A Canticle is a sacred song taken from Scripture.

CHRISTMASTIDE: A name for the twelve-day season that begins on Christmas Day (December 25) and concludes on Twelfth Night (January 5), the Vigil for the Epiphany.

COLLECT: A brief prayer, which is usually a single sentence made up of an address to God, followed by a petition, thanksgiving, or intercession, and concluded with a formulaic closing.

COMPLINE: The last prayer of the day in the Liturgy of the Hours. It is said at bedtime, and the name derives from the ancient word for "completion." Portions of this Office have been used to compose the Night Office in this book.

CONFESSION: The acknowledgment of one's sins, either publicly or privately made.

CORPUS CHRISTI (THE BODY OF CHRIST): One of the Feasts of Our Lord. It is celebrated on the Thursday after Trinity Sunday and commemorates the institution of the Holy Eucharist.

DIVINE COMPASSION, FEAST OF THE: One of the Feasts of Our Lord. It is celebrated twelve days after the Day of Pentecost.

DAILY OFFICE (OR DIVINE OFFICE): Also known variously as the canonical hours, the Liturgy of the Hours, and so forth. Originally there were eight hours: Nocturn, said with Matins and Lauds at midnight; Prime, said at 6 A.M.; Terce at 9 A.M.; Sext at noon; Nones at 3 P.M.; Vespers at 6 P.M.; and Compline at bedtime. Over the course of time, there have been various reformulations by and for different communities within the Church. Portions of these traditional Offices have been adapted and reshaped to compose the Offices (Morning, Noon, Evening, and Night) in this book within the tradition and the spirit of the original Offices.

EASTER EVE: The Saturday before Easter, which is generally marked as a day of fasting or devotion and concluded after sunset with a service known as the Vigil for the Resurrection of Our Lord.

EASTERTIDE: A popular name for the season that follows the Resurrection. The season is bound on one end by Easter Day and on the other by the Feast of Pentecost.

EASTER WEEK: The six days of the week following the Sunday of the Resurrection. They are marked by special devotion and piety.

EMBER DAYS: Days of prayer for the ministry of the Church and its people. They are traditionally observed four times each year, on the Wednesday, Friday, and Saturday following the first Sunday of Lent, the Day of Pentecost, St. Lucy's Day (December 13), and Holy Cross.

EPIPHANY: The name for a specific feast, January 6, the day on which the Church celebrates the manifestation of Christ to the Gentiles, with particular focus on the visit of the Magi and the baptism of Jesus by John the Baptist. It is also the name for the season to follow, which lasts from four to nine weeks, depending upon the date for Easter.

FEAST DAYS: Holy days that are set apart as days of rejoicing, as opposed to fasting or penance. The Feasts of the Church are classified into various groups, known as Principal Feasts (such as Easter or Christmas, Sundays, which are always Feast days), other Feasts of Our Lord (such as the Presentation or the Divine Compassion), and other major and lesser feasts (such as St. Peter's Confession or St. Francis Day). Particular traditions place more or less emphasis on certain classes of Feasts: one is advised to investigate one's own tradition fully as a way of marking feasts and fasts as an act of community prayer.

GLORIA IN EXCELSIS (GLORY TO GOD IN THE HIGHEST): An ancient hymn that is taken from the song of the angels in Luke's story of the birth of the Christ. It is used in many traditions as part of the entrance rites in worship.

GOOD FRIDAY: The day that commemorates the Crucifixion of Christ. Many communities hold a Communion service, typically at the noon hour.

GRATIA: A name given in this book to the order for prayer for use before meals.

GREAT THANKSGIVING, THE: The central prayer of the Eucharist.

HOLY CROSS, FEAST OF THE: One of the Feasts of Our Lord. It is celebrated on September 14 and is set aside for the veneration of the Cross upon which Jesus died. For the purposes of this book, it marks the end of Pentecost and the beginning of Ordinary Time.

HOLY FAMILY, FEAST OF THE: One of the Feasts of Our Lord. It is celebrated on the Sunday after Christmas Day.

HOLY SATURDAY: The day following Good Friday during Holy Week. The Eucharist is not celebrated on this day. It is generally marked during the day by acts of devotion and piety, and concludes at sunset with the Great Vigil of Easter.

HOLY WEEK: The last week of the Lenten season. It begins with Palm Sunday and concludes at sundown on the following Saturday.

HOURS: See Daily Office.

KINGDOMTIDE: A popular name used in some communions for the liturgical season that begins at All Saints' (November 1) and continues until Advent Sunday.

KYRIE ELEISON (LORD, HAVE MERCY): A brief prayer often used as a response in liturgical worship. It is also used as a breath prayer: Kyrie elesion; Christe eleison (Lord, have mercy; Christ have mercy).

LAUDS: One of the Canonical Hours from the monastic tradition. It was recited at midnight, generally along with Matins, as one Office.

LECTIO DIVINA (SACRED READING): A practice of reading the Scriptures or other sacred works in a way that the reading, through meditation and contemplation, becomes prayer itself.

LECTIONARY: A cycle of readings of Scripture used in the Church.

LENT: The season of the liturgical year that follows Epiphany and precedes Easter. It begins on Ash Wednesday and ends on the Saturday before Palm Sunday, which begins Holy Week. It is a season marked by fasting and penance, as preparation for the Easter season.

LITURGICAL CALENDAR: The Church year begins with Advent Sunday, the Sunday closest to November 30, and ends with the feast of St. Andrew the Apostle (November 30). The calendar is divided into two parts, the Temporale, which comprises the holy days and seasons of the Church year whose dates are based on the date of Easter each year; and the Sanctorale, the calendar of holy days that are on fixed dates.

LITURGY (THE WORK OF THE PEOPLE): It refers to the formulas and rites used for worship. The Liturgy for the Eucharist (The Mass) and the Liturgy of the Hours (Divine Office) are the two principal worship forms of the Church.

MAGNIFICAT: The Song of Mary, a Canticle based on the Scripture found in Luke 1: 46–55. It is the traditional Canticle used for Vespers, or evening prayer.

MATINS: One of the canonical hours, most properly recited at midnight. It is often combined with Lauds and Prime to make one Office said at daybreak.

Maundy Thursday: The Thursday of Holy Week, often commemorated with a service of foot washing.

Nones: One of the canonical hours, properly recited at 3:00 P.M.

Nunc Dimittis: The Song of Simeon, the traditional Canticle for Compline, or night prayer. It is based on the Scripture in Luke 2:29–32.

Office: See Daily Office.

Ordinary time: The name given to the liturgical season between Pentecost and Kingdomtide. The term is also used in certain communions to identify the time between Christmas and Lent, which in this book is named as Epiphany.

O sapientia (o wisdom): It refers to the seven Antiphons to the Magnificat, which are traditionally used on the days before Christmas, December 17–23. In this book it refers as well to the devotional practice of offering prayers in anticipation of the Nativity.

Palm Sunday: The Sunday before Easter. Its celebration tells of the entry of Christ into Jerusalem for the Passover. It is also known as the Sunday of the Passion.

Paschal mystery: Paschal refers to Easter, and is taken from the Hebrew word, *pesach* for Passover.

Pentecost: The fiftieth day of Easter. It marks the end of the Easter season and celebrates the day upon which the Holy Spirit was given to the disciples in the Upper Room in Jerusalem. The Feast is known as Whitsunday in the Anglican Communion.

Pho Hilaron (gracious light): An ancient Greek hymn used as a Canticle at Evening Prayer.

Prayers of the People: General intercessory prayer that consists of prayers for the Church, the nation, the world, the local community, those in need, and for the departed. The term is used in this book to refer to the intercessions and petitions that follow the Lessons in each of the Offices.

Precious Blood, Feast of the: One of the Feasts of Our Lord. It is celebrated on July 1 and honors the death of Christ, our redemption, and the sacrifice that Christ made for us. It has been dropped in some communities but is still observed in others.

Principal Feasts: A term for the major holy days of the Church year. In addition to Sundays, these days are to be observed as days of sabbath rest and devotion, and the Eucharist is to be attended. Specific Feasts can vary from one community to another. For example, in the Anglican Communion, the principal feasts are Easter, Ascension, Pentecost, Trinity Sunday, All Saints', Christmas, and Epiphany. Other traditions add one or two others to that list.

Psalter: The section of a prayerbook that incorporates the 150 Psalms of David.

Rogation days: Days set aside for prayers for agricultural seasons, and for a bountiful harvest and, more recently, the care of the earth. They are observed once each year on the Monday, Tuesday, and Wednesday preceding the Ascension.

Sanctorale: The calendar of holy days whose dates are fixed each year, such as Christmas. See Liturgical Calendar.

Simeon, Song of: See Nunc dimittis.

TEMPORALE: The calendar of the holy days and seasons whose dates vary each year according to the date for Easter. See Liturgical Calendar.

TRANSFIGURATION, FEAST OF THE: One of the Feasts of Our Lord. It is celebrated August 6 and commemorates the story of Christ's transfiguration as described in the Gospels.

TRINITY SUNDAY: The first Sunday after Pentecost (Whitsunday). It refers to the mystery of God in three persons: Father, Son, and Holy Spirit, or Creator, Redeemer, and Giver of Life.

TWELFTH NIGHT: The Vigil for the Epiphany. The name refers to the fact that it is observed on the twelfth day after Christmas.

VENITE (O COME): It refers to Psalm 95, the traditional Psalm of invitation to be recited before the day's appointed Psalm is sung or said. For the purposes of this book, it represents the opening Psalm in any of the Offices.

VERSICLE: Brief verses of Scripture that are used to begin an Office or another portion of the liturgy.

VESPERS: The sixth of the Canonical Hours, recited at 6:00 P.M.

VIGIL: A night service before an important feast in the Church year. Collects have been given in this book to be said at the Offices on such days.

WHITSUNDAY: The name given to Pentecost Sunday in the Anglican Communion of the Church. It refers to the white robes worn by those who were baptized at the preceding Easter Vigil.

ZECHARIAH, THE SONG OF: See Benedictus.

BIBLIOGRAPHY AND RESOURCE NOTES

The author would like to gratefully acknowledge the work of the hundreds of faithful and diligent scholars, editors, and publishers whose work is reflected in the list of sources below. It is those people, and the books that are a result of their work, who make it possible for any of us, and perhaps all of us, to learn to pray. More personally, they are the sources to whom this author turned time and time again throughout the nearly ten years that it took to make this book, and commends them to anyone whose journey takes them in the direction of learning to pray the prayer that sanctifies the day.

SCRIPTURE AND SCRIPTURE REFERENCE

BONHOEFFER, DIETRICH. PSALMS: THE PRAYER BOOK OF THE BIBLE. Minneapolis: Augsburg Publishing House, 1970.

THE COMPLETE PARALLEL BIBLE. New York: Oxford University Press, 1993.

CROSSAN, JOHN DOMINIC. THE ESSENTIAL JESUS. San Francisco: HarperSanFrancisco, 1994.

GAUS, ANDY, TRANS. THE UNVARNISHED GOSPELS. Putney, Vermont: Threshold Books, 1988.

JONES, JEREMIAH, AND WILLIAM WAKE, TRANS. THE LOST BOOKS OF THE BIBLE. New York: Random House, n.d.

MACK, BURTON L. THE LOST GOSPEL OF Q. San Francisco: HarperSanFrancisco, 1993.

MAYOTTE, RICKY ALAN. THE COMPLETE JESUS. South Royalton, Vermont: Steerforth Press, 1998.

MERTON, THOMAS. OPENING THE BIBLE. Collegeville, Minnesota: The Liturgical Press, 1970.

MEYER, MARVIN, TRANS. THE GOSPEL OF THOMAS: THE HIDDEN SAYINGS OF JESUS. New York: Vintage Books, 1986.

MITCHELL, STEPHEN. THE GOSPEL ACCORDING TO JESUS. New York: HarperCollins Publishers, 1991.

MITCHELL, STEPHEN. A BOOK OF PSALMS. New York: HarperCollins, 1993.

THE NEW ENGLISH BIBLE. New York: Oxford University Press, 1970.

THE OXFORD STUDY BIBLE. New York: Oxford University Press, 1992.

THROCKMORTON, BURTON C., JR., ED. GOSPEL PARALLELS. Nashville: Thomas Y. Nelson Publishers, 1992.

VAUGHAN, CURTIS, ED. THE NEW TESTAMENT FROM 26 TRANSLATIONS. Grand Rapids, Michigan: Zondervan Bible Publishers, 1967.

PRAYERBOOKS AND WORSHIP

THE BOOK OF COMMON PRAYER. New York: The Church Hymnal Corporation, 1979.

CELEBRATING COMMON PRAYER: A VERSION OF THE DAILY OFFICE (Society of Saint Francis). New York: Mowbray Publishers, 1992.

CULLMAN, OSCAR. EARLY CHRISTIAN WORSHIP. TRANS. A. S. TODD AND J. B. TORRANCE. Philadelphia: Westminster Press, 1953.

ESLINGER, ELISE, ED. THE UPPER ROOM WORSHIP BOOK: MUSIC AND LITURGIES FOR SPIRITUAL FORMATION. Nashville: The Upper Room, 1985.

GUILBERT, CHARLES MORTIMER, COMP. WORDS OF OUR WORSHIP: A PRACTICAL LITURGICAL DICTIONARY. New York: The Church Hymnal Corporation, 1988.

KAYE, JOHN. THE FIRST APOLOGY OF JUSTIN MARTYR. London: Griffith, Farran, Okeden & Welsh, n.d..

LESSER FEASTS AND FASTS, 1997 EDITION. New York: Church Publishing Incorporated, 1998.

THE LUTHERAN BOOK OF WORSHIP. Philadelphia: Lutheran Church in America, 1978.

OMAN, JORDAN. CHRISTIAN SPIRITUALITY IN THE CATHOLIC TRADITION. San Francisco: Ignatius Press, 1989.

SALIERS, DON E. WORSHIP AND SPIRITUALITY. Philadelphia: Westminster Press, 1984.

SENN, FRANK C., ED. PROTESTANT SPIRITUAL TRADITIONS. New York: Paulist Press, 1986.

TAFT, ROBERT, S. J. THE LITURGY OF THE HOURS IN EAST AND WEST: Collegeville: The Liturgical Press, 1986.

GENERAL RESOURCES

ATTWATER DONALD, WITH CATHERINE RACHEL JOHN. THE PENGUIN DICTIONARY OF SAINTS, 3RD EDITION. New York: Penguin Books, 1995.

BRODERICK, ROBERT C., ED. THE CATHOLIC ENCYCLOPEDIA, REVISED EDITION. Nashville: Thomas Nelson Publishers, 1987.

THE ESSENTIAL CATHOLIC HANDBOOK. Liguori, Missouri: Liguori Publications, 1997.

HALLAM, ELIZABETH, ED. SAINTS. New York: Simon & Schuster, 1994.

INDEX

Italics indicate words or phrases connected with the specific Offices themselves, such as *Lauds,* or *Morning Prayer;* specific titles of elements within the Offices, such as the *Venite, exultemus* (the traditional invitation to Morning Prayer); or common names for the Canticles found in the Canticles section of the book, such as the *Song of the Redeemed.* The bold type indicates principal feasts, fasts, and vigils of the Church as well as other days of special devotion. The roman type indicates persons and events found in the Remembrances section. The index is alphabetized by first name or first word in a phrase.

A

Abo, 48
Abraham of Smolensk, 75
Adamnan, 79
Adelaide, 65
Adrian, 50
Advent, 24
Aelred, 56
Agatha, 42
Agnes, 74
Agnes of Moltepulciano, 72
Aidan, 93
Alban, 76
Albert Schweitzer, 41
Albert the Great, 63
Alcuin, 72
Alexander Crummell, 53
Alexis, the Man of God, 67
All Saints, 35
All Souls, 37
Alphege, 70
Alphonsus Ligouri, 37
Ambrose, 47
Andrew Fournet, 58
Andrew the Apostle, 93
Annunciation of Our Lord, 82
Anselm, 74
Anskar, 38
Anthony of Padua, 58
Antony, 66

Antony Mary Claret, 81
Apollonia, 50
Arnulf of Metz, 69
Ascension of Our Lord, 29
Ascensiontide, 29
Ash Wednesday, 25
Athanasius, 36
Athanasius the Athonite, 43
Augsburg Confession, 82
Augustine of Canterbury, 84
Augustine of Hippo, 89
Autumn Ember Days, 31

B

Baptism of Our Lord, 25
Barnabas the Apostle, 54
Bartholomew the Apostle, 81
Basil the Great, 60
Bede the Venerable, 82
Beheading of John the Baptist, 91
Benedict, 55
Benedict of Anine, 54
Benedictus, 8
Berard and Companions, 64
Bernadette, 64
Bernard of Clairvaux, 73
Bernard of Montjoux, 88
Berthold and Brocard, 88
Bertilla Boscardin, 73

Boniface, 42
Brendan, 64
Bridget of Sweden, 79
Bruno, 55

C

Caesarius of Arles, 87
Candlemas, 34, 36
Casimir, 40
Catherine dei Ricci, 58
Catherine Labouré, 89
Catherine of Siena, 90
Cecilia, 77
Chad, 36
Charles Borromeo, 41
Charles de Foucauld, 35
Charles Simeon, 57
Charles Stuart, 92
Christopher, 87
Christmas Eve, 81
Christmastide, 24
Christ our Passover, 115
Clare, 55
Clement, 79
Clement of Alexandria, 43
Cloud, 47
Colette, 44
Columba, 50
Commemoration, 20
Communion, 18
Compline (Night Prayer), 14
Confession of St. Peter, 68
Constance and Her Companions, 51
Conversion of St. Paul, 82
Cornelius the Centurion, 40
Corpus Christi, 30
Cosmas and Damian, 85
Crispin, 83
Cuthbert, 72
Cuthburga, 39
Cyprian, 57
Cyril of Alexandria, 86

Cyril of Jerusalem, 68
Cyril and Methodius, 60

D

Dag Hammarskjöld, 69
Daniel the Stylite, 55
David, 34
Denis of Paris, 51
Dietrich Bonhoeffer, 50
Divine Compassion of Our Lord, 31
Domine, investigasti (Psalm 139), 14
Dominic, 49
Dominus, pascit me (Psalm 23), 20
Dorothy, 44
Dunstan, 70

E

Easter Eve, 27
Easter Sunday, 28
Eastertide, 29
Easter Week, 28
Edmund, 73
Edward the Confessor, 59
Egbert, 80
Elias and Companions, 64
Elijah and Elisha, 75
Elizabeth and Zechariah, 43
Elizabeth, 71
Elizabeth Bichier des Anges, 85
Elizabeth of Portugal, 49
Elizabeth Seton, 40
Ephrem, 52
Epiphany, 24, 44
Eric, 68
Eskil, 56
Euphrasia, 58
Euphrosyne of Polotsk, 78
Evelyn Underhill, 62
Evening Prayer (Vespers), 12

F

Fabian, 72
First Song (of Isaiah), 107
Florence Nightingale, 59
Florian, 44
Forty Martyrs of England and Wales, 52
Francis de Girolamo, 54
Francis de Sales, 80
Francis of Assisi, 41
Francis of Paola, 36
Francis Xavier, 39
Frideswide, 71
Frumentius, 87

G

Gabriel the Archangel, 80
Gelasius the First, 75
Genevieve, 38
George, 78
George Augustus Selwyn, 54
George Fox, 60
George Herbert, 86
George Kennedy Bell, 39
Gerard of Csanad, 81
Gildas the Wise, 90
Giles the Hermit, 35
Gloria in excelsis, 10
Godric, 74
Good Friday, 27
Gratia (Table Office), 16
Gregory of Nazianzen, 50
Gregory of Nyssa, 50
Gregory Palamas, 61
Gregory of Sinai, 87
Gregory the Great, 56
Gregory the Illuminator, 78

H

Hallvard, 62
Helen, 69

Henry Muhlenberg, 47
Hilarion, 75
Hilary, 58
Hilary of Arles, 42
Hilda, 69
Hildegard of Bingen, 67
Hipparchus and Philotheus, 51
Hippolytus, 57
Holy Cross of Our Lord, 61
Holy Family of Our Lord, 24
Holy Guardian Angels, 37
Holy Innocents, 89
Holy Name of Our Lord, 34
Holy Week, 27
Hugh of Grenoble, 34
Hugh of Lincoln, 67
Hyacinth, 55
Hyacinth of Cracow, 67

I

Ignatius, 67
Ignatius of Loyola, 93
Immaculate Conception of Mary, 49
Independence Day, 41
In quo corrigit? (Psalm 119), 10
Ireanaeus, 88
Isaac Watts, 83
Isidore the Farmer-Servant, 52
Ita, 62

J

Jackson Kemper, 80
James Hannington and Companions,
    91
James, the Brother of Our Lord, 79
James the Elder, 83
Jane Frances de Chantal, 57
Jarlath of Tuam, 44
Jerome, 93
Joan of Arc, 90

Johann S. Bach and George F. Handel, 89
John and Charles Wesley, 38
John and Paul, 84
John Baptist de la Salle, 46
John Baptist Vianney, 41
John Bosco, 92
John Calvin, 86
John Climacus, 92
John Donne, 42
John Eudes, 71
John Keble, 90
John Mason Neale, 47
John of Beverley, 46
John of Chrysostom, 86
John of Damascus, 41
John of God, 48
John of Matha, 48
John of the Cross, 61
John the Almsgiver, 78
John the Egyptian, 86
John the Evangelist, 87
John the Iberian, 57
John XXIII, 38
Jonathan Edwards, 76
Joseph, 70
Joseph of Arimethea, 35
Joseph Cafasso, 78
Julian of Antioch, 64
Julian of Norwich, 48
Justin the Martyr, 34
Justus of Lyons, 61

K

Kingdomtide, 31

L

Laudate Dominum (Psalm 146), 16
Lauds (Morning Prayer), 8
Lawrence, 53
Lawrence Giustiniani, 43

Lent, 26
Leo the Great, 53
Leo the Ninth, 68
Leonard, 45
Leonard of Port Maurice, 85
Levavi, oculos (Psalm 121), 12
Lioba, 89
Litany of Penitence, 125
Louis IX, 83
Louise de Marillac, 62
Louis Grignion de Montfort, 88
Lucian of Antioch, 46
Lucy, 59
Luke the Evangelist, 69

M

Macarius the Younger, 36
Macrina, 71
Magnificat (Mary's Song), 12
Marcellus the Righteous, 91
Margaret, 65
Margret of Cortona, 76
Marian and James, 92
Marina, 56
Mark the Apostle, 82
Martial of Limoges, 92
Martin Luther, 68
Martin Luther King, Jr., 40
Martin of Tours, 55
Martin the First, 58
Martyrs of Agaunum, 77
Martyrs of Lyons, 36
Martyrs of New Guinea, 37
Martyrs of Vietnam, 81
Mary, the Mother of Our Lord, 63
Mary di Rosa, 63
Mary Magdalene, 77
Mary, Martha, and Lazarus, 91
Mary's Song (Magnificat), 12
Matilda, 60
Matthew the Apostle, 75
Matthias the Apostle, 60
Maundy Thursday, 27

Maximilian Kolbe, 61
Melania the Younger, 48
Michael and All Angels, 91
Michelangelo, 44
Missions and Missionaries, 91
Monica, 40
Montanus, 80
Morning Prayer (Lauds), 8

N

Nativity of John the Baptist, 80
Nativity of Our Lord, 83
Nativity of the Blessed Mother, 49
Nectarius Kephalas, 51
Nicene Creed, 123
Nicholas Ferrar, 37
Nicholas of Myra, 45
Nicholas von Flüe, 74
Nicodemus of the Holy Mountain, 61
Night Prayer (Compline), 14
Ninian, 65
Nunc dimittis (Simeon's Song), 14

O

O gracious light (Phos hilaron), 16
O Sapientia, 67, 69, 71, 73, 75, 77, 79
Oliver Plunket, 35
Ordinary Time, 31
Oscar Romero, 84
Osmund, 65
Oswald of Northumbria, 51
Oswald of Worcester, 88

P

Palm Sunday, 25
Parents of the Blessed Mother, 85
Passion of Our Lord, 25
Patrick, 66
Paulinus of York, 53

Pentecost, 30
Perpetua and Felicity, 46
Peter and Paul, the Apostles, 90
Peter Eymard, 39
Petroc, 40
Philip and James, the Apostles, 34
Philip of Heraclea, 77
Philipp Nicolai, 85
Philotheus, 51
Phos hilaron (O gracious light), 16
Pierre Teilhard de Chardin, 52
Placid, 43
Polycarp, 78
Porphyry of Gaza, 84
Presentation of Our Lord, 34, 36
Protus, 55

R

Resurrection of Our Lord, 28
Richard, 38
Rita of Cascia, 76
Robert Bellarmine, 66
Robert of Chaise-Dieu, 66
Rogation Days, 29
Rose of Lima, 79

S

Saints and Martyrs of Africa, 74
Saints and Martyrs of Asia, 39
Saints and Martyrs of Europe, 46
Saints and Martyrs of the Americas, 48
Saints and Martyrs of the British Isles,
    49
Saints and Martyrs of the Pacific, 73
Saints and Martyrs of the Reformation,
    93
Saints of the Order of St. Benedict, 59
Scholastica, 52
Seattle, 46
Sergius and Bacchus, 49
Sergius of Russia, 83

Seven Brothers, 53
Seven Founders, 66
Seven Sorrows of Mary, 63
Shahdost, 72
Sigfrid, 62
Silas, 59
Simeon of Salus, 37
Simeon's Song (Nunc dimittis), 14
Simon and Jude, the Apostles, 89
Simon of Cyrene, 56
Simone Weil, 45
Sojourner Truth, 73
Song of Divine Love, 117
Song of Emmanuel, 113
Song of God's Children, 118
Song of God's Grace, 114
Song of God's Love, 120
Song of God's Mercy, 111
Song of Humility, 109
Song of Moses, 99
Song of Penitence, 110
Song of Pilgrimage, 102
Song of Praise, 98
Song of Redemption, 116
Song of Repentance, 119
Song of the Blessed, 112
Song of the Cosmic Order, 96, 97
Song of the Earth, 97
Song of the Knowledge of Wisdom, 100
Song of the Messiah, 106
Song of the New Creation, 103
Song of the Redeemed, 121
Song of the Spirit of Wisdom, 101
Song of the Wilderness, 104
Song of the Word of the Lord, 105
Song to the Lamb, 122
Sophronius, 54
Spring Ember Days, 25
Stephen Harding, 62
Stephen of Hungary, 65
Stephen of Perm, 84
Stephen the Martyr, 85
Summer Ember Days, 30
Symphorian, 77

T

Table Office (Gratia), 16
Te Deum Laudamus, 124
Teresa of the Andes, 56
Teresa of Avila, 63
Theodore of Sykeon, 76
Theodore of Tarsus, 71
Theodosius of the Caves, 38
Theodosius the Cenobite, 54
Theresa of Lisieux, 35
Third Song (of Isaiah), 108
Thomas à Kempis, 81
Thomas Aquinas, 88
Thomas Becket, 47
Thomas Cranmer, 65
Thomas Ken, 70
Thomas Merton, 53
Thomas More and John Fisher, 45
Thomas the Apostle, 39
Tiburtius, 60
Timothy and Titus, 84
Transfiguration of Our Lord, 45
Trinity Sunday, 30
Twelfth Night, 42

U

Unity of the Church, 64, 66, 68, 70, 72, 74

V

Venite, exultemus (Psalm 95), 8
Veronica Giuliani, 51
Vespers (Evening Prayer), 12
Vigil for the Ascension, 29
Vigil for the Candlemas, 34
Vigil for the Epiphany, 42
Vigil for the Holy Cross, 59
Vigil for the Holy Name, 93
Vigil for the Resurrection, 27

Vigil for the Transfiguration, 43
Vincent de Paul, 87
Vincent Ferrer, 42
Vincent of Saragossa, 76
Visitation of the Blessed Mother, 92
Vladimir of Russia, 63

W

Walburga, 82
Whitsunday, 30

Wilfrid of York, 57
William Laud, 52
William Tyndale, 45
Willibrord, 47
Winter Ember Days, 24
Wulfstan, 70

Z

Zechariah's Song (Benedictus), 8
Zita, 86

ACKNOWLEDGMENTS

The author would like to thank the many individuals and groups whose encouragement, kindness, hard work, prayers, and support over the years made this work possible, even when they may or may not have realized they were doing so. I include, but do not name, of course, the scores of people who have shown me the kindness of letting me be a part of their prayer at retreats.

They include these holy communities of which the author has been a part or who have been gracious and hospitable to the author and his friends as we learned to pray: The Academy for Spiritual Formation, Christ Church Episcopal Cathedral, West End United Methodist Church, The Upper Room, Mars Hill Dinner Club, St. Mary's Retreat Center, Camp Sumatanga, Dubose Conference Center, The Sisters of Loreto, Vision of Peace, and, as always, The Friends of Silence and of the Poor.

These people have been brother and sister, companion and teacher, angel and guardian to the author and without them this work, poor as it is, would not have been possible. The mention of their name means less to them than it does to the author, but to fail to acknowledge would be an act of ingratitude: Esther Armstrong, Bob Benson, Pat Brasher, Marilyn Brown, Stephen Bryant, Geoffrey Butcher, Dale Clem, Jim Collier, Cindy Crosby, Jeff Crosby, Ben Curtis, Lynne Deming, Bettie Durden, Father Edward Farrell, Brenda Garrett, Tom Gildemeister, Bert Goodwin, George Graham, Janice Grana, W. G. Henry, Gary Heskje, Charla Honea, Ann Horton, Katrina Hudson, Reuben Job, Emma Lytle, Hazelyn McComas, Brennan Manning, Eric Major, John Mogabgab, Danny Morris, Henri Nouwen, John Owen, Robin Pippin, Mary Lou Redding, Sarah Schaller-Linn, Peggy Scott, Wallace Siler, Matt Steinhauer, Phyllis Tickle, Jon Vance, Judith Weaver, Reuben Welch, Claude Whitehead, Dean Wilson, Nancy Wilson, Wendy Wright.

These people are the ones who make it possible for this author to make any books at all: Cindy Dupree, David Groff, Joel Fotinos, Timothy Meyer, Bo Siler, and Denise Silvestro.

Two people—Alan Petefish and Barbara Riddle—are the ones who first saw the first stumbling attempts at prayer on the part of this pilgrim, and have walked beside me faithfully from that very day.

Finally, Ms. Jones of Merigold, whose kindness and love make it possible for the author to have a place to listen and to dream and to pray.

One last note.

The author is still trying to learn to pray, and is always pleased to hear from other pilgrims, poets, and seekers who have some light to share. He can be reached by mail at 1001 Halcyon Avenue, Nashville, TN 37204.

ABOUT THE AUTHOR

Robert Benson is the author of *Living Prayer* and *Between the Dreaming and the Coming True*. He lives in Nashville.

For the Evening

You made this day for the works of the light,
    and this night for the refreshment of our minds
        and bodies:
Keep us now in Christ; grant us a peaceful evening,
      a night free from sin;
and bring us at last eternal life . . .

Before sleep

Lighten our darkness, O Lord, and by Your
      great mercy
    defend us from all perils and dangers
      of this night:
Guide us waking, and guard us sleeping,
      that awake we may watch with Christ
    and asleep we may rest in peace . . .